LIFE THROUGH THE BURNING BUSH

VOLUME ONE

An Autobiography of
DR. DAVID M. GITHII

Life through the Burning Bush

Edited by Winstone Sharrad@yahoo.co.uk

Cover Design & Layout: Winstone Sharrad
For any book order or inquiries, the author can be reached through Email:

dgithii@yahoo.com.

Local Phone contact (Kenya) 0722-659-252.

International contact +254-722-659-252 as well as WhatsApp number.

ISBN: 978-1-968966-71-3

Initial Design and Layout by Emily Mukomunene

Email: emukomunene2077@gmail.com

DISCLAIMER

The safest way not to step on anyone's toes is by not walking at all, let alone running. But because I have the desire to share my story, nothing could stop me from walking and sometimes running as I re-run my journey with the reader, for it is the right thing for me to do for a story that is long overdue. For that reason, and in advance, I apologize to any party that may feel injured by any of the content contained in this publication. I admit that I intend no harm or slight to any entity, bearing in mind that diplomacy and facts, at times, most often do clash.

JEREMIAH 1:5: "*Before I formed you in the womb, I knew you. Before you were born, I set you apart; I appointed you as a prophet to the nations.*"

Contents

ABBREVIATIONS

GA	General Assembly.
GAC	General Administrative Committee.
PCEA	Presbyterian Church of East Africa.
PUEA	Presbyterian University of East Africa.

DEDICATION

This book is dedicated to my children and grandchildren.

My children include:

Benson Githii

Sammy Gichuki

Amos Thuku

Nicholas Githang'a

Mary Wangari

Terry Njoki

My grandchildren include:

Ayoub, Lucy Githii, Glen

Jazlynn, Timothy Muhia,

Christina Wanjiku, David Muhia Gichuki, Joseph Muiruri, David Muhia Githang'a, Lucy Githang'a, Ndungi Githuku, Joshua Azande, Joseph Azande, David Muhia Njoki.

ACKNOWLEDGMENT

In writing this book, I owe much gratitude to my wife, Lucy Wanjiku and my daughter, Terry Njoki, who bore an unquantifiable amount of sacrifice in kind and psychologically as I consumed the sunlight hours. She also withstood the nights over in all the hours my eyes could remain open over the length of time I jotted what now is a *"book"*. For many hours, I could not give them nor reciprocate their rightful rights, for I was fully submerged in writing. In comradeship, they made sure that I was well-fed and that my needs were met accordingly. They ensured that the environment was conducive enough for my writing. Without their support, this book would not have been. I am also thankful to all my children (Benson Githii, Sammy Gichuki, Amos Thuku (Ndichu), Nicholas Githag'a and Mary Wangari. They were patient and took interest, thus boosting the morel that I required while I dug deep into the spirit and mind so as to bring forward every aspect to form the book. I'm grateful for all the support they have given me.

My special gratitude goes to Tabitha James, who spent so much of her time and energy wrestling with the tedious work of writing my manuscript. She selflessly offered her services and even encouraged me the many times I felt like giving up as I got overwhelmed with research and writing. She was always urging me when I struggled to recall and clear events overlapping for many years so as to publish the correct information. She is currently at Kigoco FM- an early morning show called; *'Kwiitunara Hari Ngai na Manoya'* (Pouring our hearts to God in prayer)

INTRODUCTION

Why the Burning Bush?

Why this book, "Life Through the Burning Bush?" I chose the above title because, as I meditated on my life path, I came to visualize it as the experience Moses had when he saw a bush, which *"though on fire did not burn up."* This is also referred to as *"The Burning Bush"* (Exodus 3:2). In the same scenario, I realized that my life had gone through a lot of *"fires"* that have never burnt it. In other words, it has never been extinguished by the fire as I am still walking through it. I also saw myself upholding Moses 'call of liberating people from oppression, whether politically, spiritually, economically or socially oriented.

Moses had his call, and the consequential responsibility spelt out by God, who told him;

> *"I have indeed seen the misery of my people in Egypt… So now, go. I am sending you to Pharaoh to bring the Israelites out of Egypt"* (Exodus 3:7, 10).

What Moses visualized is a call that also could be likened to the fire he had already seen burning the bush. No wonder his response to God's call was, *"Who am I, that I should go to Pharaoh and bring Israelites out of Egypt"* (Exodus 3:11). It is then that God went on to assure him that the call was likened to the burning bush he saw which though seemingly burning, was not being consumed. It is true that his life will be like passing through fire. It is in this regard that God told Moses, *"I will be with you"* (Exodus 3:12). And like Moses, throughout my obedience to my call, I have been greatly encouraged by God's Word in Luke 10:19, which

1

confirms the authority God has given to us, *"to trample on snakes and scorpions and to overcome all the power of the enemy;* and that *"nothing will harm you."* I hear the same assurance from God when he says,

> *"So do not fear, for I am with you; I will uphold you with my righteous right hand. All who rage against you will surely be ashamed and disgraced; those who oppose you will be reduced to nothing and perish.... Do not fear; I will help you"* (Isaiah 41: 10-11, 13).

One thing the reader of this book will come to agree with me is the fact that in my life, I have been through *"fire."*

What makes me possibly a little different from many other believers is the fact that very few of them are willing to endure the sufferings through which complete gentleness is obtained. Otherwise, for one to be obedient to his or her calling, he/she must die to himself/herself before one is turned into real servanthood. Through my experiences, I have come to identify two types of fires. One is the very fire we use in our everyday life for domestic activities, the fire we use in cooking, electricity, burning coals, firewood, etc. But there is another fire that, though not physically visible, is experienced in everyday life. It is that part of life in which one experiences some struggles, opposition, suffering and conflicts. Sometimes, these experiences are quite fiery.

But I have come to realize that, as much as physical fires have their own positive side, so do invisible fires through life's experience. They match with Paul's words, *"And we know that in all things God works for the good of those who love him, who have been called to his purpose"* (Romans 8:28). Paul further reminds us that we *"can do everything through Him who gives.... strength"* (Philippians 4:13).

This book sets precedence for those who are called to work in the Lord's vineyard: That they should never fear the fire that they will pass through. Whether it is severe opposition, character assassination, torture, humiliation, frustration, psychological torture or all kinds of manipulation, I hope the reader receives this appetizing aspect from the book.

A Prophetic utterance

I am calling this a prophetic message because, at the age of six years, my mother told me that, one day, she had placed a heavy load on my head to carry as we were going home after a day's work in the garden. It was then that we met an old man who, as per my mother's words prophetically said to her,

> *"Why have you placed that heavy burden on the brains in this boy's head? If only you knew how much God is intending to use that head for his glory, you would do all it takes to protect and preserve it."*

My mother, who went to be with the Lord in 1998, would have come to realize the significance of that old man's words had she lived to witness the publication of this book. As you read it, you will affirm that those words uttered by that old man or an angel for that matter, were prophetic words. Before I totally plunge into my story, it is important that I say something about my grandfather and my father as an introduction to my background.

1. FAMILY BACKGROUND

Muhia wa Githang'a was the name of my grandfather. Muhia was born and raised at Kibichoi in Kiambu County, which merges into both Githunguri and Gatundu. In his adulthood, he migrated southward in search of greener pastures for his greatly expanded flock of cattle, sheep and goats. He settled at Thogoto/Dagorreti so that he could graze his flocks in the lush greenery plains of Kibiku. From there, he went to Ngong Market, where he became friends with a Maasai family. The Maasai family later informed him that a person was needed to lead a group of people to clear the way for the brook which had been obstructed by overgrown forage and its shedding of leaves. This made it difficult for the smooth flow of the river to feed the District Commissioner (DC) premises and the residents downhill.

The person was to trace it upstream as he cleared the brook's path to the source of the spring at the Ngong Hills. This was because it had significantly dwindled in its flow, forcing people to go far and wide in search of water. The District Commissioner (DC) was looking for a person of great courage. The place was infested with wild animals that posed great danger to people involved in clearing the way downstream. It then dawned on my grandfather that this could be an opportunity for him to gain access to a wider scope of grazing areas. He therefore applied for the job. When all the applicants were considered, it was agreed that my grandfather bore the characteristics needed for the risky job. He was, therefore, instructed to go up Ngong hills to clear the undergrowth (bushes) and the soil that hindered the spring from having a smooth flow downhill. It was a long stretch between Kibichiku and Ngong. And in the course of his work, he married my grandmother Gachiruiya, who became the mother to my father. As already stated, it was not an easy job because the spring was blocked by thick bushes, soil and grass that needed to be cleared. He also had to deal with fierce wildlife that lived within the bushes and depended on that spring to quench their thirst. This is why it was not possible to get a person who would have wanted to take the risk of handling that job apart from my grandfather. He had already gained the reputation of being a very courageous person far and wide from his previous bold acts. This is why it became easy for some people to accept joining him in that endeavor. He first led this group to the uppermost part of Ngong Hills, where the source of the spring was found.

In the course of time and through his leadership, the group managed to clear and even deepen the trench through which the water flowed, making it easy for the water to flow to the government administration headquarters and the residential area. He used to chase the wild animals away in what was seen as a mysterious manner. People had nicknamed him *"Wild Life Chaser."* All said and done, many people now had ample access to the water. As said earlier, this was a very courageous act that my grandfather undertook as it meant confronting wildlife that dominated the bushes and forests that covered the Ngong Hills.

All kinds of animals lived in the forest, including leopards, lions, hyenas, buffaloes, and elephants, among others. It is said that at one point, my grandfather had to confront a buffalo that was preparing to attack them. He instructed his team to climb trees as he personally engaged the Buffalo. This happened when the calf had run in the direction of my grandfather and his people. Luckily, he managed to thwart the animal.

Another occurrence is when a lion almost knocked him down as it ran very fast chasing a Zebra. It was this kind of courage that made my grandfather's name become a household name. This was especially true when he made it possible for people to have abundant clean water. This was a great relief to them after many years of struggle without enough water. The shepherds would no longer have to drive their flocks for miles. Sometimes, they would have gone for almost two days in search of water. Women also used to walk for long distances to fetch water with jerry cans, sometimes using donkeys as the means of transportation.

Finally, my grandfather settled in Ngong, a place known as Kiwanja. In fact, if he was Maasai by blood, he would have been elected to the position of community chief. His "**DNA**" was Kikuyu. It is said that, as a result, he earned a good name within the community. He received numerous gifts in the form of cows, sheep and goats. He, therefore, became a very rich man.

He now owned a permanent residence in the neighborhood of both Gatuiku, who was the area chief and Professor Saitoti's father. Saitoti, in later years, became the vice president of the Republic of Kenya. It was while there that he married his second wife, Wanjiku. He had become very wealthy, and therefore, marrying a second wife was not a big deal. Having so much wealth, he could easily manage the dowry. In marriage, the dowry then, unlike today, was in the form of animals, alcohol, honey, various types of crops, etc. This was the environment in which my father, Benson Githii Muhia, grew up. All the same, he retained a very strong attachment to Kikuyu land, where his umbilical cord was cut. He spent much of his life in Kikuyu land as well. Allow me then to say something about my father. He had a brother in Limuru. While in Ngong, he married his second wife, Wangare.

BENSON GITHII MUHIA

Benson Githii was the name of my father. Being the son of Muhia, his full name was, therefore, Benson Githii Muhia. According to the Kikuyu clan alignment, my father was a Muithirandu. The Kikuyu tribe has ten clans, although they talk of nine, ignoring the tenth one. This is because the tenth, she never got married. This automatically makes me a Muithirandu. One characteristic of Aithirandu is the quality of being good leaders and people of great courage whom the community can depend on for successful leadership. Like many other boys of that time, my father grew in the habit of shepherding flocks of cattle, sheep and goats. But at a young age, he went to stay with his elder sister Njoki in Thogoto. Njoki was the firstborn of my father's family. Njoki had escaped from home to join the missionary school at Thogoto.

Men of that day hated their daughters joining the religion of the whites, as Christianity was referred to. They reasoned that when a girl got educated, she would not get a man to marry her, meaning the father missed the animals that could come to him in the form of dowry. They also accused the whites of having destabilized the African culture. This, to a certain extent, is true. The whites undermined any good that was part of African culture. They saw it as their duty to erode the African culture and replace it with what they referred to as *'civilization,'* which was another name for the European culture. This being the case, Njoki was inviting his brother to come and taste the new way, the civilized way that was being offered by the Scottish Missionaries who had settled at Thogoto in 1898. Those who had joined them were encouraged to bring in their close relatives. This is how the missionaries got their first converts. As already hinted, there was a distorted mentality among the Kikuyus that a girl converted to Christianity had automatically entered the gateway of *"prostitution."* Another aspect is that a Kikuyu girl is valued by the parents and clan as a source of wealth due to the dowry proceeds. Thus, a girl running away from home to become a Christian was seen as a great loss for the entire family. It was seen as a displaced wealth in terms of the flock and herds that would benefit the family after the girl's marriage. It was, therefore, treated as taboo for a girl to be associated with Christianity. No wonder such a girl was cursed by the parents and the clan. On the same note, the Kikuyus hated to see a man moving from home to go and be schooled by the whites. Men were regarded as the backbone of the home.

They took care of the flocks by shepherding them and, of more importance, protecting them from being stolen by people from other communities. They were the catalyst for the human expansion of the home because they were the ones who, after marriage, brought about children. Unlike women who married and left home, men married and remained at home. This then tells you that my grandfather would be unhappy with my father going to join the indoctrination of the whites. The other reason, and possibly the worst, was the fact that a Christian girl never went through the female circumcision *"rite of passage."* Such a woman was to Africans worse than the Gentiles were to the Jews. This was even further worsened by the fact that, by becoming a Christian, one removed the African traditional clothes and wore the Western clothes that were regarded as the attire of prostitutes. Thus, for Njoki to acquire Christian indoctrination and also attain some education, she had to escape from her parent's home to Thogoto, where the Scottish Missionaries established their first mission station in Kenya in 1898.

It was here that after attaining the attributes of a Christian, including some education, Njoki got married to a man known as Robinson Gitau, who was not only a pronounced Christian but a missionary employee- a cook. This further deepened Njoki's rejection in the Kikuyu society and of her family being sidelined. Needless to say, any girl married to a Christian was regarded as an outcast and was no longer accepted in the family. This was the background through which my father was invited by his sister at Thogoto. Many relatives had discouraged my father from visiting her, stating that he might lose some credibility in his community, but he decided to go anyway. It was in the course of his stay at Thogoto that my aunt persuaded him to join the school. He then accepted, though with some reluctance. He, therefore, got enrolled at Thogoto Primary School. At this time, education was very new to the Africans, and instead of being seen as a source of knowledge, it was viewed as foolishness and a stumbling block to acquiring wealth in the form of livestock.

Let me emphasize the fact that, among the things that made Africans dissociate themselves from Christianity was because Christianity was seen as a foreign culture that affected peoples' mentality. Africans prided themselves in their culture and wanted to remain married to it. To put it point blank, the foreign culture was seen as an enemy and a threat to the lives of Africans. To a great extent, this was true because it advocated against what was considered most sacred, like polygamy, African religion and girl or female circumcision. Africans anchored their belief in a legendary prophecy by one, Mugo wa Kibiru, who himself was considered a Kikuyu prophet or medicine man. The legend had it that Mugo had prophesied having seen many white butterflies moving from Coast Mombasa), which is next to the Indian Ocean, heading to Kisumu to Lake Victoria.

He had also foretold of a big snake swallowing people and vomiting them along the way. Breathing out fire, it would likewise coil itself from Coast to Kisumu. This later came to be interpreted as white people being the butterflies and the long snake producing fire as the railway line and the train. Thus, like all the other Africans, my grandfather bitterly hated the Europeans, especially now that they had denied him wealth that he could have attained through Njoki's marriage. By God's providence, my father came to love education as soon as he tasted it. He proved to be a person with a fertile mind, and the teachers came to like him. Nevertheless, education went hand in hand with canning for mistakes committed in school, including things to do with academic performance and lateness, among others. Such were immediately corrected through canning. It then happened that one day, my father came to school late, and he was to be punished for that.

The teacher on duty was a lady, and she was the one punishing the latecomers. My father, in his Kikuyu cultural understanding, could not tolerate being canned by a woman. Among the Kikuyus, the worst insult one could make was to liken a man to a woman. That called for an immediate apology, or a fierce fight would ensue. As it would be, the teacher insisted on canning my father, and she grabbed his hand and hit him. My father reacted violently, and the headmaster had to intervene. Even then, the lady teacher hit my father with a stick on the buttocks. Immediately after being hit, my father went out swiftly to my aunt's home and got armed with a sword, a spear and a club with the intention to go and attack the lady teacher. My aunt tried to stop him, but his fury, the burning anger, was beyond my aunt's strength. Nevertheless, she made an urgent call to neighbors and another passerby and my father was held, got disarmed and therefore blocked from going to attack the teacher. He then said, *"If I cannot beat that woman, then I will not go back to that school,"* and without mincing his words, he packed and left for Ngong. As a shepherd, he had the energy and the pace to move fast, and he managed to arrive home by around 7.00 p.m. Back at home, things were not too hospitable for him. His father had been so much angered by his escape from home and enjoining himself to his sister rather than shepherd the flock.

My grandfather, therefore, confronted him and even beat him until he promised never to go back to Thogoto. Thanks to the neighbors and relatives who persuaded my grandfather to bury the hatchet. Thus, immediately, my father went back to shepherding. However, he had a persistent thirst for education. He had tasted something that was so appetizing, and he felt the urge to continue with his education. But, alas! How was he to convince his father, who so much hated the Western education as he equally hated the Europeans and their culture? It took many relatives and close friends to convince him to allow my father to attend school in the morning and then go to rear the animals in the afternoon. Now that my grandfather had agreed, my father then joined a school at a place known as Oloolua, not far from Matasia and, at the same time, easy to walk to from home. He would wake up very early in the morning and run to school. After school at 12.00 noon, he would run to where the flock of cows, sheep, and goats were, join the other shepherds in rearing them, and then help drive the flock home. He would also help in the milking of cows. At Oloolua, my father joined class 2 as he had taken some classes at Thogoto.

After some time, the District Commissioner in Ngong was concerned that there was an advance increase in livestock, which was eating a lot of foliage and grass. This was exposing the earth to scorching sun, resulting in soil erosion. He, therefore, ordered that the flocks of non-Maasai people be minimized. He spelt out the number of animals each individual should own. This meant that half of my grandfather's herd of cows was to be removed. My grandfather approached a certain man whose name was Munge, a close relative and who lived in Kikuyu land at a place known as Thathai, near a grassy plain known as Kibichu, to allow him to move some of the flock there as there was more room with no restriction. Such a flock would then be accompanied by one to shepherd it. This shepherd was to be my father, who, like all the shepherds in that area, could be grazing the flock in the huge grazing area known as Kibiku.

Munge accepted the request, and then my father accompanied this flock. This was quite a bitter pill for my father. It meant he had to stop going to school again, a halt he hated. Could he go back to Thogoto? He wouldn't be accepted, though by now, he had yielded to the cane. He had realized that caning was an appetizer to education and that every good thing called for patience, perseverance and endurance. But the truth of the matter was that he could not be accepted at Thogoto School as he had earlier messed up. In that far place, away from home and with no brother or sisters nearby, my father became quite faithful to the care of the animals, including protecting them from the Maasai invaders. His courage as a warrior won him respect and many friends. He milked the cows both in the morning and evening. He sold the milk and kept the money, often giving it to my grandfather, who occasionally came to see how the animals were faring.

One time, my grandfather came to see the flock, and he decided to sell the bull that my father loved. My father tried to convince him not to sell that bull, but he insisted on selling it, and, in his word, he sold it. This made my father so angry that he decided not to engage in shepherding the flock anymore. In protest, he went back to Thogoto at his sister's home. It was while there that my aunt introduced my father to a relative, Stevenson Githii, who was one of the early converts to Christianity and then an ordained pastor. Stephenson was among the first African theologians to study outside Kenya. He and another clergyman, Kareri, were the first clergymen to study theology in South Africa. By the time my father went to Thogoto, Stephen was both a pastor and a teacher at Thogoto, the Church of Scotland-

14

oriented school called Mambere. Due to Stephenson's influence, my father had an opportunity to continue with schooling. My father was brainy. He worked his way through making good grades. Unfortunately, when he got to class 4, his academic progress was hindered by a lack of school fees. He was supposed to pay some money for school fees, which he did not have. Stevenson persistently persuaded my grandfather to sell at least one cow to have my father continue with education, but he categorically refused to part with it, not even one cow out of the very many he had. He insisted that my father should give up schooling and concentrate on shepherding the cows. This was a big blow to my father, who had already built great hopes for advancing his education. Whatever his dreams were, he had hit a deadlock. He, therefore, went back to Ngong.

Meanwhile, while my father was pursuing education at Thogoto, he fell in love with a lady named *Mary Wangari*. They later got married, and I became their first-born child. Mary's father was Thuku Wa Wanene. Incidentally, Thuku had a number of wives, Wabai being one of them. She was also the mother to Mary. Wabai bore seven children, six girls and one boy. The latter is David Thuku, who then turned out to be my only uncle. David has been a great blessing to Thuku's offspring as he has cohesively brought the clan together. He has managed to create a firm, solidified family unity, something only imagined in many large families in modern times. Thuku (my grandfather) was well established in terms of wealth in flocks of cattle, sheep and goats. The next move that my father took was to enroll in a typewriting training institution in Nairobi.

My aunt Njoki supported him in meeting the transportation and the payment needed for the course. But there were times when my aunt could not afford his transport. At such times, my father had to walk. He would begin his journey at 6.00 am so as to be in Nairobi by 10 am. He could then take a two-hour training class and then start walking home sometimes, arriving very late in the evening. This he did for six months.

WORLD WAR II

It was soon after completing his typing course that my father learned that the recruitment for people to be involved in Second World War 11 was ongoing. Among the people needed were clerks. Now that my father had typing skills, he was easily recruited as a clerk. He was immediately assigned to join a battalion that was heading for Ethiopia. My father was an intelligent man, industrious, and a person of great integrity, maturity, and courage. He could attempt even what others would describe as impossible. He quickly gained respect among the army officers, which in turn gave him quick and successful promotions. At one time, he was to be appointed a sergeant major, a rare rank for an African.

The rank entailed the supervision of soldiers of all races, including Europeans. Europeans, who saw the great potential in my father, were overcome by jealousy and therefore conspired on how to block him from getting to that rank. The British soldiers could not imagine an African taking charge of them. The Africans, as would be expected, were looked down upon by the European soldiers. Nevertheless, my father upheld his leadership / status. The time he spent as a shepherd and his confrontation with the cow raiders, especially the Maasai, created a deep zeal in him as a fighter and a leader.

Now, the Second World War had made him travel far and wide, going all the way to Burma. After the war, my father came home. It was very unfortunate that the Africans were never rewarded by the British government. They were abandoned. This was unlike the Europeans who took part in the war. They were all rewarded with good jobs and big ranches of land, especially in what we now call Rift Valley. Thus, my father, not knowing what to do next, got a teaching job as an untrained teacher in a missionary-oriented school in Ngong. It was around 1950. This was also at a time when the Kikuyu people were widely involved in oath-taking, specifically vowing to leave no stone unturned until the British Colonialists were expelled from Kenya. My father turned out to be one of the key administrators of this oathing. This resulted in the formation of the Mau Mau Movement in which my father was the key leader in the movement. He was a regional coordinator in Maasai, the adjacent Kikuyu land, and the Nairobi area.

In the meantime, my father proved to be good at teaching, and he was therefore recommended to join Kambui Teachers' Training College, which was a boarding school located in Kiambu County. This was sixty miles from Ngong. It was headed by a white person known as Leakey. And even while in school, my father was advancing the course of the Mau Mau Movement. He was one of the prominent agitators to drive the Europeans out of Kenya, not because they were white but because of the way they oppressed the Africans. They treated them as sub-human.

Many took the Africans to be a representation of Satan and evil due to what they call *"their black skin"* and those with what they called *"Whites"* as a representation of angels and purity. No wonder, then, my father, among others, aggressively mobilized Africans. He was so handy that, as much as he was involved in learning, he still retained his leadership position as the regional secretary and chief organizer of the movement in the areas I mentioned above. He did much of his consultations during the weekends and on holidays. Sometimes, he could sneak out of school, even at night, to carry out the agenda of the Mau Mau movement. He had a great advantage over many other people because of his education, for having been exposed to life outside Kenya, and even having interacted with people of other races in the course of his travel during the Second World War.

Oath-taking was the binding ritual. It involved taking, among other things, a slaughtered animal (uncastrated he-goat or a ram). It was ritualistic. Suffice it to say that 70% of the Kikuyus nationwide (which was and still is the largest tribe in Kenya) took the oath. It also happened that a higher percentage of Kenyans who confronted the British in land matters were the Kikuyus. It is also important to recognize that many other people from the 42 tribes in Kenya played a role in the endeavor to decolonize Kenya. Thousands of the Mau Mau fighters were killed by the British, while many ended up in various detention camps that had been purposely set up to lock up members of the Mau Mau Movement and their supporters. In the process, thousands of people died. Many others died in the forests, engaging in guerrilla warfare. Those who championed this course were the former African soldiers who had been engaged in the Second World War. Those Africans who did not end up in jails and forests were placed in concentration camps so that their movements could be monitored by the British colonialists. It was also a way of preventing the common people from supporting the Mau Mau either by food supply or ammunition. Of course, there were many other Kenyans, including some Kikuyus, who opted to be loyal to the British. Such were called loyalists and other Home Guards.

As hinted above, one of the things that really motivated the Kenyans to engage the British was the skills learnt and the exposure and experience in their involvement in the Second World War. Prior to the war, the Africans' concept of the whites was that they had the power and status of Angels. They even did not think that they had the same body as Africans. One of the common beliefs was that a white person could not die. Then, when they went to the Second World War, they witnessed many of the British soldiers wounded, crying for help and dying just like Africans. Thus, they came to realize that their bodies, apart from their white skin, were similar to that of Africans. They then understood that a white person is also vulnerable to death, fear, hunger, despair, sickness, and all other natural human occurrences. They also realized that the whites were not superior to Africans; thus, they had no reason to colonize them.

The experience of being a leader in the Second World War made my father very militant. He thus played a great role in the confrontation between the British and Freedom Fighters as they were commonly known. In fact, while my father was busy in class, he, at the same time, was monitoring the struggle for independence. Already, the Mau Mau Movement was causing havoc in the country through their guerilla war against the British. Also, at this time, many people were surrendering to the colonialists, and in doing so, they were renouncing the people who were known to be leaders in the Mau Mau Movement. In this way, all the people who surrendered in the Ngong area and some parts of Kikuyu land mentioned my father as the key leader and the person who administered the oaths. They portrayed him as a recognized, respected and a dangerous Mau Mau Movement leader. As a result, my father got blacklisted by the colonialists, and no wonder then, he turned out to be one of the most wanted of the so-called *"Mau Mau terrorists."* He was to be contained under every circumstance.

THE ARREST

As stated above, my father was one of the most wanted *"terrorists."* But this time, he was already in school and could not be picked without going through the school administration. So, they could wait for a time when they could get some evidence to have the school's administration surrender him. Such an opportunity came when one of his letters to the Mau Mau leaders was intercepted. In this letter, he encouraged the fighters to keep on and never give up. He reminded them of heroes like Kwame Nkrumah of Ghana, Mahatma Gandhi, and Indra Gandhi of India, who fought tirelessly for their country, and they made it because they loved their countries more than their own lives. That is to say, they were ready to die so long as their countries got liberated, especially for the sake of future generations. Upon learning this, the police were dispatched to go and get him from college. Already, the principal of the school had found my father a potential teacher, one able to grasp teaching skills easily, and a respectable person bearing a variety of talents. For that reason, the principal, who, of course, was a white person, refused to hand him over to the police. He could not release him, and even more so because he was the school captain.

By virtue of his being a European and, therefore, part of the government, the principal had authority over the students' protection, especially as far as school matters were concerned. This proves that among the Europeans, we had some good people who did not look down on Africans. After all of him, my father studied in a missionary-founded school at both Thogoto and Ololua at Ngong, which, in this case, were Christian schools. The principal took it for granted that my father was well-grounded in Christianity. For that reason, he even defended himself from suspicion that he was a Mau Mau leader. But the police inspector who was the leader of that group of police persisted that my father had been the chief Mau Mau organizer doing all secretarial work while he was still a teacher. This way, he could not be easily suspected. That it was while he was in the college that the government learnt of his destructive role as Mau Mau leader and that he was deeply involved in the oath-taking and the agenda to expel the British from Kenya. He told the principal that the revelation came through those who had surrendered from being members of Mau Mau to becoming loyalists to the British, including the intercepted letter. In spite of these persistent demands, the principal refused to part with my father. He told them;

"Deal with him when he is out of school. I would hate to see him go. He is one of my best students, a person with potential leadership qualities. He is very gifted. We should not destroy every African for the sake of grabbing their land. Their conscience cannot allow them to keep quiet."

This further shows that not all Europeans supported the British colonization of Africans. The government then timed my father at the time the college would close for the holiday. This was determined as the best opportune time to arrest him without any resistance. Thus, no sooner had my father arrived home for the holiday than the police came home and arrested him. I am always suspicious that the two policemen who came for him were sympathetic to the Mau Mau movement. This is because, although I was very

young, I remember overhearing one of the policemen telling
my father,

> *"If it were not for the directive from the police commander that
> we take you today, I would have let you organize things in your
> home tonight, but now that we are under the obligation to take
> you, I'm sorry that our hands are tied. I hope all will be well
> with you. Otherwise, the accusations framed against you are
> not good. I suspect that the repercussions might turn out to be
> bad. Nevertheless, we will do our best to save you even if it also
> means we're getting into trouble."*

I then heard my father's response, saying, *"I have a feeling
that my life will be different from this moment."*

He then turned to my mother and said,

> *"Have courage. If you will never see me again, remember it is
> all about this nation; it is all about this soil we are stepping on;
> it is all about the future generations. Take care of Muhia and
> Githang'a. I believe that God, who rescued me from the
> dangers of the Second World War, will, in his own miraculous
> way, bring me back to you. My greatest wish is to have Muhia
> and Githang'a attain education, and if I ever do not come back,
> God will pave the way for their education. Then he shook her
> hand, grabbing it for a while and then they left."*

By this, my mother was bitterly crying. I watched my father
as he shook my mother's hand. I could not understand it,
but I felt something was wrong, especially when I saw tears
freely flowing from my mother's eyes down her cheeks,
something that I had never seen before. Even as she
watched my father until they went out of sight, I was
uncertain of how to respond to the awkward moment.
Those last words from my father's mouth became a treasure

that I cherished. He was out of sight but not out of my mind. I had earlier heard both my father and mother talk about my getting into nursery school. I had heard them talk about some school requirements like the new slate. By then, there were no exercise books, especially for beginners; instead, pupils used slates and special chalk rather than pencils. Already, the school uniform was being tailored, and other requirements were being processed. I gathered the courage to ask my mother, *"Where has my father gone? When do I go to school?"* Little did I know that the opportunity to begin school evaporated with my father's departure that day. The only thing I remember is crying a lot and persistently asking my mother when I was to go to school. This shedding of tears was enhanced when I saw kids from my neighborhood and my playmates coming from school in uniform. I remember my mother also shedding tears, but hardly did I realize the bitterness saturating her tears was because of the high chances of being called a widow any time, for there were no known cases of people who were in my father's category of having strong involvement with Mau Mau Movement that escaped the gallows.

ESCAPE FROM POLICE CUSTODY

After being arrested, my father was taken to Ngong Police Station, where he was put in a cell for some time. Then, there was a plot to eliminate him, but in a very unsuspicious way. Thus, his enemies resolved that at a certain time at night, my father would be told that he was to be moved to a different cell. Then, as soon as he was out, he would be shot, and the report would be that he was shot as he was escaping from the police cell. What an evil plan! It was like the devil had vowed that my father should never survive. But what the devil had forgotten was that;

"Those that wait upon the Lord shall renew their strength; they shall mount up with wings as eagles; they shall run, and not be weary; and they shall walk, and not faint" (Isaiah 40:31).

God had already appointed the two policemen and the one guarding the police station gate. The two did not want to leave any stone unturned until they made way for my father's escape. They realized that unless they acted swiftly, they could soon witness the flow of my father's blood. Thus, the night that the deadly plan was to take place, one of these friendly policemen and possibly one who had taken an oath went secretly to my father and with tears flowing from his eyes. He told him:

"This night is the darkest night in your life, for you will be killed. The plan is that they will pretend to move you out of this room to another one, and as soon as you are out, you will be shot on the pretext that you were escaping. Now listen, remain on watch the whole day, and as soon as I notice that there is nobody in sight within the compound, I will cough

*three times consecutively, and since I am not locking the door
of this room, you will immediately go out and head towards the
main gate, we have also arranged that one of those trying to
save you will be manning the gate. Thus, as I will be coughing
in pretext as a sign for you to leave the room, I will at the same
time give a sign to the gatekeeper, who will then go to the toilet.
Thus, as you pass through the gate, he will not be there. In case
someone happens to ask you where you are going, tell him that
I have sent you to buy some cigarettes for me, but even as you
talk to this person, be on the move. As soon as you are out of
the gate, get into the bush and run for your life."*

Having explained to my father what was coming up and
what he had to do in the way of escape, the policeman
hugged my father as he said:

*"There are a number of us here who have vowed to save your
life. Now, I leave you in God's hands. This is the much we can
do, but God can do exceedingly more in safeguarding your life.
We have also made it work out that your escape will not be
known until that time; they will be sending someone to tell you
that you are being shifted to another room, and this will be the
early morning hours of the next day. This will give you time
to get in touch with your wife, possibly at night, and put your
domestic plans in order."*

The policeman then left, wiping tears from his eyes with a
handkerchief. At around 11 am, the police friend coughed
three times, upon which my father went out, and before
long, he was out of the gate, then got into the bushes and
ran as fast as his legs could carry him. What happened
within the police station after his escape, we have no record
of it.

LIFE IN THE FOREST

That day, in which my father escaped from the police station, he hid in the bushes but not far from our home for the home was adjacent to the forest as he waited for the darkness to envelop the environment. He stealthily went home, knocked on the window next to the bed and whispered to my mother to open the door. He was in the house for a substantial part of the night as he narrated to my mother what to do and what to watch out for.

I am sure they also talked a few other things about home and the way my brother Githang'a and I were to be brought up. The parting was difficult, painful and tearful. I did not know of his presence since I was asleep. In any case, they held their talks in a low whisper. At a certain time, deep in the night, he bid my mother goodbye. I was awakened by the sobbing of my mother as both were crying bitterly as each one of them realized that the chances of seeing each other alive again were remote. My father went out carrying some packed food and water.

The next destination that very night was his sister Nyamaiga's home. Her home was in an isolated place and next to thick bushes, so he felt safe, and he was sure that the news in regard to his escape had not yet leaked out as he was sure his friends in the police station were to keep to their words. Having reached Nyamaiga's home, he knocked on the door and whispered to her to open it. Having opened the door, my father called her out, and they went into a nearby bush. My father explained the situation, and the two made quick plans on how he was to hide. He was to spend time in a very remote part of the forest where neither shepherds nor the women who collected firewood went. It was a place that was feared for some taboo reasons. They made arrangements on how and where my father would come late at night, pick food, eat and leave the utensils there – it was a stone's throw away from my aunt's home.

After every three days, the two had to meet so that she could update him on the developments, especially the government's reaction to his escape. The news of my father's escape was relayed on the morning radio broadcast, and soldiers dispersed to hunt for him. Their first target was our home. Thus, at around 10.00 am, I was playing a game not far from home when, to my surprise, I saw men heading to our house with swords, clubs, spears and all kinds of ammunition. They were coming from every direction. I remember the two who passed where I was playing the game asked me, *"Hapa ndiye nyumbani kwa Benson Githii?* (Is this the home of Benson Githii?) And quite innocently, I replied, *"Ndio"* (Yes).

What followed was beyond my understanding. Within minutes, the entire fence surrounding our home was flattened, and many of the soldiers and policemen were already in the house. Others were busy on the roof, plowing through the grass that had thatched our house. I later learnt that the search on the roof was geared towards checking for any hidden files or documents, for that matter, that could help in learning more about the Mau Mau movement. Those inside the house were doing the same, searching for any evidence or files, money or his presence. It seemed they never found anything. The next thing I remember was my mother being whipped, kicked about, slapped and beaten with thick sticks and forcefully being asked to reveal where my father was, where the Mau Mau documents were kept, who were my father's associates, etc. I remember my mother weeping in a lot of pain as she got kicked and beaten, but she insisted that she knew nothing about the escape of my father, and she had no knowledge of his involvement in the Mau Mau leadership.

I do not remember much of what happened next - the only other thing I remember is that, after much beating and harassment, the attackers finally left our premises. I remember my mother continuing to cry for some time and nursing the wounds that had much blood oozing out of them. She was in great pain.

The next day, we were awakened very early in the morning by the area chief, whose name was Gatuiku. He knocked on the door with a lot of velocity and urgency. My mother nervously quickly opened the door. Upon getting in, the chief did not even greet my mother; instead, he shouted at her, saying,
"You are supposed to be at the District Commissioner's Office by nine this morning. So, prepare yourself like someone who is not coming back. Get ready while I and the people with me look around the house; we still think there could be some valuable documents that could help us in tracing the involvement of your husband in the Mau Mau Movement".

After some time, the chief came back and called out my mother, saying,
"Come out now. You are already getting late in making it to the DC's office by nine. Remember, you will get yourself into

more problems if you get there late." I then saw the chief stretch his hand towards my mother, saying, *"Close the house and hand over the keys to me. Also, give me the keys to your granary. I can see you have an abundant harvest. Unfortunately, you will not eat any of these. The chances are that you will not be coming back to your house."*

It was as a result of this last statement that my mother made a request that she be allowed to carry some important items from the house, but to her surprise, the chief said, *"From this moment, you own nothing in this house."* My mother then handed over both the house keys and one of the granaries. The latter was full of maize (corn), beans in sacks, potatoes, peas, sorghum, etc. The house had a lot of expensive things, some of which my father had brought from World War II. I remember my mother persistently pleading with him to allow her to take some items from the house and leave them in the neighborhood so that she could pick them up later, but the chief harshly responded,

"Get out of here, or I will as well label you a Mau Mau terrorist, which will automatically place you in jail! I am only sympathizing with these children; otherwise, I am as well aware that you have taken the Mau Mau oath. Your husband had prided himself on being a teacher; now, he will be nothing if not a corpse."

Crying bitterly, my mother handed him all the keys, meaning that from that moment, we owned nothing. The chief handed over the keys to his bodyguard. My mother was not even allowed to carry anything, not even a dress or a blanket, let alone plates, cups or working tools. Meanwhile, leaving his bodyguard to guard the house, the chief went with his other guards to flash in the nearby bushes just in case my father could be hiding there. This bodyguard was sympathetic to my mother's pathetic situation, and I also learnt later that he was a good friend of my father. It was then he opened the door and told my mother to go and get some items like money and food for the child and a few other items she could handle. Meanwhile, he was watching the movement of the chief. He had told my mother,

"If you hear me tell the chief, 'Have you also checked the bush behind the toilet?' then you will come out quickly, for by then, the chief will be coming out of the bush."

He then told my mother to get started for the DC's Office. So, by the time the chief came out of the bush, my mother had already left. I remember my mother breathing and sweating heavily as she kept on encouraging me about the serious consequences if she failed to show up at the DC's office by nine. Moreover, the DC was to leave by 10 am, and if she kept him waiting, she would be jailed without a trial. By God's providence, we made it.

The Chief also came as we arrived. Immediately we arrived, we were summoned inside. The DC was a stout, tall man. We were never given a seat. The DC seemed to be breathing fire as he cast a hostile look at my mother. After this long, hateful look, the DC asked my mother through the chief as the interpreter;

"You woman, wife of a Mau Mau terrorist, I understand you have hidden your husband - are you forgetting that the government has a long hand and that I can now order you and your children to be put in jail?" He went on, *"Do you want*

me to put you in now? Tell me the whereabouts of your husband."

My mother nervously said, *"I have no idea where he is. The last time I saw him was when he was taken away by two policemen."*

Burning with anger, the DC went on, *"Do you realize that the escape of your husband has jeopardized my position?"* Then he turned to the chief, who, throughout this time, was interpreting the communication between my mother and DC on what he was saying to her. Then the DC wrote something down, handed it to the chief and immediately the DC left vibrating in anger. Before the chief said what the DC had written on the paper, he asked my mother;

"Where do you go from here? In response, my mother said, *"We will be going to Gikambura, where my parents reside; it is my birthplace."*

The chief read and interpreted what the DC had written to my mother. He said,

"The DC has given an order that you immediately leave the Ngong area. Meanwhile, I will try to look for some means of transport to take you to the border of Ngong and Kiambu, the district you will be going to."

It was already 11 am, and no effort was being made. The chief's plan was for us to get late so that our lives would be terminated. No wonder then, he had left us there being sun baked. No one even came near us. Not even the very neighbours who happened to be around the offices. None approached us for fear of the consequences. We got very thirsty and hungry. It was at 3.00 pm that someone came and told my mother that the chief had sent him to inform us that no vehicle was available for our transportation. He was at the same time reminding us of the fact that we were expected to be out of Ngong area by 6.00 pm. Otherwise, there was the possibility of being treated as suspects of taking food to the Mau Mau terrorists who had taken their cover in the forest. When this information got to my mother's ears, she started not only breathing heavily but got into heavy sweating. I could see drops of sweat falling from her face, and even her clothes were turning wet from the sweat. I believe that it dawned on my mother the chief had no intentions of getting us a transport vehicle. Shockingly, and as if a bomb had fallen on us, my mother cried bitterly and tightly held on to my hand, saying,

"Muhia, let us go. If this is our day to say goodbye to this world, I leave everything in God's hands. I know you are hungry and thirsty, but what can we do? Our souls are already trapped for death, but God has the final word."

It was by then that I realized how precarious our lives were, and I joined my mother in crying bitterly. Remember, we had no time to have breakfast that morning, and we had no lunch, and now we were not only faced with death but also a long walk, if not a long run. Remember, as well, I was of a tender age, and even running was hard for me. My mother had carried my younger brother, Githang'a, who was just a few months old. This was in 1952. We started what looked like a marathon.

We had no shoes, and we had to pass through thorny bushes and rocky ground. The Journey was long and tough. Many times, I felt like my legs had refused to carry me, but in an attempt to sit down, my mother would revive my strength. She would say,

> *"Muhia, I know you are hungry, thirsty, tired and sweating, but remember we have to be out of Ngong area the soonest as possible, and worse still, we have to cross the Kibiku plains by 7.00 pm before the wild animals start coming out of the forest, But I know soon we shall get some food."*

Kibiku is where people let in flocks of sheep, goats and herds of cattle for grazing during the day. It was next to a huge forest. Yes, this was a dangerous journey. The area between Ngong and Gikambura was populated with wild animals, including cheetahs, buffalos, hyenas, etc. Our lives seemed held between the jaws of death. Soon after dark, they would come out into the plain. They would be wandering there looking for any carcasses of dead animals. These would include cows and goats or any animal that might have strayed from the rest of the herds and was, therefore, left behind without the shepherds' knowledge. There were also wild animals like zebras and antelopes that lived within this grassy plain, which other wild animals would come out to hunt. Tens of flocks grazed in this huge Kibiku plain during the day.

How it all happened, I cannot really tell, but after much hunger, fatigue, being tired, the fear of unknown, and what I trust to be angelic guidance, we finally arrived at my grandfather's home at around 8 in the evening. It was already dark, and they could hardly believe their eyes when they saw us. I remember my grandmother, Wabai, seemingly angry, asking my mother, *"Wangari, how dare you come here at this time of the day with your children? What if you got consumed by the wild animals? What has happened to you? Are you mentally okay?"*

My mother could not answer the series of questions immediately. She was still breathing heavily, and her body looked like she had come out of some kind of a pool. The sweating was overwhelming. They had already eaten their evening meal, yet our stomachs were empty. We had to wait for another hour before our dish could be ready. What a day! What a night!

My aunt had continued to feed my father secretly for some time, but then his being hunted became quite intensified. Many policemen and regular Home Guards were being dispersed at night to roam around the paths leading to Ngong Hills. It was then that my father advised my aunt to go to Gikambura and tell one of his age mates about his predicament and hence make arrangements for him to go and hide him.

My aunt did exactly that. She consulted with Thaba wa Tharuba, as his age mate was known. A way was then paved for the move of my father to Gikambura, not far from the present Gikambura Primary School. He was hidden in a garden somewhere far from home, where a big hole that looked like a cave was dug. It was there that he was being fed, both in the morning and evening.

He was also informed of the current political situation in the country. After some time, it became clear that someone had leaked out the presence of my father within the surroundings. One home guard who was also the age mate of my father informed Thaba that, soon, a detergent of home guards was to be released to come and intensively look for my father in the surroundings. This move could put Thaba and his family in a precarious position. For this reason, a method was urgently formulated to transfer my father back to Ngong area until the hunt had calmed down. So, with the same urgency, he was smuggled back to Ngong area. This time he would spend the day deep in the forest and valleys of Ngong Hills. He would travel late evening to collect food near my aunt's home, and as often as possible my aunt would update him on the political developments. Then, he would travel back to the bushes and ravines of Ngong Hills, where his life was at the mercy of the wild animals. He was constantly in danger of being eaten up by wild animals. While narrating his story, he told me that his main protection from the animals was a smelly soap that he had put in his trousers pocket. All animals, including lions, hated this smell.

I remember him talking of a night when he was almost knocked down by a lion that was fast chasing an antelope. The lion stepped on stones near him, and the movement of the stones was so fast that if any of the stones knocked him, it would have disabled or killed him. It was a very lonely life, in darkness and with death ever beckoning him. The reader should bear in mind that, all this time, my father had not had a shower. His life was fast turning to be like a monkey's life. He had become very hairy. Sadly, the hunting of my father intensified. By then through Thaba and my aunt, my father got connected to a man who had slipped from the government's hands and was as well hiding in the bushes. For lack of his name, I will just call him Mwitengia. Mwitengia had a sister who was married to a Maasai and lived far beyond the Ngong Hills. A way was paved and this man and my father got connected. My father then moved from Ngong area and went to hide in the company of Mwitengia, now far beyond Ngong Hills.

Mwitengia's sister would wrap food in a container with fermented milk and sometimes porridge. This was in a sack that she would then tie with a rope hanging it at her back. She would then walk into the bushes pretending that she was going to fetch firewood. She would go deep in the bushes, meet the two at an appointed spot, feed them and also update them on the political mood of the country. Other times, she could leave the food in a designated place where the two would come at night and feed on it. Then, after some time, they would shift to the surroundings of my aunt's, where she would feed them for some time. Then, after a while, they would revert to being in the hands of the Mwitengia's sister. This went on for a long period, like a game of hide and seek.

By then, and by use of helicopters that flew over the forests and the bushy areas, the government was dropping pamphlets making appeals to those hiding in the forests to come out, indicating total forgiveness for any of the people in the forests who would surrender. Whoever surrendered would come out holding a green branch. Such a person would be pardoned and continue to carry on the normal life. Mwitengia had six sisters who then conspired to persuade their brother to surrender. They accompanied the sister who fed them, and calling their brother aside, they could persistently plead with him to surrender and, at times, cried bitterly. He resisted their call for him to surrender but finally yielded when they brought their parents to speak to Mwitengia. He could not resist the tears, and he, therefore, surrendered, leaving my father alone in the forest.

MY FATHER'S FINAL ARREST

Upon the surrender, Mwitengia was told by the government,
"We have learned that you were in the company of Benson Githii. This is the deal, while we appreciate your surrendering, we cannot forgive you unless you give us tips that will lead to the arrest of Benson Githii. Otherwise, failure to do that, you will end up in the gallows."

Having said that, he was handcuffed, put in the police vehicle and taken to a Police Station. While there, he was so much tortured to the point of death. Again, his sisters and parents persistently urged him to reveal the whereabouts of my father. Finally, the man gave in and said, *"The person who can lead you to capturing Benson is his sister, known as Nyamaiga."* That was enough to trigger my father's arrest. He was one of the most wanted Mau Mau terrorists in Maasai and Kikuyu land, and it was felt that his arrest and killing would be a great blow and demoralization of the Mau Mau Movement, which was still gaining strength day by day.

The government equated my father with other Mau Mau terrorists like Dedan Kimathi, who were too slippery to arrest, yet they were the catalysts for the Mau Mau Movement. No sooner was this vital information released by the Mwitengia's than policemen were immediately sent to my aunt's home. They met her peeling some potatoes for the evening meal, which also included my father's meal. The first question they put to her was, *"Where is your brother Githii?"* In response she said, *"I have never seen him since the time he got arrested.*" It was then that the policemen grabbed her by the neck and pulled her to the ground, inflicting pain on her whole body by kicking, slapping and clubbing. She was even threatened with being slashed into pieces as she was being shown swords that had been drawn out. She was beaten, and she kept on asking, "*Riu murahurira ki, mwoiga munjurage tuhu? Ngai wakwa nduke uturute ukomboini wa athungu, ndakua tiiri! ndakua tiiri!?*" (Why are you beating me with no reason, why kill me for nothing, oh my God come and liberate us from this oppressive spirit of colonialism, am dying because of soil).

It was when she became almost unconscious that their leader, fuming with anger and lifting the sword up, ready to strike on the well-spread-out throat that the other policemen, said to my aunt, "*Say no and die or say yes and live - do you know where Benson your brother is?*"

Then he said, "*I will count up to ten and by the tenth time, if you will not have said yes, I will slash your throat.*" And true to his word, he started counting, "*One… two…three…*" It was at the eighth counting that my aunt said, "*Yes.*"

Then the policeman said, "*Leave her alone.*" He then commanded all other police to retreat, and he and other police went on interrogating my aunt. She confessed that she did feed my father, and then she took them to where she used to feed him. She was bitterly crying even as she responded to their question, "*Niaroka utuku wa umuthi na akoruo niguori, eguka thaa cigana? ("Is he coming here today, and if so, at what time?")* She responded, "*Eguka thaa ithatu cia utuku*" (He will come at 9.00 pm").

They then went with her to the Police Station, and all police - including those on leave, were summoned. The Officer Commanding the Police Station said,

> *"At long last, we are on the verge of capturing one of the most wanted gangsters in Maasai and Kikuyu land. Each of you has to play his role diligently to rule off any mistake that would hinder his capture, dead or alive. The implicated person for that hindrance will be condemned to die. What I mean is missing to take that life will result in taking your life."*

By 8.00 pm, the entire police force in Ngong was strategically aligned, surrounding the place where my father was to appear within the next hour. Every policeman was burning with anger, and all thirsted for my father's blood. The only strip of ground that was not guarded was the one which he would come through. The path was well trodden, as he had come there several times. In any case, there would be people to immediately occupy that path immediately after he had passed. My aunt was under very strict instructions not to tell him anything apart from asking him loudly, *"Niwoka?"* (Have you come?). She was also under instruction to speak to him from afar and then move very quickly after my father had responded to her greetings; otherwise, she would be killed as well. At exactly 9 in the evening, innocently and unsuspecting, my father came in and sat down under the hedge, which somehow hid him from the surrounding view.

My aunt was then released to go and talk to him just for an assurance that he was really there. She had to be very careful; otherwise, her blood would mingle with her brother's blood. And so off she went. As instructed, as she approached him, she shouted from afar, *"Niwoka?"* (You have come?) No sooner had my father said, *"Yes,"* than all the surrounding bushes vibrated with rapid movements. It was like all the bushes and grasses were being uprooted. The ground vibrated with swords, spears, and clubs raised high in the air, ready to strike. But alas! A plot had already been carried out by those who did not want my father killed but rather to be arrested alive. One thing that is worth noting is that, my father was recognized as a strong leader and one who commanded a lot of respect among the people, both Maasai and Kikuyus.

There was also the other vital aspect that even among the police force, there were those who had secretly taken the oath to the effect that one would never kill anyone fighting for the course of freedom. Most of such policemen were at the forefront of the arrangements on how my father would be killed, yet it was only on the pretext that their agenda was to save his life. All those who were after saving my father were placed to be the closest ones to where my father was to appear. Thus, some of these loyal policemen had been instructed to fall upon my father as a cover. They were to do this; immediately, my father's voice had come out of his mouth. The others were to fight back those who would aggressively be thirsting for my father's blood. The strategy was that the person known to be very fierce, one who could strike immediately, was given two or three people to stop him from acting, i.e., immediately one could move to strike, such was to be guarded by two or even three people. As soon as the aggressor lifted his weapon to strike, the defenders would place the sword on the aggressive man's neck while at the same time, another person would be pointing at his heart with a spear, telling him, "*Make a move, and then I strike you.*"

It then happened that, immediately after my father spoke, about five policemen without their weapons drawn rushed very fast and lay on top of my father, giving him total protection such that there was no way a sword, spear or club would have reached him. The people fighting to save my father had formed a hedge around the five lying on top of him, something that made it difficult for the killer group to penetrate and reach the victim. The fighting went on for about thirty minutes. Many became wounded, though none died. It was then the Police Provincial Commanding Officer (PPCO) arrived and hurriedly ran to the scene. Upon arrival, he said, "*Is he dead or alive?*" The officer in charge said, "*He is still alive.*"

Then the PPCO said, "*Stop! Everyone retreats from the scene.*" Then, every policeman moved out. The PPCO, accompanied by Ngong Police Commanding Officer, then went to where my father was lying. To their disbelief, there then was my father lying on the ground but still breathing normally and safely. The officer looked at him and asked him, "*Are you the real Benson we have been hunting like a lion?*" My father responded, "*Yes, my name is Benson Githii.*" He asked him, "*Have you been hurt?*" My father responded, "*No.*" The officer then said to him, "*Neither am I going to hurt you.*" He then asked the policeman who had accompanied him to handcuff him. The PPCO then placed my father in the hands of two faithful policemen to take him to the chief's camp. That policeman chose two of the policemen who had acted as his cover when he was under attack. All the other

44

policemen were told to go back to their respective police posts. The two policemen started for the chief's camp.

The two of them were really kind to him. They even encouraged him for the course he was fighting for. One of them told him,

"Don't take us as enemies. We are also in this fight but in disguise. If all of us were in the forest or in the detention camps, who would be taking care of the wounded, secretly delivering weapons to those in the forest, including some medical facilities and food, and passing the thoughts and plans of the colonialists to the freedom fighters and if all African men die who then would raise the flag after the Mzungu (white man) goes home? It is important that we have people in all faculties of life, in prisons, hospitals, police force, among the chiefs, teachers, home guards, etc."

When they asked how my father was feeling, he stated that he was feeling pangs of hunger. Hence, on the way, the two policemen stopped in one of pro-Mau Mau's homes, where they had my father fed with milk and Ugali (thick porridge). The party arrived at the chief's camp shortly before midnight. My father was placed in a room. In the morning, at around 10.00 am, he was made to sit in an open place guarded by four armed people who were positioned at a distance. Don't forget that the chief here is the very Gatuiku who had grabbed all that my father had after demanding the keys to both the house and the granary from my mother. It also means it was in our former home neighborhood. By this time, our house had been demolished. Then, the worst almost happened two days after my father got arrested. As usual my father had been placed in the open space under some guards armed with arrows. He was enjoying the sunshine. At around noon, two people came cycling very fast towards him. These people were possibly sponsored by some people in authority to kill him. They seemed to be in a business that had to be finished really quickly, and without waiting for the bicycles to stop, they just jumped, pulled out each a glittering sword, and hurriedly ran towards him with the swords raised up and ready to strike. But just a few steps from him, my father saw death, and immediately he shouted to them;

"What is the problem and yet the DC has just finished interrogating me here, and he has authorized that no one should touch me; otherwise, such a person will be severely punished?"

Then one of them rather hesitantly said, *"Where is he?"* My father replied, *"He has just left and authorized the chief that no one should touch me."* As if a kind of a switch had been applied for a stop, the two men quickly returned their swords to the sheaths and hurriedly cycled away. The mention of DC (District Commissioner} and what he had authorized saved my father from death. Thank God who gave wisdom to my father to be able to manipulate these two would-be killers. The truth of the matter is that my father just made up that story! He had not seen the DC, but God gave him that insight, for his soul was in God's hands. This fits well with God's Word in Jeremiah 29, verse 11, which says, *"For I know the plans I have for you...plans to prosper you and not to harm you."* It also reminds me of Psalm 138:7, *"Though I walk in the midst of trouble, you preserve my life; you stretch out your hand against the anger of my foes, with your hand you save me."*

Meanwhile, the day came when my father was to appear in the court of law. My father's enemies had already plotted to leave no stone unturned until my father's blood was poured to the last drop. The police and the administration were especially angered by the way many of the policemen got wounded during my father's arrest. Some were seriously wounded. They did not want to stop from anything other than to see my father undergoing a death sentence. One of the so angered persons was the court prosecutor. He was to implicate my father by distorting whatever my father would say in response to the judge's inquiries. The judge was to carry on the interrogation in English, and the court prosecutor would carry out the interpretation in both Kikuyu and English. My father was to communicate through Kikuyu language. The judge was a white man. The case began at around ten in the morning. This then was the flow of the case:

Judge: *"How many years have you been a Mau Mau Leader?"*

Githii: *"Ndiri ndakorwo ndi wa Mau Mau" (I have never been associated with Mau Mau).*

Court Judge: *Court "I have been a Mau Mau since the movement started."*

Judge: *"What has been your main contribution to the Mau Mau movement?"*

Githii: *"Ta uguo ndoiga ndiri ndakorwo nginyitanira na Mau Mau na nii ndiri undu njui wigie Mau Mau" (As I have said, I have not been collaborating with the Mau Mau and I know nothing about that movement). "*

Court: *"I have been one of their key leaders, and we managed to cause quite some harassment to the British government and that has always been my agenda."*

By now, the judge's anger was building up even as he asked my father the next question, saying,

Judge: *"Is it you who led Mau Mau terrorists that attacked Ngong Police Post, killing a home guard and running away with a gun?"*

Githii: *"Nii onandiui kana kwi post ya Ngong yahuritwo."* (I am not even aware that there was any attack in Ngong police post).

Court: *"Yes, I recall that as one of our most successful raids, but I was not directly involved in the killing of the policeman, neither did I take the gun."*

The judge, burning with anger, with both his lips and hands trembling due to anger, said,

Judge: *"I don't want any further evidence. You are the kind of Mau terrorists that the government should get rid of and in this case (he was now bending to write down the judgment) I declare that you have been found guilty and I..."*

At this point, my father interjected, but this time speaking in English.

Githii: *"Sir, before you pass the judgment, please allow me to say something."*

Looking at my father and, more than anything else, amazed that he could speak English. The judge had all this time taken him as a totally typical illiterate African, especially because he had his ears roped. The judge, gazing surprisingly at my father, then put the pen down and took a position that really indicated that he was eager to listen to this seemingly learned African.

It was then that my father went through all the questions the judge had earlier asked him through the court prosecutor, plus the prosecutor's explanation. Now, the judge's anger turned to the court prosecutor. Fuming with anger, he said to him,

Judge: *"Do you deny that is what he said? And if so, why tell lies in the court? What benefit would you attain if this man is condemned to death. Your case does not end here; I will pursue it further"* (Now with less hostile face he addressed my father) *"Meanwhile, Mr. Benson, I have liked your courage in defending yourself but since I also believe that you have some deep involvement in the Mau Mau Movement, I have reverted my earlier intention to condemn you to die. This time my judgment is that you be detained for seven years with hard labour."* At that point, the judge stood and left.

My father was then handcuffed and was led outside to board a police vehicle to start his detention. Meanwhile, the court prosecutor had followed him to the vehicle, and as my father was getting ready to get into the vehicle, the court prosecutor, fuming with anger and at the same time, raising high a very thick stick, said to my father, *"How dare you question my interpretation to the judge?"* It was then that he forcefully brought down the thick stick, hitting my father so hard that he knocked him to the ground. My father was helped to his feet by the vehicle driver and others who rushed to his rescue even as they confronted the court prosecutor for that horrible action. One of them told him,

"This man is innocent; otherwise, you are guilty of wanting him to die. Your day is coming. You have greatly manipulated peoples' cases, and by that, you have shed a lot of blood. That blood continues to cry from the soil."

From there, the driver got into the steering wheel and finally stopped at the doors of MacKinnon Road Prison, where my father started seven years' imprisonment with hard labour. I am always thankful to God in that in spite of the widely opened jaws of death that was to swallow my father. God blocked the mouths of lions as he did for Daniel. I always figured out that as much as God wanted to save my father, he did it with some focus on my father's offspring, including me and our children and that generation that would emerge from my father's DNA. Looking back and also looking at the establishment of my call so far, I can see why God preserved my father's life as a way to preserve my life as well.

At the same time, knowing that God's call at times involves crucifixion, which is wrapped up by suffering without bitterness. It is one that is geared only by determination in total trust and faith in God. It will mean experiencing genuine breaking and crushing of self, which will be used to afflict the heart and conquer the fear of the unknown. Many Christians fail to trust God through His word that says,

"I have summoned you by name…. you are mine. When you walk through the fire, you will not be burned; the flames will not set you ablaze" (Isaiah 43:1-2).

God has a very profound mission he has assigned to me. Some of it has been accomplished, but there is still more to come.

2. LIFE IN MY GRANDFATHER'S HOMESTEAD

As my father went through the forest ordeal, we were slowly settling at my grandfather's homestead at Gikambura. This was my maternal grandfather, Thuku Wa Wanene. We were, therefore, living with my mother's relatives at my grandfather's homestead. During this time, I would accompany a certain old man every day to shepherd my grandfather's huge herd of cattle and a flock of goats and sheep. I always remember how every evening, I would meet my grandfather at the home entrance, waiting for the animals to come. Every day, he praised me for being such a good shepherd. All the animals' stomachs bulged out, indicating that they were not only well looked after but also grazed in green pastures. My mother also used to help in the garden. Unfortunately, this was very short-lived. My father was still in the bush.

Then, it happened that my grandfather's homestead was adjacent to a huge forest that extended from Gikambura to the outskirts of Ngong. This forest had become the habitation of many Mau Mau fighters. These fighters used to come out for hit-and-run guerrilla warfare. At the same time, they targeted the homes with big goats and rams. They used to invade such homes in order to take some animals which they would slaughter for meat to feed them as a way to sustain themselves and gain physical strength from the fat and meat of such animals.

It then happened that my grandfather's home became a target. Twice, they attacked our home, but they could not manage to penetrate. My mother and two other aunts who were housed there made noise calling for help, something that made the intruders leave. Nevertheless, in their third attempt, they were very determined. They pushed the door from outside even as my grandfather pushed it from inside. As much as the intruders pushed the door, they were at the same time trying to cut the door into pieces. It was then that one of the swords came into contact with my grandfather's fingers, cutting off three of them. But then, they left having not made an entry.

It was unfortunate that in the midst of his pain, my grandfather turned his anger to my mother. He now claimed that it was my father who was leading these Mau Mau people into his homestead. He told my mother, "*How on earth can Githii bring these people here to dine on my animals? I can no longer house you here.*" Remember, my father had sought his habitation among the Ngong Hills and, sometimes, far beyond these hills, hiding in the bushes in Maasai land. My mother tried to explain that my father was not among the Mau Mau fighters hiding in the Gikambura forest, but my grandfather could hear none of it.

It was then that my grandfather took a knife and threw it at my mother, aiming to hit her right into her face. By God's providence, the knife did not land on her face on the side with the sharp blade. It landed on its wooden handle. It only made a deep cut. In a quick move, my grandfather took a thick but long stick and was fast coming to hit my mother, who then took to her heels, running for her life but carrying my young brother, Githang'a. My grandfather ran after her even as he persistently cursed her. My mother ran fast and at the same time shouted as she called upon the neighbours to come to her help. Luckily, she managed to get into the home of Muthungu Wa Mbucho, who was known to be an African medicine man. As soon as my grandfather came back into the house, I sneaked out and went to a neighbour's, from where I was led to connect with my mother. My grandfather was threatening to come there but Muthungu sent some elderly men to go and warn my grandfather not to dare to go to his homestead.

After two to three weeks of being homeless, we were offered accommodation by my mother's stepbrother, Karuma. This was in a place known as Mai-a-Ihii. I do not remember the exact duration we stayed there, but it was possibly one year. It was early in 1954 that the government decided to have all people assembled into concentration villages as one of the ways to control the movement of the Mau Mau spirit. By now, hundreds of men were in the forests, and they were carrying out guerilla warfare, which was causing a lot of damage, including the killing of white people and many of those Africans who were loyal to the British Government. There were also two types of villages, those of the loyal families (hence known as loyal villages) and those of the families suspected as not being loyal, more so because some of their members were detained for being anti-British government. The individual families were allocated a space to build.

LIFE IN THE VILLAGE

My mother was allocated a place to build in at Gikambura. It was a non-loyal village and this was where I would spend most of my life. My mother had to construct the house, as there were no men to do that. This was very anti-African since the building is considered to be purely men's work. The men in the loyal villages could not help as they greatly avoided being connected with Mau Mau associates. Even with people in these concentration villages, the Mau Mau fighters intensified the war. To prevent these fighters from getting into chiefs' camps, deep trenches were dug all around the government's administration posts as Mau Mau fighters were invading them, causing a lot of manslaughter. This was more so because the Mau Mau warriors had invented ways of making homemade guns; there was also a lot of smuggling of guns and bullets, and even the police and army uniforms. With these, the Mau Mau warriors used to disguise themselves, making them sometimes get into government institutions like police stations, chief's camps and some barazas (public meetings) without being noticed. This is why the Africans finally overcame the white people.

The whites thought and treated the Africans as fools and unlettered people, but Africans were very intelligent people. Much of the knowledge, especially the military combat techniques, had been acquired from the Second World War. The British were blind to the contribution the Second World had made, especially in opening the Africans' mindset. The exposure Africans got then widened the scope of their mind.

When Mau Mau fighters persistently attacked the colonialists, the latter introduced what was known as curfew, whereby everybody was supposed to remain indoors from 6.00 pm to 7.00 am. There were set out times when women were to rush to their gardens to get food to cook for the family but it was a very short time. This was strictly to take place during the day. As if this was not enough, the government introduced hard labour for all those people who dwelt in the non-loyal villages.

I remember times when my mother could get out of the house at 5.00 am, and she would never come back until 7.00 pm. This was meant to humiliate the women and make them weak, stressed and depressed so that they could intercede with their husbands to give up the struggle. What the government did not know is that, the oaths these people had taken had so much bound them together. This bondage was far more powerful than the guns. They had vowed to fight until the last drop of their blood dropped in the soil to redeem their soil. Death was easier for them than surrendering. When one was hit by a bullet or hit by an object that would kill, before one died, he/she would grasp the soil to die with it in his/her hand. This was to encourage those left to fight on and also as a reminder that the person had died fighting for the course that was their soil, a course all freedom fighters were to pursue without surrendering.

Life became very difficult for us all, but my portion was quite a bitter pill. When my mother went for communal labour, I was the one to sweep the house. The floor of our house was earthen and I had to first splash some water on the floor before sweeping so as to calm down the dust. I used some green tree branches for sweeping especially one known as 'Mubangi' whose smell could drive away or kill the fleas. The fleas were so many that one could see them jumping about and climbing on one's legs and arms. Many would hibernate on one's clothes. It is hard to imagine how much of my blood these tiny creatures would suck out of my body each day – they were irritatingly too many. Having swept and after heaping the rubbish together near the entrance, I would first search for any grain of maize (corn) or bean in it that might have fallen, even if it is some days back. That I could pick and chew since hunger was the order of the day.

I would then afterwards fetch firewood. I had to walk for three to five miles to do this. I would carry the rope and go to places where trees had been cut down for posts, timber and charcoal burning and collect the already dry branches. I would tie a huge bundle and carry it on my back or on top of my head or shoulder. Other times, I would go to the uncultivated gardens with tall and thick growth that had already dried up. Other times, accompanied by other boys, we would get into the forest, climb trees and pull down the already dry branches. Sometimes, one had to climb a number of trees to get enough wood. Where the tree was too tall to climb and had many dried branches, we did cut down such trees.

I had to draw water for domestic use. In the beginning, there were no cans that could be used for drawing water. So, I used a cooking pot (sufuria). I would walk a distance of about three kilometers and queue for about 30 minutes to one hour for my turn before getting to where the tap was located. There was only one tap from where many people drew the water, I am talking of an approximate figure of like 3,000 families who depended on that tap for water. This place was called Riu. Thus, at any given time of the twelve-day sunshine, there would always be a big queue. I could draw like six pots, which means I made 6 trips. In later years, there were cans available that I could carry with my hands, sometimes 2 on each hand. This reduced the number of trips. Later, the boys invented a kind of wooden cart on which one could manage to carry a full tin or two of water, each containing 20 liters of water. Also, around this time, the number of taps had increased to six. I had also to go to fetch vegetables.

During these years, by God's provision, a variety of natural vegetables had grown even in the uncultivated gardens. Since we did not own a garden, I would go to these uncultivated gardens and beside the roads to pluck as much vegetables as I could. I would come home, put all of them in a big cooking pot and let them be cooked. When my mother came in the evening, she would add a little maize flour, mash it, and then we could eat. We called this *"Ngunjagutu"*. The vegetables I am talking of here were of different varieties including amaranth. Other times, there could be one or two cans of maize that I would cook in a pot, after which I would put the vegetables which my mother later mashed. Sometimes, the maize grains were too few such that one would eat a full plate of vegetables and occasionally see only two grains of maize (corn) in a whole meal. There were many times that we ate the vegetables alone, for we could not afford either the maize flour or the maize grains. But the worst time was the time of the year when there would be a prolonged drought. Sometimes, we could go for three to four days without food, while other times, we could only afford a little porridge.

There were times that my mother would hide herself so as not to be involved in communal labour. Other times, they were free not to go. In such times, we would go with my mother all the way to Kiraraponi where she could acquire an opportunity for a day's work. This place was at the outcasts of Ngong. The labour was available from a Maasai whose name was Bauru. To get there, there were two routes. One and the shorter one was through the forest that spread between Gikambura and Ngong. It took close to one hour to get to our destination. The other route was to circumvent from Gikabura via Dagorret and Karinde, which took us three hours. Unfortunately, there were those days when we could not use the shorter route through the forest.

This way was prohibited by the government. Remember, this was the dwelling place of the Mau Mau fighters and anybody passing through it was suspected of taking food or ammunition to them, which in most cases would be true. Thus, in order to get to Bauru's home at 7 am, we had to start our journey around 5.00 am so as to be there by 8.00 am and therefore be sure of getting the job. There are times we would arrive after 7.00 am and we missed the job. At such times, we would sleep hungry and be on the road the following day. There are even times we arrived on time but found the queue quite long. Thus, if, for example, on a given day, the number of people needed on that day were 20. When the number was counted from the front, there were those times we fell out of the bracket. There are people who arrived there by 6 am. One of the joys of getting the job was that one was sure of getting porridge at lunchtime – the whole day's pay from 8.00 am to 4.00 pm was one shilling. By then, seven shillings was equal to one dollar. Any time we missed the job, we were a laughing stock to our able neighbors, some of whom were relatives. They would say something like, "*Aya nimekuumira?*" (Are these one's going to survive?) Having said that, they would laugh loudly at us.

OTHER PROBLEMS I ENCOUNTERED

As already hinted, I was in constant attack by various insects/parasites for 24 hours a day, 7 days a week, 30 days a month and 12 months a year. These included the lice, fleas and bed bugs. My one and only shirt and one pair of shorts were occupied by territories of these insects. The lice formed an unbroken line under the hemline, and in many cases, they carried each other in groups of two, three and four. It's possible that some of my readers cannot grasp this because some have never seen an assembly of lice, fleas and bed bugs. One cannot even imagine this kind of environment. Such a mental picture is unimaginable. But whatever distorted picture one may have, this was the whole truth. The hair was another habitation of lice, and so was the habitation of jiggers in all the toes. Sometimes, the toes would bleed when the jiggers were taken off. Also note that, for seven years, I had never owned two shirts or pairs of shorts. Moreover, even the ones I had were full of patches. I had never won shoes. The first pair of shoes I wore was the year I joined Kirangari High School. It was mandatory that one had to have a pair of shoes, and even when I wore them, I had to learn how to walk in shoes.

When I wanted to wash the clothes, I would pick up lots of Adam's apples (ndongus). I would then wait until the time people went to sleep, when I would boil water in a basin, then cut the (ndongu's) into small pieces. I would then put them in the boiling water and stir for some time. I would then remove all those remains of (ndongu), and the water would be left looking soapy. I would then dip the clothes in boiling hot water for a while to kill the insects before washing them. The reason for using the 'ndongus' was that we could not afford to buy soap. So, the juice from the 'ndongus' acted as the soap. After washing them, I would place a wooden stool near the fire and leave them to dry so that I could wear them in the morning. Meanwhile, I would sleep naked. I had not worn underwear until I joined high school. The reason behind boiling the water to a very high degree was to kill the lice and fleas and their numerous eggs. It was also to make the 'ndongu' juice come out as they got tossed about while boiling. Due to the intense high boiling point of water, many of the fleas and lice would die, but what surprised many of us was the fact that many seemed to have a lot of resistance. They would look dead, but after coming into contact with the body's warmth and sucking blood, they would soon resurrect, and by the end of one week, they would be a multitude.

For many years, I did not know the warmth of a bed. My bed and blanket were the sacks that my mother would use during the day in her daily labour. This was the sack I would get into at the time of sleeping. I had to sleep next to the fire hearth so that I could have some added warmth from the embers of the fire. Even in the evening, I had to wash my clothes, I would just get in the sack and thank God that, apart from the days the hunger pangs were notorious, I slept soundly. But I had to wake up very early because my mother had to go with the sack. It was very hard for us to own two sacks - yet even the one we owned had holes that would let in a lot of cold air as I slept in it. Don't forget that the floor which acted as the floor of my bed was flooded with fleas, and my shirt and shorts were as well flooded by lice. Thus, as I slept, I had become a blood donor to lice, fleas and sometimes the bedbugs which had invaded the sack.

As already implied, the problem of jiggers had so much formed concentrated villages in my fingers, toes and the sidelines of the feet. Most of the time, they would be too close to each other, such that after removing them, those areas bled, leading to the formation of wounds. Being barefooted, it became so cumbersome to walk on the very rough paths, sometimes covered by stones, sand, and even thorns and dry grass. So, there were times I was tempted not to take the jiggers off because the consequences of having removed them caused a lot of pain. Incidentally, the pain caused by their eating up was more bearable than the pain inflicted as I walked in the woods. I had to try to walk with my toes raised and turning my feet sideways, forming a one-degree angle facing outwards. No wonder my feet have never been straight, even to date. They acquired that shape in the course of those years I was under the oppression of the jiggers. The other problem was that we had no land or nothing of our own, for the plenty we had was robbed as we were chased from my father's house in Ngong. We lived from hand to mouth in spite, of some of our relatives still owning large tracks of land.

The other problem was rats. The poor, unhygienic conditions in the village, both outside and inside the houses, created an environment whereby the rats bred rapidly. They fed on the leftovers in various homes and also in the pit latrines (many of which were filled up). These pit latrines were so full that if one relieved themselves, one could see the steaming of the excreta because it was just at the surface. One could even see and count the number of worms in the excreta. The worms were a big problem as there was no medicine. If at all it was there, there were not many people who could afford it. The worst thing was that these rats ate and played over the food that might be left as morning breakfast (though not many times would such food be available in our houses), after which they went back to their dwelling places in the toilets and the thatched roofs and in some dark corners in the house. So, how on earth did I survive? Only God knows why and how He preserved my life. Not one day do I remember falling sick.

I remember a day we had gone to fetch some firewood in the forest with many other young boys. We had the habit of felling mature trees just to get the dry branches as firewood, but at other times, we were just after a few feet of the tree's topmost part, the tip. This we sold for some coins, which we could use to buy maize flour. Other times, we would fell a tree just to get a seven-foot post for selling, in order to get money for use, or as already stated, to get the dry branches for firewood. We had done this for many days and it had so much angered the forester and the forest guards. They were instructed to either arrest those who were recklessly destroying the forests or they would get fired. This had made them so worked out that they even thirsted for our blood. This was during the time of emergency, and to kill an African was not a big deal. No one would have been accused in court of killing an African. In fact, the Africans were regarded as of a lower caliber than a dog.

So, on the day in question, we were deep in the forest collecting firewood. I had gone deeper in the forest than anyone else but I could hear others talking. The next thing I heard was the pounding of feet on the dry leaves of people running fast, and soon, it was so quiet that I could feel my breathing. I then realized that something wrong had happened. I was all alone in the forest. I did not need to be told that the forest guards had chased away my comrades. I then tiptoed towards the road that separated the forest we were in and another one. Upon reaching the edge of the forest, I glanced to the right side, and very far, I saw my comrades running very fast but were being pursued by two forest guards.

I watched until they disappeared at the corner of the road. Now, here I was, lonely and fearful. Standing there and pondering the next step to take, I saw one of the forest guards coming back and furiously raising and tossing a well-designed club that he had. I could tell his anger because, from the look of it, I could see that he was talking to himself. I decided not to move but to wait for him to get back into the forest, and then I could run towards the way he was coming from because that was the homeward way. The man continued coming, and the closer he moved, the clearer I could read his anger. He kept coming on, and I watched his every step, expecting him to get into the forest within the next few steps. But alas! He kept coming on until he reached a point where I now realized that he was not getting into the forest. If I tried moving back into the forest, the man would hear me because the dry leaves covering the ground would betray me as I stepped on them, and also, if he managed to catch me, he would kill me, and it would take months before my body was discovered. The other option was to get to the road and run fast along the road that continued leading into the depths of the forest, but at least I would be seeing myself. And if I happened to be killed, the corpse would be visible. And also, who knows? The man might not be fast enough, or he would give up after getting tired. In a lightening thought, I decided to take the second option.

I got to the road and took fast on my heels. No sooner had the man seen me than he got to his heels. The first thing I remember is the sound of the club as it whizzed in my ears. It landed in front of me. I automatically realized that this man wanted to crush my head and kill me. At first, I thought of picking up the club, but then I realized that that would be a catalyst for him to keep on pursuing me. So, I jumped over the club. The man took the club, and with an added speed and strength, he aimed the club at me. And it hit hard behind me, almost on my heels, for the only thing I saw was a cloud of dust with some ploughed pieces of earth falling in front of me.

By now, my energy was fading, more so because that week I had fed very poorly and worse still, I had not eaten the previous night. Now, for the third time, the club missed my head by an inch as it flew over my head and fell in front of me again, producing a cloud of dust that almost blinded me. I now started staggering since my legs were giving up, my breath was laboured, and my heart was beating up very fast. I was approaching a sharp corner of the road, and at that point, all my strength had departed. I lost control at a sharp corner of the road, and I staggered, falling, luckily, on two men walking on the same corner. The two men held and supported me to prevent my fall.

But then, the men saw this forest guard who was running fast after me and fuming with anger. Immediately, one of the men released me and ran towards the forest guard who was now holding up the club to give me one and final blow on my head. The man held him tightly and caught the club, which the forest guard kept on furiously trying to wrestle himself out of the man's tight grip. As he struggled with him, the charcoal banner kept on pleading with him, "*Oh please, don't kill him; oh man, don't you also have children? Why do you want to shed innocent blood? Oh, for God's sake, don't kill this boy.*"

Meanwhile, the second man was shielding me, saying, "*You better kill me, but not this boy.*" Then the other man released me, and both of them held the man and finally managed to snatch the club from him. The forest guard was by now shedding tears and shouting loudly, saying, "*This boy must die! They have destroyed the forest, and they are almost making me jobless; let me kill him.*" Then one of the men held me by the hand, drawing me closer to his chest, and walked a short distance with me and then left me again to go and help his friend to calm down the forest guard, as the other man was trying, by all means, to calm him down. After some time, he calmed down and seemed to have reluctantly accepted the pleas of the charcoal burners. One of them came to me, held my hand, and we started walking, keeping a distance from the guard and the other man. To me the two men were angels sent by God to rescue me. The two followed us, and when we reached the spot where I emerged from the forest and started running, the forest guard made a sign for us to stop. When he got to us, he addressed the two men, saying,

"I did drop my whistle and sword when we were running after this boy's friends. So, I will go inside and pick them up. Meanwhile, walk with this boy and when you get to the shopping center, wait for me there. I will call for some transportation so that this boy and a few others in his company, who were also caught, will be taken to the Forest Post, and the forester will then decide their fate. Make sure I get this boy with you at the shopping center."

The shopping center was about two kilometers away. The men were no longer holding me. Rather, they were asking me questions, trying to find out who my parents were. I was grateful that the two men rescued me from death, but my concern was that I was not sure what would transpire in the forest station. I feared extreme torture where I was likely to be maimed in the torture, or alternatively, they could as well summon my mother, claiming that she encouraged me to cut down mature trees for sale so as to get her income and even firewood. Again, I started looking for options. One was to go with these men, who would then hand me over to people who could possibly torture me to death. I was also concerned that they could end up demanding some kind of fine from my mother, who, upon failure to pay, could end up in jail. The second option was to run away before we arrived at the shopping center. I obeyed the second option. As the two men walked relaxed and as we negotiated a corner in our path, I kind of walked behind them as the path had narrowed, and off, I ran away. I overheard the two men saying, "*You have gone? Why have you decided to jeopardize our lives?*" Whatever transpired after the man found them at the shopping center, I do not know. But I always assume that they also went their way rather than waiting for the forest guard.

There is also this day that I cannot forget. It was a day that we had to wake up very early to be at Keraraponi by 7.00 am in order to register for the day's work and earn the one-shilling pay. We had spent the previous three days without food. Thanks to a neighbor who, the previous night had given us a handful of maize flour that we had used to prepare very light porridge. I remember this porridge was so watery that it left the can so clean after the porridge was taken.

This day, my mother seemed not to have slept long. Her mind was focused on making sure that we would be at Keraraponi, if possible, far, much earlier than 7.00 am. She could not imagine us going for another day without a substantial bite. I was somehow deeply asleep when I heard my mother call me on a very high note, "*Muhia! Muhia! Wake up; we are already late, and we ought to have travelled up to Dagoreti by now.*"

I then quickly got out of the sack which she hurriedly folded together with a hole and a bottle of water and put them into the basket (Kiondo). I was feeling so sleepy, so much so that I kept on wondering how short my sleeping time was.

Nevertheless, my mother quickly locked the door, and we were on our way. The night was cold, and my sleep quickly got suppressed, and before long, I was shivering terribly in the night's cold. The sky was cloudy but giving some light which seemingly indicated the early morning. My mother's mind was really focused on moving quickly, as fast as our legs could carry us. She kept on shouting at me, "*Muhia, widen your stride; what if we miss work today? I know you are cold and hungry, but there is no alternative; we've got to hurry up.*"

The atmosphere was really quiet; the dogs could be heard backing far from the village we had left. Some donkeys were braying once in a while. It was in this kind of atmosphere that my mother seemed to have awoken from a deep sleep in the middle of the night, dreaming about work. There was yet no sound of birds. There was no voice of a human being. She recalled how the government had issued a stern warning that nobody was supposed to be outside the house after 6.00 pm and before 5.30 am. The government had ordered that anybody found in between was to be shot dead because such a person was either a Mau Mau terrorist or one of those feeding the terrorists with food, information or ammunition. No wonder some people have lost their lives this way. It was by then that my mother realized that it was such a silent night because dawn was far from coming. As I would later figure it out, it was around 1.00 am. We were now far from home. We were at what is today the entrance to Thogoto Teachers Collage from Gikambura/Thogoto highway. With a lot of agonies and much desperation, my mother said to me, "*Muhia, we are doomed unless God intervenes; we are dead."* Then she said what sounded like a prayer, *"God, if I have to die, please God, spare Muhia, and have mercy on him."* The next thing I remember hearing was her sobs in agony. But one thing remained clear: we had come all that way without being noticed by the government.

At first, my mother thought of getting into the bush and remaining there until dawn, but then she withdrew the thought because if we found out, we would be killed there, and possibly our relatives would never know what happened to us. This was common because when people got killed in such circumstances, they would be buried in the same spot or left for dogs and other wild animals to feed on them. Then, the government would announce That a woman and her son got shot as they were taking ammunition to Mau Mau terrorists. This was meant to scare the Mau Mau sympathizers and discourage those who were strategizing how to attack the government. Alternatively, in their announcement, the government would not have said a woman and her young boy; they would have said that two terrorists got killed at around 1.00 am as they were heading to spy out the surroundings of the government post.

My mother decided that we move on, heading to Wanyoro's home, which was like three kilometers away. Wanyoro was her sister and, therefore, my aunt. My aunt lived in the neighborhood of Thogoto shopping center. She took this decision with great trust in God. She knew that God would send us angels to guide and protect us. She realized that before we arrived at my aunt's home, we would have to pass next to a chief's camp, which was located at the place we now call Kiamburi and not far from Thogoto shopping center. Nevertheless, she did not have any other choice.

We moved on. By now, she was very quiet, but once in a while, I could hear her lips moving about, producing very controlled whispers, and I knew that she was praying to God to come up with a miracle for our protection and possibly at the same time praying that if the worst was to happen that God to accept us in his heavenly glory. She knew that a bullet would hit any time. At one time, I overheard her say, "*Please, God, don't let Muhia be part of this ordeal, and if it is your will, let us cross this sea even as you helped the children of Israel.*" By then, we were approaching the chief's camp. My mother was aware that in that camp, there was a tower raised many feet above the ground, on which there was an armed watchman keeping watch in the surroundings of the camp for twenty-four hours. Thus, for my mother, there was no way we would pass without being noticed. After all, the moon was no longer curtained by the clouds. It was so bright that one would pick a pin on the ground.

The worst moment came as we were passing the camp. The dogs from the surrounding homes seemed to have been summoned to bark. They barked as if they were either crying over our blood or praying for us, with two or three donkeys joining them in braying. If there was any time my mother had ever smelt death, it was this time. Her legs were vibrating in fear, a clear indication that they were being forced to carry her. I also, for the first time, realized how dangerous the situation was and why my mother was mentioning my name in her talk with God. I overheard her say, *"If this is the time, God, I commit my life and the life of Muhia to you."*

My mother was raised next to Kikuyu Mission, where the pioneer Presbyterian Missionaries founded the mission in 1898. It was around this time of its founding that her father was born. Thus, my mother had grown up in a Christian environment, and she had undergone catechism, been baptized and confirmed. So, she knew all about Christianity and man's relationship with God. She knew that there was eternal life after this present life. Hence, she knew where she would go in case she died. She also knew from the Bible that God had the power to save. She was well versed with Biblical stories such as those of Daniel in the den of lions; Meshach, Abednego and Shadrach in the fiery furnace; the way God, in many instances, rescued the Israelites from their enemies, and the way He rescued people like Paul, Peter and Silas. This is why, even at that point of total desperation, she had not lost hope.

As if we were dreaming, we found ourselves passing the chief's camp's main entrance, and before long, we had surpassed it. The barking of the dogs started calming down, and the legs gained some strength. This reminds me of Isaiah's words in Isaiah 40:28-31:

"Hast thou not known? Hast thou not heard that the everlasting God, the Lord, the Creator of the ends of the earth, fainteth not, neither is weary? There is no searching of his understanding. He giveth power to the faint, and to them that have no might, he increases strength. Even the youths shall

74

faint and be weary, and the young men shall utterly fall: but they that wait upon the Lord shall renew their strength; they shall mount up with wings as eagles; they shall run, and not be weary; and they shall walk, and not faint "(Isaiah 40:28-31-KJV).

As miraculously as it turned out, before long, my mother knocked at our aunt's door. She seemed to me to have taken very long before opening the door, although no sooner had she heard her sister's voice then she rushed to open the door. My mother was still praying as we waited for the door to open; she had realized that even here at the door, the bullets could perform their work. What if we were being followed? Finally, the door opened, and much to our relief, we got in, and the warmth in the house was also so relieving. As one would expect, we were really cold. The warmth of the Lord's protection flowed in our hearts. It was unbelievable that the ordeal was over. My aunt had so much panicked that, at first, she stammered as she asked my mother,

"Wangari, what really happened that you walked by night knowing how risky it is? How on earth did you manage to reach here? Tell me, tell me, surely the angel of the Lord must have been with you. I cannot believe what I am seeing, but one thing I know is that I am not dreaming."

My mother then narrated all that had transpired: she told her of how we had spent three days without food, how she was so eager to be at Keraraponi before 7.00 am and how the bright moonlight deceived her as it was covered by the black clouds which made it seem like the early hours of the day. Having noticed how cold we were, my aunt quickly prepared a cup of tea and then prepared a place for us to sleep. This cup of tea also relieved the pangs of hunger in my stomach. We slept until 5.00 am, after which we started for Keraraponi. I remember that that day we got the job, and I could hardly wait for the 1.00 pm plate of porridge.

I had expected that my aunt's husband could have sympathized with us and given us some help, but he, being a home guard, could not help the family of a Mau Mau man. When we came back in the evening, we found that news had spread like fire. A few had heard our door close, and one neighbor confessed that she had heard my mother telling me to widen my strides, for it was already late for our departure. The other source of information was from one of our family friends who would have accompanied my mother to Keraraponi. We had stopped by her house in that early morning to pick her up, but she was not going that day as she was unwell. This was to our advantage because had she joined us, the two would have walked conversing on the way, and chances were that their talking would have betrayed us. Also, three people would have been a crowd, making it easier for someone to notice us. It was also fortunate because her being left behind made it possible for my brother, Githang'a, to be left with her. Otherwise, what used to happen was that every time we left, we would part company with Githang'a, and he would walk alone to the village where my grandparents lived. This was about 4 miles away.

In fact, most of the time, we got late in leaving for Keraraponi because we had to wait until it was clear enough for him to be able to walk to the grandparents. This would have been the same scenario in this fateful morning. We would have parted company, asking him to follow the same path as our grandparents. What do you think would have happened to Githang'a if this woman was also joining us for work that day? Anything would have happened. Among the dangers my brother would have encountered include being killed by some crooks for what would have been described as a means of delivering information to the terrorists as he would not be easily suspected because he was a small child; he would also have been eaten up by dogs or wild animals; he would have gone astray and gotten lost in the bushes and died there as he was so weak and hungry. In any case, my mother would have been arrested and accused of child neglect, which would have ended her in jail. This could be very devastating to my life. Does this not also tell you how God's hand embraces us and protects us in all faculties of our lives? If you are like me, you do. The other surprising thing is that I do not remember any other time this woman failed to go to Keraraponi. It was either she went earlier than my mother, or they would go together. So, by God's grace, all things worked together for our good. Suffice it to say that I led a very difficult life while growing up – words fail me to explain the bitter pill in my life.

At one time, my mother had managed to get me into class one at Mai–A–Ihii school. I learnt for one year, and I completed class one. I was excitedly looking forward to joining standard two, but this became impossible because my mother could not afford the six shillings needed for school fees. By then, one dollar was equal to seven shillings. This then means that I failed to continue with schooling because my mother couldn't manage money equivalent to less than a dollar. I was out of school for two years.

3. MY FATHER'S RELEASE

One day late in 1958, my mother told me to wash my only shirt and shorts, which were so torn. The reason given for this was that the following day, she wanted me to meet a very important person in my life. She wanted to surprise me. Thus, the following day, I accompanied her to Dagoreti, where all those who had served their jail terms would be first kept for some time before they were finally granted full freedom. When we arrived at Dagoreti, I noticed a group of men whom I had not seen before. As I accompanied my mother towards them, there was a long silence as the men looked at us. As I looked at them, my eyes could not register recognition of any of them. But to my surprise, these were all thin people with shaggy hair, eyes retreating into their sockets and yellowish unclean teeth packed in their mouths. Before we reached them, a policeman stopped us, and then he talked to my mother as he asked her,

"Whom have you come to see, and what is your relationship with him? My mother replied, "We have come to see Benson Githii. I am his wife, and this is Muhia, his firstborn."

As the two talked, I noticed that one man kept on looking at us uncontrollably.

I also noticed that some of those men were glancing at this curious-looking man. My eyes also seemed to be magnetically fixed on him. His eyes were wet with tears. Meanwhile, the policeman went and called out the name

"Githii!". I then saw the very man who had been watching with some excitement rise up and start coming towards us with tears running down his crumbled cheeks. He hugged my mother in a tight grip and then said to her,

"God is so great; at long last, He has re-united us. At one time, this looked so impossible."

My mother responded,

"How else can we know the greatness of God? Welcome back. The fruits of your labour and many others will soon be here as the independence of this country is almost here with us."

My father then turned to me. He held me tightly and said in a loud voice, *"Muhia, my son! I had always longed to see you again! It always looked impossible. Thank you, my God."*

He continued, *"Muhia, I am your father."* Tears of joy and disbelief rolled down my weak cheeks as I enjoyed the warmth of my father's body and his tears wetting both my hair and neck. It was all clear. But what if I was dreaming? I looked at my mother for clarification, only to notice that she was busy wiping away her tears, too. Meanwhile, a few men whom I assumed were my father's friends had joined us and they were comforting my mother. I heard one of them say, *"This is great! It is wonderful! It is unbelievable. It is one of those God's miracles."* I also looked at the men for clarification; they were crying, and one man who seemed to understand me said, *"Yes, this is your father; you are his firstborn. Seven years is a long time. I imagine you were too young when he got arrested."* Yet another one addressed me, saying, *"Thank God. You will now be in good hands."* Before long, the men were summoned aggressively by the policeman. My father kept on holding my shoulders and pulling me softly and lovingly to his chest.

It was not until the policeman came and said to him, "*The thirty minutes allocated time is over. You need to bid your family goodbye; otherwise, you will soon be with them.*"

My father then hugged my mother and whispered something to her. He then shook my hand as he said, "*Muhia you will go to school. One month more, and I will be part of the family.*" I kept on watching him as he walked away, and he, likewise, kept on looking back at us until he disappeared behind the fence. The next one month seemed a very long time for me. I longed for two things: to be in the presence of my father and to go to school. As I lived prior to the coming of my father, as much as I hungered for food, I also psychologically greatly hungered for education. It was such a relief to realize that with the survival of my father, I would have the two hunger pangs satisfied. I had an unexplainable natural hunger for education. I knew that, this was good for me and for my children and my community at large. One challenge that faced my father so as to satisfy my hunger was getting a job. The government was still in the colonial hands. There were rumors that Africans were to be independent, but people like Kenyatta were not yet released. Thus, all those labeled as Mau Mau terrorists were seen as great enemies. These were people who needed further monitoring, even when one was out of jail. They were looked at with a lot of suspicion and could hardly get a job. But my father needed a job as soon as possible so that I could join the primary school during next January's intake. In his pursuit of a job, he would walk for fifteen miles to Nairobi city. At times, he would be at a point of being offered a job, but when asked for the identification, it betrayed him as a Mau Mau terrorist, and nobody would want to be associated with him. He trekked for two weeks consecutively until he felt he could do it no more. We have to remember that his body was too weak after seven years of hard labour, torture and underfeeding. In any case even for an energetic person, we are talking of thirty miles, both ways. These were not the old days in the 1940s when he would walk almost the same distance going for typing courses in Nairobi.

It was at this point of desperation he learnt that his former principal at Kambui Teachers' Training College, Mr. Leakey, was now the principal at Thogoto Teachers College, which was a walking distance from our home. He knew that all Europeans had the same negative mentality towards the Africans, but he tried to think positively by recalling how this same principal had refused to hand him over to the police when they had come to arrest him at school until he was arrested when he went home for the holidays.

So, he gathered the courage to go and meet Mr. Leakey and tell him of his desperate need for a job and the need for his son to get an education. When he finally came face to face with Mr. Leakey and having introduced himself, Mr. Leakey looked at him with disbelieve as he asked him,
"How do you claim to be Benson Githii? We all read in the newspaper that Benson got arrested and killed at Ngong as one

of the most wanted Mau Mau terrorists around Ngong and Kikuyu land. Benson was a man I greatly admired, and this is why I still have that newspaper cutting in the file."

He went to the shelve, pulled out a file and showed him the newspaper cutting with his picture in it. To this, my father responded,

"Yes, that was a headline in one of the widely read newspapers, but you know very well that such propaganda was highlighted so that those in the forefront of the Mau Mau movement would be discouraged and be vulnerable to surrender. Remember, this was the time the government poured down pamphlets from the air using helicopters and planes pleading with Mau Mau freedom fighters to surrender and come out from the forest, lifting up green branches as a sign of surrender. It was all a matter of propaganda."

To this, Mr. Leakey replied,

"You are attempting to make me believe that you are Mr. Benson. Could you possibly remind me of some incidences that took place in the school or between you and me so that I can be fully convinced that you are the Benson Githii I knew and loved?"

It was then that my father reminded him of many incidences ranging from classrooms, dining hall and sports. He even reminded him that he was the class prefect, the captain of Boys Scouts and was among the top three students in the class. He also narrated to him how the policemen had come to arrest him at school and how he (Leakey) had refused to hand him over to them. After a long pause and with his eyes wetting with tears, Leakey rose from his chair, gave my father a good handshake and said, "*Truly God is wonderful. Yes, you are Benson.*"

He then called his secretary and introduced my father to her, saying,

"*This is a very important man and a hero in the African eyes. Once, he was my student in this very college before it transferred from Kambui to this place; please, bring a cup of tea for him and something that he can eat.*"

As my father enjoyed the cup of tea and a loaf of bread Leakey kept himself busy in responding to some calls and notes. After this, the two spent quality time together as my father narrated to him his experiences in the Second World War, the way he was arrested, how he escaped, his life in the forest and his seven years of ordeal in prison. Leakey, having intensively listened to all this, finally said, "*What an experience with God's total protection! Now, Mr. Benson, tell me, what can I do for you?*"

This is the moment my father had long waited for. He then told Leakey,

"*Please, provide me with a job. I have met my family so impoverished and of greater importance; I want my son to begin school this coming January. He is already quite aged for school because he is now twelve years old.*"

To this, Leak exclaimed, "*Twelve years! And what class is he to join?*" my father replied, "*Standard one,*" Then Leakey said, "*Mr. Benson, are you aware that your son should be in class five at that age?*"

To this, my father responded,

"In fact, this is why I need a job so as to help him begin school. I am sure he will catch up. I have even noticed that he loves education. He keeps on reminding me of the importance of being in school. Please bear with me as you are aware that if it were not for the imprisonment, my son would have by now advanced so much in education."

It was then that Leakey called the accountant and told him,

"This is Benson Githii who is my former student at Kambui. He is a man with a story to tell. We need to help him; tell me, what are the possibilities of getting him a job, taking into consideration his academic background and health status? He is not well educated to work in the faculty, and his typing skills cannot fit here. After all, I think we have enough typists."

Then the accountant, who I am sure looked down on my father, said, *"The only vacancy available at the moment is in trimming the grass by the mower."* Leakey then, looking at my father sympathetically, said, *"Mr. Benson, do you think you can do that?"* To this, my father replied, *"Yes sir, if it is the only job available, tell me when to start."* Leakey then instructed the accountant to go with my father, give him the instructions, and enter him into the payroll.

My father now had a job! He was happy in that now, at least his family would be sure of their daily meals, the school fees would be available, as well as the uniform and the books. Thus, he embarked on the job. But alas! By the end of the first month, he had become so exhausted, weak and even thinner to the extent that he could no longer manage the high-powered engine grass cutter. It was sapping a lot of his energy from his already wrecked body. It was then the accountant went to the principal and informed him that there was no need to retain my father's name in the payroll because his health was getting worse and worse. Each day, the portion he worked on was getting smaller and smaller, as most often, he would be either sitting down or lying on the grass. The accountant explained that my father was portraying a lot of physical weakness and recommended that he be paid for the work he had done so far and then have his services terminated. He said, *"He keeps on reminding me of the importance of his son being in school and that I should bear with him and that it was not for you, Mr. Principle, he would not have been considered to work here."*

The principal then summoned my father. When he looked at him, he said,

> *"Surely, Benson, this kind of work will kill you. I am not sure that I can be of much help to you; I would hate to see you die here in the college. I thought that by getting a job, your health would improve, but surprisingly, you have continually become weaker than when you first came here."*

To this my father replied:

"Yes, sir, I feel so much weakened by the machine. But as you are aware, I am a man of great dedication to my work. When I was a teacher, I was known for my great devotion to my duties. Moreover, the British government had almost made me attain the position of sergeant major in the army, the highest rank for an African to attain. At Kambui, you had come to like me because of my dedication to the school and studies. Please sir, could you authorize that I be given another job, one that will

not make my body strain so much, a job that will give my body an opportunity to recover?"

Even as my father said this, Leakey's eyes were wet with tears. He called the accountant and authorized him to squeeze my father into the workforce in the store, saying,

"Let him be responsible for distributing the towels, soaps, toilet papers, working tools and sports equipment to the students. He will also be in charge of giving out the daily food rationing as required by those in the kitchen."

The accountant had no way but to abide by his boss's instructions. Having now attained the job, my father worked so devotedly that the College Board came to honor him. Due to his trustworthiness and efficiency in working, he greatly surpassed those who formerly managed the kitchen and the supervision of the subordinate staff. The college life rejuvenated in many ways after his getting the job. There had been a lot of corruption going on in the management of the store. So many things used to disappear. This led him to be upgraded in his job group with commendable allowances and other benefits. He was even allowed to sell some items to outsiders and even to students. Leakey, with all the trust he had in my father, gave him added responsibilities, including being the manager of college vehicles and in the buying of all food stuffs related to the college. Since the college owned a big land most of which was rented to the outsiders and others given to the workers, my father was given the responsibility to let these lands on behalf of the college and also dish out pieces of land to the workers. This way, we also came to own much land in which we grew various kinds of crops, including sweet potatoes, maize, Irish potatoes, beans, peas, etc. After some time, he was even allowed to keep a canteen on the campus. He was so much liked by the faculty staff, subordinate staff and all the students. He worked under several principals who equally liked him until he retired in 1986. Thus, he worked in Thogoto college from 1959-1986. My father went to be with the Lord in 2006.

PRIMARY EDUCATION

As already stated, my mother had put me in school at Mai – A- Ihii Primary School, but I could not proceed to Standard Two since she could not afford 6 shillings, which was less than one dollar since a dollar was equal to 7 shillings for my school fees. My lack of opportunity to go to school was a great disappointment such that it is hard for me to forget. I remember the bitterness and sorrow that held me captive in the morning and evening as I watched children going and coming back from schools with their books in bags hung on their shoulders or at their backs. But then things changed with the release of my father from detention. He kept to the words that he had said to me as he bade me farewell that first time I saw him at Dagoretti, when he told me, *"Muhia, you will go to school."* I was getting very disappointed those two weeks that my father traveled to Nairobi and came back with the negative report that he had failed to acquire a job.

Under the instructions of my father, my mother went with me to request my school admission. When we reached school, the deputy who was in charge of school admission said that I was over age and late for school. That I could, therefore, not be admitted. My mother then decided to speak to the head teacher. When we got to her office, my mother explained that I had gone to class one in Mai-ihii but missed joining class 2 for lack of school fees. The headmaster exclaimed, *"Is this David Githii, the one I taught in class one!? He is bright and qualified for class two."* She then called her deputy, explained the situation, and requested her to have me admitted to school. I have no words to explain the ever-treasured joy I felt at the time at twelve years of age. I was fitted with a new uniform (though no shoes), and then, for the first time, with surety of continuing with my education, I walked proudly to Gikambura Primary School. To crown it all, it was headed by Miss Wambui Gituku my former teacher, who I held a lot of admiration for. Wambui was a stout energetic lady and hardworking. She owned a bicycle, which was a wonder to me, for I had not personally known someone who owned a bicycle. I had hardly known any person owning a car. If bicycles were a rare commodity that only a rare head teacher could afford, then how rare were the vehicles? It was not even uncommon to find teachers who had no shoes. Even those who owned shoes had no more than one pair, and it would be of very poor quality. I do not remember any teacher who owned a suit. Very few teachers even owned ties, and even then, they were of unimaginably poor quality. At school, we sat on wooden desks that accommodated mostly three pupils. Like our homes, the floors of the classes were earthen - it was all dirt. The walls were made of posts and mud. Many of these walls had many holes that let in a lot of cold. In reality, those days were cold, especially in the months of June and July. It was only short of having snow. The cold flexed our fingers to the extent that sometimes it became difficult to hold even a pencil. Yet one positive thing about the cold was the fact that it made the palms rather numb, which helped in controlling the piercing pain from the many canes one would get from teachers in the course of the day. The teachers seemed to do it as though it was part of their training. There were so many *"don'ts"* such that one would hardly go home without having been caned. One would be caned for failing;

- ➤ *To arrive on time. Many students walked long distances to get to school one way.*
- ➤ *Failing to carry water in a can or a big bottle. Water was important because before classes were swept, a lot of water was sprinkled on the floor to calm down the dust. There were also flowers and young trees to be watered.*
- ➤ *Failing to comb one's hair or having lice in it.*
- ➤ *Failing to clean one's body. In many homes, water was being rationed.*
- ➤ *Failing to keep the clothes clean, especially from Wednesday after wearing them for two days, as no parent would have afforded two pairs of uniforms.*
- ➤ *Failing to brush teeth. There was no toothpaste or brush. One was to chew one end of a fresh green stick from some undergrowth. By chewing the tip of the stick, it formed a kind of brush with which one then brushed the teeth continuously.*
- ➤ *Failing to finish the homework. One reason for this was because there was no electricity, and people were supposed to use a small can fixed with a wick, which got socked in the paraffin contained in the can and then gave light. Unfortunately, not many families can afford paraffin. At times, we used the light of the firewood, and yet even firewood was not always available. Therefore, some people would fail to have done the homework.*
- ➤ *Failing to attend Sunday school for kids on Sunday as it was compulsory to do so.*
- ➤ *Failure to have the materials for handwork or not coming up with a good handwork. Usually, handworks were based*

on carvings cum modeling from the clay soils, making of various items from sisal threads like mats and ropes, etc.

➤ *Making noise in the class, it was the work of the prefects to write down and hand in the noisemakers to the teacher.*

➤ *Failing to bring tools for working around the campus. Such included pangas (a large broad-bladed African knife), spades, hoes, slashes, axes, etc.*

➤ *Failing to stand when a teacher passes by. Any me a teacher would be passing by, and the student was seated, it was mandatory for one to stand up as a sign of honoring the teacher.*

➤ *Failing to carry a packed lunch. Again, it was mandatory that every student carry a packed lunch. Unfortunately, some could not afford it.*

➤ *The most common canning was through failing to attain the required marks per subject.*

➤ *We would also be caned for failing to copy the notes at the same speed as the teacher, and most of them wrote very fast on the blackboard.*

➤ *Failing to recite memory work assigned by the various teachers.*

➤ *Failing to come up with one's parents when required in school.*

➤ *Failing to contribute to the harmonious life in the school. For example, if you bullied or abused other students.*

➤ *Failing to honor the recommended schedule for the school. One was not supposed to leave earlier than the recommended time.*

THE PRIMARY SCHOOL DAY'S PROGRAMME

The school reporting time was 7.30 am, and since many people came from far away, many in a radius of 20kms, the time between 5.30 am and 7.30 am was a time when all roads and paths were full of pupils running to different schools. In our neighborhood, there were those going to Mai-a-Ihii, Gikambura and Gicharani Primary Schools. The teachers were expected to be at school by 8.00 am, apart from the teacher on duty, who had to report earlier than 7.30 am. I remember we were loaded as we hurried to school. I used to carry water and a broom. Depending on the activities of the day, there were times I had to have a hoe, a panga (sword), the materials for handiwork and even sometimes four to five pieces of wood, including books and food. From 7.30 am to 8.00 am, the school was a beehive of activities. There were those sweeping the toilets, classrooms and pathways. Others were cutting grass, others taking care of flower gardens, etc. It was at this time that the latecomers were also punished. The prefects would be busy helping the teacher on duty with supervision.

At 8.00 am, the bell rang for the parade. All could rush to the parade ground, where they formed queues according to individual classes. The standard one class is in front, and the senior classes at the rear. It is here that scrutiny on cleanliness took place. This included checking the size of the nails and cleanliness of the hair and clothes. In simple terms, the general cleanliness was checked. Those who were not up to the set standards got their beatings, or they were told to report to the office during the break time. After checking for general cleanliness, we sang one or two Christian songs, after which a teacher expounded the gospel, and the parade concluded with a prayer. It usually ended around 8.30 am. Then the classes would begin, mostly with Mathematics or English.

Most of the teachers were devoted to their work. But I remember a few who came unprepared, and they would give pupils something that would lead to an eruption of beatings. Such a teacher would spend the whole lesson beating the students. There were others who taught really well, and I fondly remember them. They also instilled some good discipline in us. One particular teacher I fondly remember and that I highly regard and respect was Mr. John Ng'ethe. I first met him while I was in standard four. He taught me Mathematics up to standard seven. He is a teacher I have emulated a lot. Other than teaching, he involved us in many extracurricular activities. One activity that we all liked and were greatly motivated by his encouragement was known as Ng'onya. One group was to try to steal a stick while the other tried to protect it. Another activity was the rounder, which is more or less like American baseball. Another teacher whom I remember and who also contributed a lot to my academic life in the Primary School was Lawrence Ndung'u Kiruku. He taught us English.

The break bell usually rang around 10.30 am. All the pupils got out playing, and the noise was so high that it could be heard about two miles away. Many pupils rushed to the toilets then, although most of them had no doors. Others would urinate on the floor and on walls, and the whole floor would be flooded with urine. The worst were the boys' toilets. While some were in the toilets, others would engage in some simple games. Of course, there were those especially in the senior classes, who did not feel the need for wasting me. They would remain in class doing homework or preparing for the next lesson. I remember when I was in the senior classes, I never wasted time. Then, the bell to resume classes would sound. The classes continued up to 1.00 pm when pupils broke up for lunch. About 60% of the school went out for lunch, some to their homes and others to their nearby relatives. The forty percent that remained had either carried food or would rush to the nearby gardens to roast Irish potatoes, sweet potatoes or even maize. Of course, there were those without anything to eat, and they sat down in the class and talked and shared stories and some experiences. There were those who laid on the grass waiting for the afternoon session to start. It was mandatory for the senior class pupils to carry a packed lunch.

When the afternoon session resumed at 2.00 pm, different classes had different activities. There were times some would go for handwork, others to gardening (Agriculture), but there would be others doing academic lessons. In most cases, we had different activities in the afternoon, depending on the individual class's timetable.

When the bell rang at 4.00 pm, the learners would assemble at the assembly ground, where the announcements would be made by the teacher on duty. This would be followed by a Christian song and prayers.

Saturday was always a free day. I spent this day working in the garden at Thogoto Teachers' College. Sunday was a day that every pupil was expected to go to Sunday school. This always took place from 1.00 pm to 3.00 pm. We were mainly taught by students from Alliance Boys High School. This was a school founded by missionaries (1926) from different denominations, mainly the Presbyterians, Methodists, Anglicans and African Inland Mission, hence the name Alliance. It was for many years considered the best high school in East Africa. The students coming to this school were supposed to be well molded on the Christian foundation. Students from the school were distributed to various schools to conduct kids Sunday school on Sundays. My Christian roots can be traced back then. I especially remember one Sunday school teacher whose name was Kanyotu. He not only taught Christian values but music as well.

The school calendar ran from January to the end of March and we had the month of April as a holiday. It would then resume in May to the end of July for the August holiday. The last term began in September and ended in November, likewise for the December holiday. The holidays came as a relief due to the enormous load of learning, but more so because there were no longer the caning and other punishments inflicted by the teachers. Talking of other punishments, I remember many times we had to uproot big stumps of trees, sometimes taking up to five days. Other times, one would be forced to run around the field a number of times, depending on the crime committed. Looking at it positively, the school discipline refined the character of the person. It looked harsh, but it really shaped pupils for adult responsibilities.

The school year also had well-marked activities during which January to March was meant to be a purely academic term; May to July was a term for athletic sports. Classes were subdivided into houses, in which different houses took turns doing activities individually, then in pairs and finally, there were the inter-house competitions to which the parents were invited. Important to note here is that practice was held twice per week, and it was after classes, meaning pupils left at around 5.00 pm on sports days. The inter-house competitions were meant to select the team to represent the school in the inter-school competitions, which took place just before the end of the second term.

The third term (September-November) was reserved for soccer and netball competitions. The same process of recruitment went on, and the inter-school competitions took place in early November. I was recognized for my taking part in both soccer and long-distance races. I had many certificates from my primary and secondary schools and in Teacher Training College.

I personally walked through a very challenging academic path. We did not have electricity (of course, no one's house had installation of electricity in the whole village, including teachers' houses). Paraffin was the most commonly used means of light at night. Thus, I used a homemade lamp, which was a can filled with a wick/paraffin, as earlier stated. There were those days when paraffin was not available. At such times, I carried my studies through the firewood light. Otherwise, when paraffin was available, I would study until very late at night, sometimes going beyond midnight and even to 1.00 am, especially when preparing for the final exams. Sometimes, we combined forces and studied as a group. My group is composed of people like Duncan Muthiora, John Kirata, Edward Jomo and Joseph Mbiu. Duncan was a really good student. He constantly led the class in almost every subject. He led our class many times as the number one student, and at no time did anyone beat him in Mathematics. As for me, I was among the top five students. Duncan was, and still is, a good friend of mine. We have shared many things and have a lot in common. We both attended Kirangari High School. At the time of my wedding, Lucy, my wife, wore Duncan's wife's wedding dress since we could not afford one.

TEACHING ON CATECHISM

One of the other things that Duncan Muchai Muthiora, John Kirata, Edward Gacomo, and I had in common was the catechism class. We had to travel from Gikambura Primary School to the Church of the Torch (ten miles away) every Wednesday for a period of three years. This, including Sunday School, is really the foundation of my Christianity. We were baptized in 1962 by the Late Rev. Crispus Kiongo, who was, at one time, the Moderator of the General Assembly. It was not until late 1963 that we were confirmed and, hence, qualified for the Lord's Table. By then, to be recognized as a full Church member meant being a well-grounded Christian, one who had mastered most of the Christian Biblical teachings. The tests carried on before baptism, and the confirmation was both written and oral. The questions covered both old and new testaments. The Evangelist played a big role in both the catechism and confirmation classes. In no way could one participate in the sacraments if one was not fully qualified. No wonder, then, there were some who remained in catechism class for four to five years. Unfortunately, this kind of Christianity was more academic than spiritual. It left a lot to be desired when it comes to matters to do with spirituality. Nevertheless, it did give a foundation in Christianity and the understanding of the Bible's content.

Religion was also intensely taught as a subject right from standard one (grade one) to high school. I remember in standard three, we had a religiously oriented set book to aid in learning how to read the Kikuyu language. It was called

"Mohoro Ma Tene" (The Old Biblical Stories). This was a collection of Old Testament stories from Genesis to Malachi. Therefore, all that is contained in the Bible was so much treasured in my mind. The Bible became such a treasure to me that I also took it as a subject in all four years of high school and in both my undergraduate and postgraduate studies. I grew up being a Presbyterian all through. I always felt a natural attachment to the Word of God. I loved, and I still love, this denomination. As a historian, I really cherish the founder, John Calvin.

As I advanced to higher classes, standard six and seven, I became quite a regular Church attendant. I used to walk for about three to four miles to Church, and I do not remember any one day that I failed to turn up for the Sunday Service or the Sunday school. One thing I cannot forget is how it felt to sit and watch the minister preach from the pulpit. It always triggered some kind of excitement in me, especially when the minister expounded the Word of God to the people. I could taste its sweetness. Little did I know that there was the seed of priesthood in me. It was only later, when I felt the need to join the ministry, that it was revealed to me that God had called me right from my mother's womb. This was the reason why I really admired those standing on the pulpit and preaching the Word right at a very tender age. When I think of it now and trace my calling, the way God calls people is sometimes like a whisper that one does not automatically realize is a special calling. It is revealed later. God had called Moses far, much earlier than the time he had the experience of the burning bush. God told Jeremiah that he had called him even before he was formed in his mother's womb. When God calls, He never revokes the call despite the long duration it might take. It took David many years, from the time he was anointed as a king to being the king of Israel.

LIFE IN HIGH SCHOOL

My primary education came to an end in 1965. It was this year that I sat for the Kenya African Primary Education (KAPE). The results came out before the end of the year. In January of the following year, I received a letter admitting me to Kirangari High School. Though a day school, Kirangari was known for its academic excellence, discipline and its strong Christian values. It was more of an Anglican Church-oriented school, but one could hardly feel locked out as it embraced all denominations. I chose this school because of its characteristics, academic excellence and its Christian affiliation. I also felt good to join my friend Duncan who had earlier been admitted there.

The completion of the Primary School had two significant marks in one's life. Firstly, it signified that one had climbed to a higher ladder in academic life. It was a kind of rite of passage promising some good status in the society. It was also a path to getting a job of one's choice. The second mark in one's life at this stage was the attainment of manhood. This was through undergoing circumcision. This was the recommended way by the Kikuyu tribe for one to be recognized as having entered into the state of maturity. It was an unwritten law, but one had to undergo this rite of passage before joining high school. There was no way one would have joined high school before getting circumcised. This ritual was undertaken between the time of the final exam (end of November) and the admission to high school in January. Circumcision for both boys and girls was highly valued as a rite of passage. Thus, this was the rite of passage that I had to undergo in December 1965 in preparation to join high school early in 1966. As I have already stated, my Kikuyu people valued and still value the circumcision of men. Otherwise, as I write, female circumcision is experiencing a death that will completely remove it from being a story to rest in the books of history. As for male circumcision, it continues to retain its tribal status and is currently associated with male health, even though it has lost a lot of its former attachment to the Kikuyu tradition.

Thus, having undergone the circumcision, I joined Kirangari High School in February 1966. One of my greatest joys was not that I had joined high school but the fact that, for the first time in my life, I wore shoes. My legs had not known shoes since birth. Just imagine that! Thus, the warmth of the socks and the leather shoes made me feel like I was in a different world. In fact, it took some time for me to learn how to walk in shoes. There was also the added advantage of having a new pair of shorts, a shirt, a pullover and underwear. For the first time ever, I was now wearing underwear. There was so much pride in me. Again, there was the school tie, yet another property I had never owned. I am sure you can see my smartness, and therefore, you do not blame me for my pride. There was no way I would have covered it under a bushel. It was meant to shine. I wanted my community to see and admire me, and for sure, I glowed, illuminating all the darkness of my early childhood.

But there was a negative side to my secondary school life. As I had indicated, the school was a day school far from home. This meant that I could not commute every day to and from school. We, therefore, rented a house where we were living with others, including Duncan Muthiora, Arthur Mukirae, Thairu and another student, bringing the number to five. We had to draw water from a distance of half a mile, shop for groceries, cook for ourselves, sweep the house, wash the utensils, and light up a fire, which sometimes took a long time as we had to depend on the wind to light up the charcoal. We also had to wash our clothes and do the homework using paraffin lamps as there was no electricity. In doing all these, we had come up with a daily schedule on who would do what, and at what time and which day. This was important as we were living about two miles from school in a village known as Gikuni.

Nevertheless, life for me became brighter when, after three years, I was asked by a step-aunt to stay in their home. These were well-up people and it was justified because Mr. Dedan Githegi was among the first lot that went to Alliance High School when it opened its doors in 1926. Githegi had a big herd of cattle and reared poultry. He delivered tens of gallons of milk to the Kenya Creameries Company (KCC) each day. The family also delivered tens of trays of eggs. This was my first time living in a wealthy home. It was also my first time to sleep in a home fitted with electricity. Also, it was the first time for me to live in a home where nutritious food was in plenty.

One advantage I had with this family was that they were very kind. I found a lot of love from my aunt Juliet, her husband Dedan Githegi and from all their children, Mbuka,

Wairigu, Wanene and Wairimu. I will never forget the wonderful treatment I received from these people. Each one of them felt the responsibility to lift up my spirit as they understood the fact that I suffered from an inferiority complex. They showed me how to handle the fork, spoon and knife and appropriate table etiquette within the house, especially around the dining table. These were, and still are, wonderful cousins. Mr. Dedan used to give me lifts (ride) from home to school as it was on his way to Nairobi where he worked as the chairman of the Child Welfare Society. I recall the friendliness, politeness, love and care that Dedan exposed me to. He was such a tender and loving man, and so was his wife, Juliet. Wanene, who was somehow my age mate, was so loving, and his jokes made me feel like one of their family members.

No words can really express the love and tenderness that I received from Wairimu. Wairimu was the youngest, but unlike children of her age from many other families I had met, she was so kind to me. Wairigu was full of love and concern for me. I pray that God will forever bless them, their families and their children of all generations. Dedan and Juliet were staunch Presbyterians. They were Christians right from their youth. They devoted much of their lives and wealth to the Church. Dedan was himself a Church elder for most of his life. They were born-again Christians, and it was in that atmosphere that they raised their children. No wonder each one of them was so warm and loving.

In their neighborhood was Dedan's son-in-law, Mr. Amos Nganga. He was married to Mary, the daughter of Dedan and Juliet. Amos was at one time a member of parliament. I also visited their family quite often. I found their children so kind, especially their firstborn, Nguyai, who later followed in his father's footsteps by becoming Kikuyu Constituency Member of Parliament. We used to play together both outside their home and inside. Their mother, Mary, was also so kind to me.

The head teacher of Kirangari High School in my years was Mr. Wang'ombe. He was tall, energetic and tough when it came to discipline. I remember on a Saturday when we had the Parents' Day in the school, the toilets were cleaned, and students were prohibited from using them that day. Unfortunately for me, I forgot the prohibition, or rather, I had not heard the announcement. Hence, I went inside the toilets. I was seen by one of the prefects, who honored his office by reporting me to Mr. Wang'ombe. I remember receiving five strokes of the cane. It did not matter that I was no longer a primary school kid. For Mr. Wang'ombe, discipline was to be maintained under all circumstances.

In high school, I belonged to the drama club. Immediately I joined it; people learnt that I had lived at Ngong among the Maasai; hence, they nicknamed me '*Kwavi*', i.e., the Maasai from the Diaspora. I took this opportunity to perform in dramas where I pretended to speak the Maasai Language in order to interpret what they were saying. I would collaborate with someone who would also pretend to say what I was saying. I remember the students enjoying my scenes very much. I was also social with a great concern for other students' welfare. For whatever reason, students wanted to be near me such that wherever I was, there would be a group of students laughing as they enjoyed my humor and advice.

As for sports, I was well-known in the areas of soccer and long-distance races. There was this race we called *"Marathon"* that took place almost every Friday, especially in the second term when we had athletic sports. In this race all students were to be involved. It was a long-distance race in which one meandered far from school. In this race, there was no way I could be below number three. I used to acquire a lot of points for my house, Mount Kenya. I also represented both the house and the school as a soccer player in the position of the center forward/number 10. My duty was to score, and scoring indeed, I did. I remember the time our school played against Thika High School, and I carried the day among the spectators. Even today, I have a big heart for sports, and I can sit for long hours watching sports, especially soccer, athletics and basketball. There was an American who taught us how to play basketball. Not that I was good at it, and after all, my height is 5'2' and below the height of basketball players, but I enjoyed watching it. During my studies in America, I was very keen on watching basketball. I remember the joy that flooded my heart when a friend of mine, Mr. Fred, and his wife Joan, took me to watch basketball finals that were held in California. This time, I had the privilege to watch people like Michael Jordan in close quarters, and my heart was puffed up with joy.

As for the religious life at Kirangari, I continued my commitment to striving to lead a moral life. The students we had rented the house with at Gikuni had come to nickname me *"Mwana"* (child). They found me too soft and so unsuitable for the adolescent mobile life. For most of the weekends, I remained indoors instead of joining others as they went out to *"breathe fresh air,"* as they called it. As they moved out of the house, they would say, *"We do not need to worry about leaving the house unlocked because "Mwana" is here."* Of all the students I lived with, I was the only one who never failed to go to Church. There was no Presbyterian Church around Kirangari, and therefore, I attended the Anglican Church. I could not follow their liturgical creed, but I did enjoy the singing and the sermons. Otherwise, wherever I was at home on a given weekend or holiday, I would attend the Church of the Torch, which happened to be the first permanent structure of the pioneer missionaries' sanctuary that opened its door in 1933.

Speaking of going home over the weekends, I remember we had to walk the long distance. Surprisingly, this would be on Fridays, and it was after the games that ended at 5.00 pm. There was no way for one to leave earlier than that. If one did, he would meet the wrath of the principal. We had to walk home because, unlike today, there were no transport vehicles operating between Kirangari and my home area, Gikambura. There were only a few buses that operated irregularly between Kirangari and Nairobi, which was a totally different direction from my home. We really never walked. To be specific, it would be safe to say that we ran all the way. Even what would be termed as walking would not qualify as it was always a wide and fast pace.

Usually, we arrived home around 8.00 pm. The struggle was even more on Sundays when I had to return to school. The main purpose for going home over the weekends was to carry foodstuff that could be used that week before going back home again for the few weeks that followed. This food was mainly a mixture of dry maize grains and beans, some potatoes and even two or three types of vegetables. This time, there was no running but a struggle to walk. I would be carrying this load in a sack, hanging it on my back and hanging others at my shoulder. This made me walk, bending a little bit forward and releasing the strain from each shoulder by keeping on shifting the load from one shoulder to another after every other short distance.

Having started from home at around 1.00 pm, I always made it to Gikuni around 7.00 pm. This tells you how much I was relieved when I got accommodation at Dedan's home. It relieved me from running home for the house rent and the struggle to carry a load of raw food, the involvement in cooking, washing utensils, lighting up the charcoal fire, sweeping the earthen floor and drawing water for daily use.

My major subjects in school were History, Geography and Religious Education. However, I also did other subjects related to science (Physics, Chemistry and Biology), and also Mathematics and English/literature.

I developed a special liking for history from my primary education. The learning of the Greek and Roman Empires, especially the conquests of Alexander the Great and the discovery and occupation of the new lands, among others, inspired me. In high school, the impact of the slave trade and British colonialism, with its impact on nations, further motivated me. Speaking of the study on New Lands, I loved the studies on the United States of America and I felt a great desire to go there in the course of my life. Thank God, he gave me the desire of my heart. I did most of my post-graduate studies in that country. I love America with all my heart. I, in particular, love the American's love for mankind, their hospitality and concern for the needy and their harmonious governance.

Before people sat for the final exam, two things happened. On a set day, people would be given forms that contained a list of schools that offered what was known as "A" Level, that is, Advanced Level. This was a two-year study prior to joining the university. Another section in these forms contained tens of jobs, training institutions, parastatals, industries, firms, etc. By this time, jobs were more than the available manpower. I knew exactly what I wanted, and therefore, as many of my colleagues took as much as two hours to choose and decide on their choices, it took me ten minutes to shade the area on *"Teacher Training."* I had taken a decision right from my childhood that I would be a teacher. This being the case, mine was to find out where Teacher Training colleges were located. It was in the forms, and I shaded it. I did not want to attempt reading others because I had to avoid any temptation to switch on to something else. There were those who opted to choose careers and nothing else. One was given three choices. I made my first choice to be Thogoto Teachers College more so because it was near home and my father also worked there. I also chose Igonji Teacher Training and Kilima Mbogo Teacher Training. There were two other things that motivated me to take teaching as my career. They include:

A great ambition to advance my education, and the only reliable avenue that could help me pursue that in the future, was teaching. The language here is academic. In teaching, the mind is kept academically awake through reading and making notes. This instilled in me a great passion for teaching. It acted as a motivation for my childhood wish to be a teacher. The second reason for liking teaching was the fact that, it was the main avenue that one would spread the Word of God. I was really motivated by my primary school teachers who preached to us in the morning during the parade and the way they helped us spiritually as they taught the Religious Education subject. I also admired the way teachers taught us in Sunday school, especially during the holidays when the boys from Alliance Boys High School were out for the school holidays. I, in particular, remember one named Njomo. As I have repeatedly said earlier, these were instincts and unconscious symptoms of God's calling in me, but I never understood it at the time.

Another reason behind my picking on teaching is because my father earned not much that could educate the other children behind me. Thus, I thought that by becoming a teacher I would be in a position to help in educating my brothers and sister out of the salary that I would be earning.

Immediately, we went out of the classroom after filling out the career forms; every student was curious to know what the other had chosen. From what I learned, every person had filled the most colorful job or training one had dreamt of. Almost every student expected me to choose one of those admired firms, parastatals, or government institutions. They knew that I had a great advantage in getting to the best there was. This was because my host, Dedan, was a widely known man and very influential in all faculties in the country. His son-in-law, Amos Ng'ang'a, was also my friend and relative and equally influential in all government circles. What a surprise it was to my fellow students to learn that of all the careers in those forms, I had picked teaching, which no person in my class would have thought of! I became a laughing stock and the talk of the season. Some were even advising me to go and change before the forms got delivered back to the ministry. I decided not to yield to this pressure from my friends. Between that time and the closure of the school, my classmates mocked me by calling me *"Mwalimu"* (teacher). On the closing day, we had a farewell party prepared by the school with wonderful speeches from both teachers and students. We then bade each other farewell and parted ways.

Since then, I have never seen most of my former classmates and the ones I have met are leading moderate lives with some seemingly struggling so much in life. I met one of those classmates who said to me,

"David, you are what we never dreamt of you becoming; God is so much on your side. In fact, when we mocked you, we never knew that God could bless one through teaching. We all thought of very colourful jobs because such were available. Unfortunately, many of us ended up being alcohol addicts."

Another one I met commented, "'*Kwavi*,' *your dreams and visions have become so much accomplished*." This was a colleague in the school where I was referred to as '*Kwavi*,' meaning a Maasai from the Diaspora. Usually, I respond to them by saying something like,

> "*You know if one's desires and dreams are God-oriented, they will at one time be accomplished. I am always thankful to God who has aligned my life in accordance with his will.*"

I then encouraged such to have a vision and goals in their lives and ask God to be with them as they work through them. I reminded them that there is no lift to success; one has to follow the stairs. I also remind them that "*Blessings come clothed in overalls and disguised as hard and impossible encounters.*" I tell them to always take the first step, and one will be surprised how the overalls will roll down on the ground, exposing the hidden treasures of life.

4. TEACHER TRAINING

After the Form Four examination, there was a long time of waiting before the results came out in the month of March, the following year, 1970. No sooner had the results come out than I got a letter of admission at Thogoto Teachers' College for two years for a P1 training course. P1 was the highest grade attainable in that college. It was the highest grade for a primary school/elementary teacher. The school was opening its doors that month of March.

The first term meant great humiliation, frustration, and torture of the newcomers through what the seniors called "*monolization.*" The seniors called themselves "*Miaka,*" indicating that they had already been made tough by the years; they considered themselves as the mature ones. The newcomers were referred to as "*njuka,*" meaning the fresh ones who, according to "*miakas,*" needed some discipline so as to be acclimatized with the college life and environment. And so, there was this "*miaka*" man who looked brutal, merciless and untamable. He approached me one day and demanded money to buy some cigarettes. I told him I did not have money, which was the whole truth. In response, he said, "*I have given you between now and 8.00 pm, and if you don't give me money, you will face the music this evening.*" I did not take him seriously, possibly because I had not learnt the seriousness of "*miakas.*" In any case, where could I have gotten the money from? The same man came up to where I was, taking the evening meal and looked at me with eyes revealing a lot of anger and hatred, and he said, "*There is still time to save yourself before the doomed hour comes.*" Then he left. As I went outside the dining hall, I saw the very man with a crowd of old students, and as I walked past them, I could tell there was trouble cooking. This is because he aggressively pointed at me, and all the others gazed at me, with one of them shouting, "*You think your father Benson is the king of the college. This is why you think he can have us expelled if we monolize you. If only you know what is awaiting, you.*" Another one followed by saying, "*We will see who has power, your father or the "miakas."*

That evening, my "*miaka,*" an enemy student, went to all the seven men's dormitories and mobilized students, at the same time maliciously spreading the propaganda that I had boasted that no "*miaka*" would touch me because my father held the position of the storekeeper in the college. It had been reported that I claimed that anybody who dared to mistreat me or demand anything from me would be reported to the principal immediately and expelled without any prior notice. In solidarity, he mobilized students who flocked into the dorm where my room was located. It was like they had taken an oath that there should be news of my death or being seriously maimed in one way or the other. This move was kept secret among the "*miakas,*" so much so that even two of them, who were very close to me as we had come from the same neighborhood, never hinted anything to me. At 8.00 pm, a large number of around thirty invaded my room. At first, I thought something horrible was taking place outside. Maybe someone like a thief had been caught. The noise outside was too much and it continued to pick up as many people seemed to be coming towards our dormitory. Then I heard the door of our dorm open, and people came in forcefully and aggressively. I heard them ask, "*Where is he? Where is that "Njuka?*" It was by then I realized that I was the one now to be treated like a thief. Someone had already hurriedly and brutally come rushing to me carrying a big bucket of water. He poured it on me, making me immediately become all wet. No sooner had he acted like this than other twenty people or so descended upon me with kicks, fists and sticks.

I was now shouting loudly and pleading for mercy. In the midst of much noise and bright torches, I was pleading, "*Please, don't kill me! Don't kill me! Have mercy on me!*" Nevertheless, my voice was getting lost in the noise. I could hear others trying to come in through the windows.

I now knew my time had come. They were thirsty for my blood. I tried to fight my way to escape, but every bit of the ground was occupied by my enemies. If only I had a way to escape, I would have gone, never to come back for the training. Now, I was falling unconscious, but I kind of felt two or three people lying on me. It turned out that three watchmen had fought their way to where I was. They had already noticed some of the students and had called them by names and threatened that they would report them to the principal the following day. One of them added, "*After all, we have alerted the principal, and he is on his way here.*"

Upon hearing this, all the students left in a hurry, and before long, it was all quiet. The watchmen and two sympathetic student *"miaka"* neighbors started nursing me. They changed my clothes and the blankets and had me lie on my bed. The college nurse was called, and he gave me some first aid including treating the bruises. Some medicine that I was given turned me into a deep sleep. Fortunately, even with a lot of bruises, my body was intact. I do not know what followed, but I only felt myself in the morning. From the college clinic, I was given some ointment to apply to the bruises and by the end of one week, I was fine.

My father tried to play that matter calmly as per the advice of the watchmen and some students. They had advised him not to pursue the matter; otherwise, the victims would further seek ways of harming me. Later, the students who had participated in attacking me came to learn the fabrication of the story that I had boasted that if anyone attacked me, my father would intervene. A number of them came to me asking for forgiveness. Many of them became good and very helpful friends. They were happy because I did not pursue the matter, which otherwise would have made them undergo harsh punishment, including even being expelled from school. I am happy because God made it possible for me not to get an opportunity to escape that night of the ordeal, for if ever I did, I would never have undergone the training, and my dreams and visions would have been doomed.

In college, I was a member of the soccer team wearing number 10, and I also represented both my house, Mt. Elgon, and the college in the long-distance races in the Inter

Colleges Athletics Competitions. I had acquired so many certificates in these races. Once in a while, I went to the Christian Union club, but I spent most of my time in the library. My goal was to privately sit for the A-Level examination as soon as I graduated from college. One time, I met a lady at Thika who was my classmate back in college. We had not met since our graduation day, which was over thirty years ago. As she introduced me to her colleagues, she said,

"Back in college, if someone asked you whether you had seen Githii, the immediate response was, 'Have you checked for him in the library?"

She went on;

"Githii was a man of books, and I am not surprised that he has come to attain that title of doctor. He also portrayed potential attributes in leadership. So again, I am not surprised that he did not only become a headmaster of both primary and secondary schools but had as well become the head of the Presbyterian Church of East Africa, commonly known as PCEA."

I was really a library person. That is where I spent most of the time while other students warmed themselves on the grass, roamed about in the surroundings, or joined together in groups as they built castles in the air. As for me, I knew that while building castles was another fashion of dreams, they would not go into the sky unless there was a firm foundation, and that was only possible if it was preceded by an action. I really thirsted for a good education as a means to a good foundation for a family and a stepping stone to go places for the bearer. It is the only commodity that none will be able to robe from you. It is the main key opener to a better life for oneself and the offspring.

TEACHING PRACTICE

Teaching practice was one of those areas that students had to be involved in at least four times before the end of the two years that the training took. The schools I took my practices in included Mai-a-Ihii, Muguga Primary School and Ndurarua Primary School. The first two are located in Kiambu County but the latter is located in Nairobi County. It is also where I had my final assessment under Miss Wokabi, who, after marriage, acquired the name Mrs. Mugo. Miss Wokabi was a lovely teacher. She was kind to all students and a wonderful lady with a lot of love and concern for both male and female students. She was also a very staunch Christian and a Church leader. Her subject was physical education which she was very competent in. She was a hero to many of her students and fellow staff members. Among my teachers from Thogoto, she was the only one who attended my wedding and gave us a gift of a kettle.

The teaching practice period was very uncomfortable for many students. It involved the preparation of work schemes, lesson plans, teaching aids (the apparatus) and, in many instances, frustrations from the staff members, depending on who became one's mentor. There were some tutors who behaved very harshly to the students. One could have taken two weeks to make all kinds of preparations, only to have their apparatus torn or thrown away or even destroyed by the tutor. The student would then have to do the work all over again. Some teachers claimed that they were training the students to have patience and to prepare them for the frustrating teaching problems that they would encounter in the future, but from the human perspective, that was not the right way to treat the students. This is why the teaching practice was an anathema to the students. Nevertheless, there were those teachers like Miss Mugo who had a lot of understanding and who labored with the students in trying to shape them to be good teachers. There were some of those negative tutors who even frustrated the students in front of the pupils by scolding and aggressively correcting them while the children listened with amazement, for they regarded a teacher as a very important person. Unfortunately, some of those staff members were alcohol addicts. Others took advantage of female students who bribed them sexually.

During the teaching practice days, we used to wake up at 5.00 am, take a shower, dress up and then rush to the dining hall for breakfast. The mood among the students and the general environment was rushed and full of anxiety. We used to scramble for tea and the pieces of available loaves. Both tea and loaves were never enough because the first lot of students to get into the dining hall took as much tea and as many pieces of loaves as they could. So, there were some students who missed either tea or loaves and sometimes both. No wonder there was a lot of scrambling over the breakfast, where a lot of tea got spilled on the floor in the process. There was also scrambling as people got into the buses. In many cases, the buses were not enough and many students had to travel while standing inside holding their books and their teaching kits. There was also the danger of being left by one's assigned bus. We were expected to be in schools by 8.00 am so that we could participate in the morning assembly, yet some schools were around fifty miles away. It was such a relief and celebration when a teaching practice term came to an end. Unfortunately, for many male students, such celebrations meant going on a drinking spree. Many of them went either to the Thogoto shopping center or Kikuyu town and drank all kinds of locally brewed alcohol, much of which would be prepared in a very unhygienic environment. Some of it would also be mixed with harmful chemicals. No wonder after such a drinking spree, most of the male students would be vomiting and experience quite some health discomfort. This was also something that happened, though to a lesser degree, during the weekends as the students went to drink around.

Fortunately for me, if there was something that I hated, it was alcohol. I had come to hate it more because of the Bible teachings, especially during the catechism classes. I had also come to hate the way drunkards behaved in school and in our neighborhood. I witnessed such, beating up their wives and their children and always at loggerheads with their neighbors. I also knew a number of kids, some of whom we grew up with, who never managed to complete their education because their father misused money through the addictive habit of alcohol drinking. Thus, instead of being influenced by my friends into drinking alcohol, I spent my time studying in the library. I would have qualified as a born-again Christian, but I lacked a testimony of the same.

END OF TEACHER TRAINING

The two years went fast, and before the final examination, we were given forms to fill out. One was expected to make a choice of three districts that he/she would have wanted to work in. I had always longed to be posted in a place where I could acquire a piece of land. The aspiration to acquire a personal piece of land was a great urge in me; I needed to find my way to prosper. We had only a quarter of an acre that had taken my father a long time to financially recover from after buying it at the cost of 250 shillings. By then, this was a great amount of money. He had to get a loan. We were four siblings in the family, together with my parents.

This was especially so because I felt that I had matured. I was also contemplating getting married. In that case, land acquisition was one of my priorities, a prerequisite to marriage and settling. This meant that I had to get out of Kiambu County and go further afield to look for land. Land was not a readily available commodity in Kiambu and when available, it was too expensive. Two areas seemed to me as the likely places to get a substantial piece of land with less money. These were Nakuru and Nyandarua Districts. These districts were more favorable because, after independence, the white settlers who had acquired the lands as gifts from the British Government as a result of their contribution to World War 2 were selling their ranches and farms in readiness to leave the country. They had expected retaliation from the African Government. Some had opted to go back to Britain, while others went to South Africa, where apartheid was the order of the day.

As they left, the Africans formed companies and societies to combine their resources and buy these farms and ranches to get shares for a certain amount of money. Later on, the farms would be subdivided among the members in accordance with the number of shares one had paid for. My father had paid some money to a company known as Mukungugu Land Buying Company. This farm was not yet subdivided, but it was to happen sometime in the future, and if it did while I was near, I would add some shares and reside there. Thus, I took Nakuru District as my first choice and just in case this bounced, I picked the second choice, Nakuru Municipality (which was independent as an urban area) and then had Nyandarua as the third choice.

Not long afterwards, the final exams were over, and then we had a big farewell party and parted company with some, never to meet again in life. If they did, maybe after a couple of years, their lives would have changed so much that they would easily bypass one another without recognition. I recently met someone with whom I was a very close friend, and he could not recognize me. But I recognized him standing at a bus stage in Nyeri, stopped and asked him where he was going and whether he needed a lift (a ride) and I waited a bit to see whether he would recognize me. After a while, I told him, "*If I am not wrong, you are Wambugu, and you took your teachers' training at Thogoto Teachers College.*" Then, with surprise, he said, "*Oh yes, that is my name, but I do not seem to have the slightest idea of who you are.*" I said, "*I am David Githii.*" The mention of my name stirred a lot of memories and we talked for some time until he reached his destination, a short distance before Nyeri town. Before the end of December, the anxiously awaited postings were released by the Ministry of Education. I was posted to Nakuru District without knowing the name of the place and school that the District Education Office was to post me to. Not long afterwards, I traveled to Nakuru, visited the DEO's offices and found names of the posted teachers on the notice board, and besides my name read *"Olmanyatta Primary School, located in Subukia."* I also noticed that one of my school college mates, Simon Kinyanjui was posted in the same school.

TEACHING CAREER

In the second week of January 1972, I boarded a bus that would take me to Nakuru Town, from where I would connect to Olmanyatta in Subukia. My father had been so drained financially in meeting the school fees of the four of us and was also still being deducted money from his salary towards his pension, land buying and a cow he had bought for milk. He had even bought a bicycle. Thus, he was not able to buy the things I required for my new appointment, and neither did he have money to give me to buy any utensils, beddings, chairs and other basics I required. I had with me one cooking pot (sufuria), one can, and a small bed with an old mattress, two blankets and no bed sheets. As for the clothes, I had the three pairs of trousers that I used in college (one of them was so faded that it had somehow lost its original color after undergoing many washings), and there were two shirts. I also had two ties that I used in college. Worse still, I was not able to get any salary for the first three months. All starters had to wait for that duration as it took time for their names to be fixed in the payroll. This is mainly because as there were no computers, every bit of work at the Teachers Service Commission offices was done manually.

Upon arrival in Nakuru, I enquired about the bus to Subukia. I was told that there was only one bus that passed by Olmanyatta from Nakuru. This bus used to leave Subukia, which was thirty miles North of Olmanyatta, at around 5.30 am and reached Nakuru town around 8.30 am. It then served other routes and started its journey back to

Subukia around 5.00 pm. I was further told that it always got to Olmanya very late in the evening because when it reached a place known as Solai, the driver and the conductor got out to enjoy some beer drinking, and it was like they didn't care when people would arrive at their destinations. They would drink and make a lot of noise, calling each other names. Having arrived at Nakuru at 10.00 am, I had then to wait until 5.00 pm before I boarded the bus to Subukia, yet I could not walk about to see the surroundings because my two pots, the mattress and the small spring bed would be stolen. Thus, it turned out to be a long day. That day, I remember I went through hunger, thirst, fear of the unknown and uncertainty of the future, whose beginning seemed to be rough. The hawkers kept passing near me and stopping many times to enquire whether I could buy bananas, bread, biscuits, mandazi, sweets, toothpaste, shoe polish, matchboxes, etc. To each one of these, I shook my head, for I had no money to buy anything. The only money I possessed in the whole world was the bus fare from Nakuru to Olmanyatta.

Despite all the waiting, with accompanying hunger, thirst and other worries, the joy of knowing that I had already accomplished one of my goals in life, being a teacher, really energized me. I was now visualizing myself standing in front of the pupils with the world map, going to the wall and pointing to places as I emphasized my points in the teaching of Geography, History or some biblical places. I could also visualize teaching other subjects like English, Mathematics, or Science-related subjects. From far away, I could visualize the beauty of Olmanyatta School, its roofs of brightly shinning iron sheets, the stone-built walls with cemented floors, a well-kept library, and well-fixed, wide blackboards, on which I could write notes with all pupils' heads going up and down as they copied my notes from the blackboard. I visualized my school house being well selected and kept, possibly with flowers around, as some other beautiful flowers were laid on the table and strategically placed to catch my eyes, saying, "*Welcome home David.*" I saw myself seated on a well-constructed chair matching the table as I prepared my schemes of work and lesson plans. I could visualize the well-kept field with the soccer pitch being well-marked. I really longed to be the game master. I could see Olmanyatta School participating in the interschool soccer competitions' and winning and getting trophies, even in athletics.

Finally, the bus came at around 4.30 pm, and by 5.00 pm, we were on our way. We had followed a road with some settlements where life looked quite promising, but this was just the first ten miles. After this, we turned left and got on a very dusty and rough road. The driver seemed to be in a hurry, and that was good for me, but, in the course of that, we were tossed up, down, right, left, all sides! Sometimes, banging our heads on the bus windows. This was quite uncomfortable for me as my stomach was so empty, and the dust increased my thirst. The road twisted and meandered along bushes, and I hardly could trace any human activities in the outside world except that once in a while, I could see an old man with a flock of sheep and goats driving them home. There were also one or two shepherds who were driving cows only.

The more we moved, the more I seemed to be getting out of touch with urbanized life. Never in my life had I seen such deserted places with no houses nor human life in sight. I had lived all my life surrounded by many busy people, smart people, good roads, green gardens, shopping centers, etc. As I was still wandering, the bus stopped and looking outside, I saw two small houses; instantly, I heard the bus conductor say, *"This is Solai Center; those who are alighting here can do so."*

As he was coming to the end of that sentence, he was halfway towards the two buildings with rusty iron sheets and walls bending at 40 degrees. I just wondered what prevented the walls from falling. As I wondered, the person sitting next spoke rather angrily in a language I had not heard before. I later learnt that was Kipsigis language. I enquired from a person sitting behind me in Swahili, *"Huyu mama amesemaje?"* (What has this woman said?) *"Amesema eti tutangoja hapa kwa masaa mawili ata zaidi."* (She has said we will wait here for at least two hours or more). Then I asked him, *"Why?"* He responded, *"Hawa watu watakuja wakishashiba pombe"* (These people will come back after they have drunk beer to their satisfaction). I had my eyes opened for a little while, and then I fell asleep. I was awakened by the noise that the driver and the conductor made as they had the bus started. Other drunkards were as well boarding the bus and were an added asset to the noise.

To my surprise, darkness had engulfed the environment. I could see nothing, for it was all dark outside. Before long, the bus was rattling about as it tossed us about. Now, I could not tell whether we were heading North or South, but by the dim headlights of the bus, I could tell that it was only the road that separated us from widespread bushes. Here and there, a rabbit, an antelope or a zebra would cross the road. Everybody was quiet, apart from the bus conductor, the driver and other drunkards. They were shouting to their loudest as they bragged about how much alcohol each had taken. They could even talk of their women lovers. At some point, one of them vomited and the entire bus was stinking. We had gone for some time when the conductor said, *"Those alighting at White Rocks can start coming towards the door."* After about fifteen minutes, the bus stopped.

The White Rocks residents got out. I tried to trace for any life through the window, but it was only bushes that responded to the curiosity of my eyes. When the bus started again, the conductor said, *"The next stage is Nyamamithi."*

Yes, after another fifteen minutes, the bus stopped. Quite a group of people alighted. Then the conductor said, *"Those alighting at Olmanyatta stage ought to start coming to the door."* My heartbeat now raised, my breathing system changed, and sharp panic struck me. Then, before long, the bus slowed down and stopped. The conductor said, *"This is Olmanyatta stage."* I was now standing next to the door and behind me were a man and a woman whom I could tell were not Kikuyus. No sooner did the three of us touch the ground, than the bus was whisked away.

With the light from the bus gone, everything turned dark. It was by then that I remembered that I did not claim my properties from the bus, the only property I owned had gone. I was muddled and confused. I then looked around as my eyes were wooing the darkness, thinking that the man and woman were also around, muddled and confused like me, but alas, they had gone - then, not knowing what I was doing, I followed the only road I found branching from the main road and went on calling, *"Hey! Hey! Mko wapi? Tafadhali ningojeeni! Ningojeeni! (Hey! Hey! Where are you? Please wait for me. Wait for me)* Then, very far in front, I had someone ask, *"Iko nini?"* (What is wrong?) I gathered the energy and responded, *"Nimepotea."* (I'm lost)

The same horrible images ambushed my mind. What if a leopard or a lion comes out of these bushes? What if I step on a huge snake? The man then said, *"Basi, twakungoja"* (We are waiting for you). The man shone a torch in my direction, and I felt relieved as I could estimate the distance between them and me. The closer I drew to them, the brighter the torch lit my way. When I got to them, I was really red, panicked and frustrated. It was like I left Kenya and I was in another world all together. I finally caught up with the two. The man shook my hand and asked me, *"Unaenda wapi?"* (Where are you going?) *"Ninaelekea Olmanyatta Primary School."* (I'm on my way to Olmanyatta Primary School). The man then said, *"Utatembea kama dakika thelathini."* (You will walk for about thirty minutes). I did not believe my ears, and to re-affirm, I asked him, *"Unasema dakika ngapi?"* (You said how many minutes?) He repeated, *"Thelathini (thirty)."* He then added, *"Ikiwa utanipa ata chai, nitakupeleka* (If you give me something, I will take you). I then explained to him the fact that I did not have money, and to make matters worse, my luggage was left on the bus. I told him *"I am a new teacher posted to that school."* It is by having said that that the man turned so friendly that he offered to take me there. He said, *"Mtoto wangu anasomea huko"* (my child is a pupil there). He then talked for a while with the woman whom I had already concluded to be his wife, handed a small package he had to her, and then we started walking but making wider strides.

To me, that was an angel that God had given me. We never talked much. I hope the man realized that I had really panicked since my breathing was audible, and I seemed to stammer while we talked. At one point, a vehicle showed up behind us, and as it passed, the man said,

"Huyo ni Bwana Labert, ako na shamba hapo mbele. Nimumoja ya wale walikuwa colonial masters Hii ghali lake ndiye pekee inapa kana hapa. Tunaishi mahali hakuna maghali ka ka mbarambara setu" (that is Mr. Labert, he has a farm not very far from here. He is one of the colonial imperialists. His is the only vehicle you will see in our surroundings. We live in such a remote place that you hardly find vehicles on our roads. After what looked like less than thirty minutes, we came to an open ground with long thatched buildings.)

I automatically knew that this was where Mr. Labert kept his horses. We seemed to pass the buildings when the man turned right and went straight to a thatched house where I could see a dim lamp light through some house cracks in the walls. He knocked on the door, and a male voice answered the knock by saying, *"A minute, please."* The door opened from inside, and the man shook my friend's hand, saying, "*Habari yako Kipsang?*" (How are you, Kipsang?) The man responded, "*Sijambo, mwalimu Charles,*" and he continued, "*Nimekuletea mwalimu mgeni*" (I have brought you a new teacher). Then, with a wide smile, Mr. Charles shook my hand, held it tightly, embraced me and asked, "*You are Mr. David Githii?*" I said, "Yes." He then said, "*Welcome and feel at home; do not be threatened by the bushes.*" The man then left, and Charles closed the door.

As Charles gave me a stool to sit on, he said, "*I am sure you are red and hungry; what time did you leave Nakuru?*" I said, "*Around 5.00 pm, but we had a long delay somewhere on the way,*" and Charles interrupted, "*We are used to that. In fact, they are early today; there are times they get here at 10.00 pm, and then you can imagine one walking all that way, especially when one is carrying luggage. As you will come to learn, we do most of our shopping in Nakuru and only once a month when we go to collect salaries. Otherwise, the only other place we can do any shopping is Subukia, which is ten miles away. Mind you, one has to walk that distance as there is no other means of transportation.*" Then Charles said, "*Let me first give you food as I would expect that you are very hungry after that long journey.*" It was while I was eating that I asked Charles, "*By the way, how far is it from here to school?*" Charles asked, "*Which school?*" I said, "*Olmanyatta Primary.*" Charles looked at me with a big surprise and amazement and said, "*I thought you saw the classes. You are already in the Olmanyatta Primary School Campus. The tall thatched building, with muddy and hollow walls, are the classes.*" With all disbelief written on both my face and voice I asked Charles, "*You mean what I thought are the dwelling places for the horses are the classes?*" Without further elaboration, he said, "*Yes,*" and then quickly, as if to cut short that subject, he said, "*You know, today I sat here taking lunch and then a snake coiled around the door frame of this house, and I called the boys, and they killed it.*"

He then had a long laugh. And then, as if to close that topic as well, he said,

"*David, you will come to like this place. You will love the people; they are very friendly and hospitable. We have a staff of fifteen teachers. The school deputy and the headmaster left in December; I am the new headmaster. Anyway, let me show you where you will lay down your head; we shall talk more tomorrow.*"

Inhibited by silence, I was shown a small bed and no sooner did I cover myself tightly so that no snake would get to me than I fell asleep. I was awakened by Charles as he prepared some tea. Before long, he called me, "*David, the day is with us here; wake up, wash your face with this warm water and sit up for a cup of tea.*"

I reluctantly woke up. I still felt so red, confused and unbelieving. I put on the pair of trousers and moved to where the water was and bent to wash my face, but alas, the water looked so brownish, as though it had been tapped from flooding water. I then said to Charles, "*I am sorry, Charles, this water is quite dirty.*" Charles then laughed and said,

"*That is the water we use here; I will take you to where it is drawn. I can understand what you are feeling because I had undergone the same confused mood when I arrived here, but like me, you will get used to it.*" and then he laughed.

By then, I had already learnt that Charles was a very jolly man and a man of great faith in God.

After I had washed my face (which to me looked like dirtying it), Charles asked me to follow him. We first visited the houses of some teachers to whom he introduced me. They all looked cheerful and respectful. Then, he led me to the classes. I could hardly believe my eyes, but here I was. Like the teacher's houses, all the classes were thatched, with the roof gaping in some areas, and other areas had some kind of weeds growing on them. The classes were partitioned with grass, which in many places left wide openings. Children in adjacent classes could easily share pencils, books or ink through these holes. The walls had gaping holes that one could see through, and some of the walls were supported with posts, which were so much eaten by white ants. The whole thing looked so threatening. The toilets for the children were a bit far from the classrooms. They were pit latrines whose walls were thatched up.

Finally, I was taken to where the water was drawn from. It was a narrow stream originating many miles north of the school and passing through very thin soil that was easily eroded, turning the water brown. It was also the stream the wildlife drank from and the cattle, sheep and goats. People also bathed in it within its course. It was also in this stream that people washed their clothes. The totality of the environment depressed me, but the joy in the kids, teachers and community, the hospitality and hope that they gave me, very soon dressed my heart with joy and acceptance and as a godly chosen way to spring up my dreams and goals. Mr.

Charles assigned me to teach English, History and Geography in standard seven. The students here were in their final year, and they needed thorough preparation for the final exams at the end of the year - that was my understanding.

The teaching profession that I had waited for many years had finally come. This was what I had aspired for. It became regular for standard seven to be in class by 7.00 am instead of getting into the class at 8.45 am. It so happened that by the time the pupils arrived, they always found me in the class and having ready work on the blackboard. I also made it mandatory that classes six and seven would not be leaving school at the usual time that the school ended, at 4.00 pm. They would remain in after the other pupils had gone home until 5.30 pm. I distributed the standard six work to be done in groups while I handled standard seven. It also became mandatory that the standard seven class was to report on Saturdays from 8.00 am to 12.00 noon. All this time, I was physically in. Many times, as I walked towards the classes, I could see teachers looking at me as they wondered what on earth I was doing, devoting myself so much, yet I was not paid, not even a shilling, for that extra teaching. I bet no teacher would have attempted to extend a lesson.

Many of them went by the bell, and even if one was writing a sentence on the blackboard, as soon as the bell rang, he/she could not complete it. Many times, I could see teachers talking in groups, even after the bell for class resumption had rung. The worst part was when the headmaster was not in school. Some of them would remain in their houses, leaving the children to make all the noise they could. At such times, I made a quick round to all classes authorizing the prefects to silence the pupils. I even went to the extent of telling the prefects to hand in the names of the noise makers to me. When I was with class seven pupils on Saturdays, all the male teachers were roaming in the surrounding places, drinking homemade beer. Reports reaching me from some parents indicated that these teachers talked evil of me, saying how foolish I was in giving all my time to pupils and yet there was no payment. This did not deter me from carrying on my duties very devotedly and without reservation.

One day at the end of February 1972 (less than two months since I started teaching), the headmaster called me in his office. He told me,

"David, I do very much appreciate the work you are doing. In fact, you are doing it for me because all credit will be mine when the kids pass well. And you know what?"

He pulled a letter from an envelope and handed it to me, saying, *"Read this. It is from the District Education Officer."* I read the letter, but I could hardly believe my eyes, for it read,

"Congratulations! You have been appointed the deputy headmaster of Olmanyatta Primary School with immediate effect. This office wishes you all the best as you engage in this kind of leadership. Charles has talked very highly of your tireless commitment to your work. We believe him and this is

why we have approved his proposal to appoint you as his deputy, a position you deserve."

I was unbelievably gazing at this letter when Charles broke the silence by saying, *"Yes, it is true; you are now the deputy headmaster of this school."*

In response, I told Charles,

"Thank you. I really don't work with an eye on promotions, but since it has come, I have accepted it. In any case, I am too green in this field, and I would have expected a more experienced teacher to receive such a favour."

Then Charles said,

"The EO's Office is aware of the kind of teachers we have here, teachers who lean on their salaries more than the welfare of the children. It is also aware of the drunken behavior of these teachers. He has letters of complaint from the parents in his file. Thus, when the DEO asked me to recommend one of my staff, I could not find a better person than you among the staff I have here. I am sure God will continue to shower favours in your teaching profession if only you maintain that attitude in the handling of your duties. Let's meet here on Friday to lay down the strategy through which you and I can uphold to promote this school both academically and physically."

Charles went on to say,

"As you will note, the records indicate that over several years, the best candidate is the one who would get two 'D's with one 'E.' Otherwise, the results are always EEE, EDE, and DEE. I believe that these children were born by women like all others

138

who scored an A or a B in other schools." Having said that, I left him.

By that evening, all the teachers had learnt that I was the deputy headmaster. One of the teachers dared to confront the headmaster and asked him;

"How can you recommend David to be your deputy yet he is so green, while some of us have been in teaching for over fifteen years, and some in the Olmanyatta campus for over ten years?"

To that, Charles said, *"I will explain that in the staff meeting tomorrow."* True to his word, he summoned a staff meeting and explained that he went to the DEO's office to collect the books, and he was given a letter that indicated that David had been appointed the deputy. One experienced teacher said,

"Of course, the DEO appoints whoever the headmaster recommends. I have been in this profession for many years, yet you overlooked my name."

In response, Charles said,

"It is no hidden truth that the DEO's Office is aware of the poor academic results that this school has attained over the years. He has in his file a number of complaints from the parents complaining about your negligence and poor attitude towards your duties. There is even an accusation of some of you sexually abusing school girls. No wonder they could not approve a teacher that has been here for long."

Doesn't the Bible say, *"You will know them by their fruits?"* And because Charles could read the written anger towards him on the faces of all teachers except me, he abruptly ended the meeting.

We carried on teaching in spite of the tension that persisted. But I hardly knew that Charles had already worked out his way for a transfer to Nakuru Municipality. He had just made a hint when one day he said to me, *"Surprisingly, David, I might not be here for long, but time will tell."* The school then closed for the April holidays. True to his words, he had already worked out his transfer in early March, but he kept it a secret.

There was this day then when a vehicle pulled into the school campus at around 10.00 am. It had some house furniture and then came out a very smartly dressed man. Mr. Charles greeted him, and they chatted a bit, then he beckoned me to join them. I was outside the classroom as it was break time. When I reached them, Charles, with his broad smile, told the new man, *"Meet Mr. David Githii, the Deputy Headmaster. He is a wonderful man to work with. He works in season and out of season."*

Then he turned to me and said,

"Mr. David, meet Mr. Gedraph Kimata, the new Olmanyatta Primary School headmaster. I know this takes you by surprise but I did not want to let the cat out of the bag until I was sure this had worked out. In fact, even before I had come here, I had already started working out for a transfer to Nakuru Municipality where I am going to be teaching henceforth."

I did put on a relaxed look as I responded to Charles, saying, "*Yes, it has taken me by surprise, but if the going has benefits for you and your family, it is more profitable to go that way.*" Turning to Kimata, I said, "*Welcome to Olmanyatta. It is a good place in spite of the poor look of its environment.*"

The two of them got into the office, where Charles started handing over to Kimata. Meanwhile, I supervised the removal of Charles's furniture and getting Kimata's furniture in the house. The vehicle that had transported Kimata's furniture was to transport Charles's furniture to his home at Bahati. Thus, Kimata's furniture was then entered as Charles' property was being loaded in the same vehicle. After about one hour, Charles and Kimata were through, and I was then instructed to call all teachers for an urgent staff meeting. Mr. Kimata was introduced to the staff as the new headmaster, something that seemed to make the staff happy.

One could read that between the lines. Then Mr. Kimata made a brief speech, but he finally said,
   "*I would like everybody to understand that being so new in this school, I will very much be dependent on my deputy in running the school affairs. In fact, he will be my eyes.*"

Then Charles called upon me to make the final remarks. I thanked Mr. Charles for his devotion to running the school within the short time that he had been there and then said,
   "*In conclusion, Mr. Kimata, remain assured that you have full support from the teachers, and as you have stated, I promise to be your good eye.*"

The meeting ended, and Charles, Kimata and I remained for two hours in the office as they made the final touches on the handing-over process. After this, Charles boarded the truck and off he went.

Now, with Charles gone, the teachers' anger was focused on me. It is like my promotion became a poison to my relationship with them. The good news was that I persistently stuck to my daily routine which by now had become so much part of me. My presence was being felt by all the pupils, and even now the staff could no longer take French leave just because the headmaster was not in. They no longer wasted time discussing trivial things as the children remained in the classes alone. They could no longer release children on time or start classes late. Each one of them became cautious because no one wanted to be reported to the headmaster. After all, the headmaster had categorically said that what I was to recommend was what he would go by.

Every teacher became active, and there seemed to be a new life in the school. The headmaster was quite often away as if he was after something in the offices. He would come to me in the morning and tell me,

"David, even today, I will not be in; there is something that is keeping me on my toes. Possibly, you will know its outcome by the month of May."

I was never concerned with his activities, and after all, when he was in, he really taught. He was such a talented teacher and speaker. Moreover, much of the ongoing teaching focused on the end-term examination revisions.

Kimata was the Nakuru District Kenya National Union of Teachers chairman. This kind of position was held by very influential people because it meant winning the hearts of most of the teachers in Nakuru District. He was well known by all those in authority, especially in the circles of education. He was a very persuasive person with a commendable personality. So, his absenteeism could be understood on that basis. We had agreed that I could make use of the time his subject would come in the timetable so that when he was in, he could use mine as well. Again, the month of March went fast. The end-of-the-term exams were done, results were handed over to the pupils and parents, and the school closed for the April vacation. I never met Kimata until the final week prior to the opening of the school in the month of May. It was towards the end of April, when I sat outside my house, that I saw a truck coming and stood next to Kimata's house. Kimata came out having a big smile and embraced me with a lot of love. I could not understand why he was so happy. He then handed me a letter and told me, *"This letter hails from the DEO's Office; please read it."*

The contents of the letter read,

"Congratulations to you, Mr. Githii. I am hereby informing you that you have been appointed the Headmaster of Olmanyatta Primary School with immediate effect. We have seen your great dedication to your teaching profession. We

have great faith in you, and we will do all it takes to support you."

This was only the second term. I had been in the school for four months only, but here I was - a headmaster. At first, I missed words to respond to Mr. Kimata, but I remember saying to him,

"Thank you. But why have you left us so soon?" He said, *"I have decided to move out of Nakuru District to work in Nakuru Municipality, which, of course, gives me good access to my family."*

If you can recall, it is for the same reason that Charles had also moved from Nakuru District to Nakuru Municipality so that he may be near his family. And who knows, God is purposely doing these things to reward you for your devotion.

Mr. Kimata then called five boys who were playing on the school field. They got into his house and started loading his furniture onto the truck. Meanwhile, we sent for the chairman of the school, whose home was next to the school, and within one-and-half hours, we had completed the handing-over ceremony. Since teachers were housed in the school compound, they were around. A teacher who had overheard Kimata speaking to me about his transfer had already whispered to the teachers of Kimata's transfer but he had not heard of my being appointed the headmaster. Of course, they would not have thought that I could be appointed the headmaster, because I was too green and I had not even finished three months as a deputy headmaster.

But soon, they got it right. As the chairman left the office, one teacher stopped him, and I am sure he asked what was happening. The chairman told him that Kimata had gone for a transfer and the fact that, I had been appointed as the headmaster. Mr. Kimata then sent for the teachers for an urgent staff meeting. Unfortunately, the teachers refused to respond to his call. Kimata waited for them for more than one hour. He could not wait anymore as he was concerned that the waiting charges for the truck would be very high. He, therefore, bade me goodbye, saying, "*I wish you all the best.*" I also waved him back, saying, "*I will look for you soon.*" As the vehicle left the school compound, Kimata waved at me, and I waved back at him.

My entire life had now taken a totally different dimension. That was around Friday when Mr. Kimata left. The school was to open in a week's time. I decided to remain indoors, for I could discern that the teachers were very angry with me, and I was not sure the direction their anger would take. But my fears were affirmed three days after Kimata left. It was around 4.00 pm while sitting outside my house when I saw a group of teachers coming. They were really drunk. They headed straight to my house with each holding a bottle of beer (Tusker) and having fixed others in their armpits, and some others in their pockets. They were making a lot of noise and calling me all kinds of dirty names. I heard one say,

"*What we need today is his head; he cannot be the headmaster over us. We will have his head detached from his body.*"

On hearing this, I realized that they were coming to attack me.

I could not wait anymore as they were coming very fast, though they were staggering since they were drunk. I got into the house and locked the door tightly. I now remembered the midnight ordeal at Thogoto College, when all *'Miaka"* students almost killed me. Other images started ambushing my mind - what if they burn the house? What if they broke the weak doors or windows of my house?

Before I had finished thinking about the *"what ifs,"* I had a big bang! Someone hit the water tank that was placed outside my house with a bottle full of beer. It sounded like an explosion! Then, immediately following this, someone else hit the door mightily with his foot. By then, they were making a lot of noise and shouting such things like,

"You 'Juka' (freshman), you cannot practice your stupidity and inexperience over us. We cannot withstand you. Who do you think you are? You are nothing! You are Just the most inexperienced teacher on this campus! Open, we need your head, and we don't want your highheadedness here."

The bottles went bang! Bang! Bang! The only advantage I had was that when each of them lifted one leg to hit the door hard, he staggered and, therefore, never applied the full force on the door. As the shouting and the beating of the drum and the door continued to gain momentum, the chairman of the school was alerted by some women who were drawing water from the nearby stream. He and three other men came, and I heard the chairman say,

"Sasa walimu, kitu gani mnafanya? Si mwalimu ni madaraka amepawa na serikali? Nyinyi nyote hamwezi kuwa headmaster; mkiendelea nitaita polisi" (Now teachers, what are you doing? Your colleague was just promoted by the government; you cannot all be headmasters. If you continue with this behavior, then I will call the police).

After this, many more people came and threatened to fight the teachers. I heard one person say,

"How can you dare to fight our new and very dedicated teacher? You have been here over the years, and your work is to roam about drinking and carrying out rampant immorality, including sexually abusing school girls. And for many years, this school had had no child admitted to a sound government school. Does it mean we have all given birth to fools?"

The chairman then asked me to come out of the house. No sooner had I come out than all the teachers retreated to their houses.

Soon, the school opened. From this point, the teachers had what looked like a go-slow strike. They were reluctant to go into the classes to teach. They would get into the class later than the time stipulated in the timetable and even then, they did not carry on any serious teaching. The resistance continued, and this degree of bitterness was expressed in depth during the staff meetings.

Any agenda that I floated was negatively handled to the extent that we sometimes had some bitter exchange of words, especially with one teacher whose name was Kariuki, an untrained teacher who was the mastermind of the attacks against me. With bitterness, he hated seeing me. The other teachers who were highly charged with hostility were Michael and Kipkoech. These could hardly keep their hatred in control. In fact, they forced me to be always armed with a whip that I hid in the inner pocket of my jacket. I hardly kept this jacket down even while in my house.

I remember one day when these three teachers went on a drinking spree and boasted that they were to beat me that evening. Fortunately, as they were drunk, they made suspicious noises as they entered the school campus. I was not sure that they were heading for my house; hence, I never bothered to close the door. I had just placed some water in a cooking pot on the fire in readiness to make some dinner. Before I realized, they pushed the door open without knocking and just before I rushed to close the door, they had already found their way into the house. They were right there facing me. As usual, Mr. Kariuki was the most aggressive. As he came towards me, he was saying,
"What do you think you are? You think this is your kingdom, and we are your children. Today, we will teach you a lesson."

Then he dug in his jacket for a whip; another one had his sword drawn out, and yet a third one had a small axe.

I sensed the seriousness of the ordeal, and I had to act quickly. I speedily got hold of the pot that I had placed on the fire and quickly splashed the warm water on their faces. Before they managed to wipe the water from their faces, I got to my bedroom and slammed the door, locking from inside. I then threatened them, saying,

"If you think you are more circumcised than me, dare to come in! I am now well armed; whoever gets in here will turn into pieces of human flesh. Come on!"

I was just trying to pretend that I was really courageous; otherwise, by now, every organ that constituted my body and self was shaking in knee-knocking fear. But one thing I knew was that whoever tried to come in would taste their salty blood from my whip works. But then, what is a whip compared with a sword and an axe? I was aware that by the time I would be lifting my whip for the second time to bring it down, the sword or the axe would be on me. That is why I kept on threatening them in order to arouse their imagination about what kind of weapon I had with me,

"Do you think you are the only one with swords and axes? I also have all that and a spear as well. Let any one of you dare come in, and you will carry his corpse out."

I then started shouting through the window, calling for some help. Immediately, some passersby responded, and my attackers ran into their respective houses. I then came out of hiding and explained my predicament to my rescuers. I told them it was all about my being promoted to the position of headmaster, something they had not expected. They had expected one of them to take that position, but the government could not do that, for they are known to be irresponsible drunkards and very mean in handling their teaching duties. Then one of them said,

"We have seen these teachers roaming about even during working hours, going for alcohol-drinking sprees. How, then, do they expect any of them to be given a viable responsibility,

like being appointed to be a headmaster? We are there to protect you, Mr. Headmaster. Just keep us updated. We have already enjoyed your presence in this school. All the children are talking very positively about you. God brought you here with a purpose and a mission for you to accomplish. Just be assured that you have the support of all the parents."

As soon as the two left, I heard two teachers talking to Mr. Kariuki, who had come out having noticed the departure of the passersby;

"For sure, you cannot do this; let us bury the hatchet and work. What image do you think we are painting to both parents and the children?"

With these words, Mr. Kariuki took a deep breath and said,

"It's not over. No! We are men; we cannot give in so easily. We have to let him learn a lesson. Meanwhile, let's go to Kipkoech's house for further strategies."

I could hear their pounding steps as they marched away. Before long, my former college mate, Mr. Kinyanjui came to my house and seemingly had come to my side. He encouraged me but he at the same time cautioned me to do my best to avoid any confrontation with Mr. Kariuki. This, he said, was because he had kept on vowing to injure me one way or another. I now became very concerned with Mr. Kariuki and his group's behavior, such that I could not go outside my house after 6.00 pm. Someone had whispered to me that one or two teachers were making a lot of regular movements at night around my house in the pretense of going to the toilet, which was near my house. This confrontational mood went on for a while.

In the midst of all this turmoil, it came to my notice that Mr. Kariuki had abruptly become very quiet. I took this to mean he was quietly plotting on how to deal with me as he was thirsting for my blood, and it was for this reason that I was always armed with my whip because I never knew where we would meet and what he would decide to do. Then, one evening, Mr. Kinyanjui came to me and said,

"I am sure you have noticed that Mr. Kariuki has become unusually quiet. The reason for this is that he has impregnated a schoolgirl by the name of Warigia. This is why he is so depressed, and he has been cautioned by the other teachers that he cannot escape from your wrath now. They have all convinced him that you will see him interdicted, especially because he is an untrained teacher. This could lead him to jail. Worse still, the Whiteman - Mr. Labert has a long relationship with Warigia's sister. He treats her as his second wife. Thus, this white man has a very close association with the family, and he has already consulted his lawyer, ready to file a case against Kariuki tomorrow."

This being the case, the teachers have already helped Kariuki in writing a letter of resignation which he has to deliver to the District Education Office tomorrow before Mr. Labert files the legal case in the court of law. At this juncture, I asked Mr. Kinyanjui, *"Do you think he has the intention of marrying Warigia?"* To this, Kinyanjui responded;

"I am not sure. But Warigia's family is saying that he is a pretender and they will not listen to him; they want him to face the law."

Having given me this information Kinyanjui left because he needed to prepare for his lesson for the following day.

I then wore my heavy coat because the night was approaching and being July, it was a bit cold. I went straight to Kariuki's house. I knocked on the door, and after he had said, "*Yes, come in*" I then entered. He had his head on the table. He even did not look up immediately, I guess he had assumed that it was his usual friends coming to comfort him. I said, "*Good evening, Mr. Kariuki?*" He looked up and gazed at me and I could tell his body was shivering as the lips betrayed it. He never answered my greetings. Instead, he quickly and in an open hostility moved into his bedroom. He left me there. I then pulled a chair and sat down facing the bedroom door. I remember saying to him,

"*Mr. Kariuki, I am very sorry for your current situation. I have come so that we can work out a strategy that will give us a positive solution. In this case, you don't have to have that withdrawn mood. I am sure you would not expect such a gesture, given what has been going on between you and me. But whatever the case, we are human beings and we fall into errors at one time or another. Please give me the benefit of the doubt and, at the same time, try to test the waters. I want to get you out of this dilemma, and I mean what I say.*"

Kariuki remained quiet, and I could only hear his heavy breathing. I kept on persuading him, and I was almost to the point of giving up when he emerged from the room. He gave me a prolonged look and finally said, "*What do you want me to do?*" I said, "*First, please tell me, do you want to marry the girl?*" He had his face brightened up, and with his lips now stable, he said, 'Yes.' I could tell from his look that he could not believe me, and possibly somewhere in his heart, he took me as a spy for his enemies. For this reason, I did not want to talk about the issue with him. I just told him;

"*Okay, let's go to Warigia's parents, and your work is only to tell them that you are very much willing to marry the girl.*" Then he said, "*But they have refused to talk to me.*"

Then I continued;

"*It is for that reason that I am taking you. That family, like many other parents, respects me as the headmaster, and even for me to be in their house will be a great honour for them. I am sure they will not let me down.*"

Kariuki then got into his room, wore a warm jacket, and before long, we were on our way trekking on the 30-minute' walk. None of us uttered a word. We just walked silently.

When we arrived, I knocked on the door. A child opened the door and rushed inside, saying, "*It's the headmaster.*" Then there was a quick rearrangement of the sitting pattern, and with a lot of excitement, the mother came to the door and said, "*Come in, headmaster, what joy to have you here.*" By then, she had not seen Kariuki, who was behind me. As I got into the house, I said, "*I also have another teacher with me and a good friend of mine.*" As soon as they saw Kariuki's face, the atmosphere became deadly silent. The mother's mood and that of all others got smeared with hatred. They glanced at Kariuki with eyes that cursed him for stepping into their home. Nevertheless, we were offered a seat. Before long, we were served with some food. Once in a while, I tried to break the silence by asking the kids about their school life, their performances, of their subjects of interest. Finally, we completed eating.

It is in African culture that, when visitors get into one's home, the first thing is to feed them before one even enquires about the purpose of the visit. Hence, we have this Kikuyu proverb that says, '*Ngaragu ndihoyagwo uhoro*' (you don't seek information from a hungry person). It was after eating that I informed the family that I had come because I had something to share with them, and if it were possible, we could share it on camera. Then, the children were asked to go to another house. Then, I explained the fact that, Mr. Kariuki was one of my very good and supportive staff and the fact that he was a very reliable teacher. Also, as far as I was concerned, he could make a good husband and father.

I explained that, though it was not intentional that Warigia got pregnant, Mr. Kariuki loved her and was just waiting for her to finish primary school and then marry her. It is for that reason that he did not feel so much bothered because, after all, she was to sit for her final exam in November. Therefore, although he could not openly say that, for him, the pregnancy was timely. I then said, "*Please, give Kariuki the opportunity to tell it all for himself.*" Kariuki then explained at length the fact that he loved Warigia and his intention has always anchored on marrying her;

> "*We had already laid strategic ways to deal with this man, and our aim was to have him jailed because he has spoilt the life of our daughter. The assurance that he will marry our daughter has saved the situation, but we also want to know the date he will bring his parents here. We want to meet them to*

make sure that they are in agreement and our daughter will be in good hands."

Turning to me, the mother said,

"I believe you because of the great trust we and all other parents have in you." She continued to explain to Kariuki how bitter they had been because they thought that his intention was to spoil their daughter. They also told him that they had been told malicious things about him, but they had learnt more about him from the headmaster whose word they would always embrace. In conclusion, Kariuki, whose face had so much brightened and was no longer looking down, said,

"I deeply love your daughter; I have always counted her as my wife since I came to know her; about my parents coming, I will bring them here any time you want, even if you say this coming weekend."

The mother called the two sons and asked them to go to Labert's home and, through his sister, to let Labert be told to refrain from taking the legal path in dealing with kariuki. After some discussions, it was decided that Mr. Kariuki's parents pay this family a visit after one month as in accordance with the Kikuyu traditions, they had to be accompanied by a few other people and the hosts had also to have a few other people as the discussion would dwell more on the required dowry and its subsequent payment. After this, the family bade us farewell. As soon as we were outside the house, Kariuki tightly grasped my hand, and he warmly said,

"Thank you so much; I really never expected anything like that. I was really nervous. I had even written a letter of resignation that I was to personally take to the DEO's office tomorrow. Even worse still, Mr. Labert was to file a case against me and there was no way I could have overcome that, for as you know, he could have used money because he has it."

In response, I said, *"It is my pleasure. I actually acted in accordance with the spirit of non-retaliation, a gift that God has bestowed upon me."* We chatted for a while, and before we knew it, we got into the school compound; as we parted company, Kariuki said to me,

"Please, Mr. Githii, forgive me for my arrogance and agitated spirit. I am very sorry for the inconvenience I have caused you and your good administration."

I went straight to my house, had a cup of tea and then slept. I later learned that, as soon as I had parted company with Kariuki, he went ahead to assemble all teachers in his house. He explained to them all that had taken place, how I took him to Warigia's parents and the outcome of that visit. The consequence was that all the teachers wholly and totally came to my support. To show their solidarity, all the teachers laboriously got involved in teaching. And for the first time in the history of that school, that year's examination results did not consist of the usual pattern of some D's and E's. There was a remarkable appearance of a number of B's and majority C's, with one or two D's.'

THE SCHOOL INFRASTRUCTURE

As I have already hinted, Olmanyatta school building had all the roofs thatched with grass. My dream focused on such a time when the school would have decent buildings. It is for this reason that no sooner had I become the headmaster than I started a campaign to have all the thatched roofs replaced with iron sheets. I held consecutive parents meetings and did my best to encourage them to contribute towards this project. I organized fundraisings and invited members of parliament like Babu Wood, Kihika Kimani and Koigi wa Wamwere. I also realized that most of the parents were reluctant to give out money, and the only thing that would have made them part with money was alcohol. So, one time, I summoned a parent's meeting in which I Influenced them to pave the way for making some local beer that could then be sold and the proceeds used to construct school buildings. In making this kind of proposal, the parents had to contribute both maize and millet. These were then to be grounded, mixed with water and then allowed to ferment for a full week. You can imagine how much the parents contributed, given that some parents contributed even a full bag of maize and like ten kilograms of millet.

There was a rich harvest of these two grains; hence, this wasn't a loss. We set the deadline for handing in the maize and millet. After this, I called for a school committee meeting which laid out the strategy of having the maize ground and for the preparation of alcohol. I informed the parents that the alcohol would be sold to the entire community near and far. That they should, therefore carry out the campaigns for the big day. The money would be used to buy iron sheets to replace the thatched roofs of the staff houses. The mention of alcohol was enough to have these people unanimously support the idea and with some sense of urgency.

They easily volunteered to give the drums. Women were to draw water and the firewood to roast the mixed flour which would then be put in drums of water. It would then be left for seven days to ferment. By then, it would turn into an alcoholic drink (buzaa). The general population liked this stuff. This kind of brewing alcohol could attract people because it had the chief's permit.

Now, with the scheduled days set for selling the alcohol, parents, pupils and friends in the community became good agents in spreading this news far and wide. The news spread like a bonfire. The selling of this alcohol took three days. The one thing that attracted people was the fact that I had received the permit for this occasion from the area chief, otherwise, the law forbade people to assemble in a drinking spree unless there was a permit for such gathering from the chief. This is why many people came because they could not fear being arrested. In this way, I was able to collect a lot of money. This I did every year and sometimes twice a year. I also, with the help of the committee, assigned every parent what we called a 'building fund.' The parents became very excited because the reflection of the iron sheets could be seen from very far away. Or else, all the buildings within the community had thatched roofs. I also influenced the kids during the morning assemblies to talk good of the school and the good changes that were taking place. Yes, I had to do some kind of campaign. I had to take every opportunity to have a breakthrough. The parents especially rallied behind me after my first year's KCPE results came out. This, with the renewed support from the teachers, really boosted the school construction project. The school had become so famous that many parents were transferring their children from other schools to Olmanyatta.

I first concentrated on the teachers' houses, the first being the headmaster's house. I was the first to enjoy a newly constructed house with three rooms. Before long, all the teachers' houses were iron-roofed. Later, I built another headmaster's house with six rooms and gave the former to the deputy headmaster, who happened to be Mr. Kinyanjui, my former college mate. With me, we had all classes reconstructed and roofed with iron sheets. We dug and built better toilets, separated between girls and boys. By the time I left in 1974, we had roofs in all school building brightly shining with iron sheets. Roofs were no longer leaking; teachers were no longer shifting their beds when it started raining; rats could no longer hide in the thatched roofs, and the fear of thatched roofs catching fire was no more. This was all through the selling of alcohol, organizing occasional dances where people spent the whole night dancing for a fee, parents' contributions through the allocated payments of building funds, and occasionally organized fundraisings by then known as "*Harambee*." Some of the people who really came to our support were Koigi Wa Mwere, Labert and other patriotic personalities.

If I didn't talk about my indulgence in alcohol, I would not have fully told my life story at Olmanyatta. Of how with all this success, my life changed negatively, especially from my second year as a headmaster. As I have indicated above, my name has become a household name. The parents came to like me so much that they longed for me to visit their homes. Some took the courage and sent their children to me saying, *"Baba anauliza kama unaweza kutembea kwetu jumapili au Jumamosi ijao?"* (*My father requests that you visit our home this weekend*). Upon my visit, I found that the parents had invited other people, especially their close relatives and friends. As a sign of respect, the man of the home would have slaughtered a he-goat or a ram and had the meat well roasted.

The thick porridge, which they call *'Kimie,'* was ready. I enjoyed the company of these people who were talking highly of me and praising me for bringing them *'maendeleo'* (*progress*) both in the academic discipline among the students and the newly roofed school residential houses. They also talked of the loving atmosphere I had initiated between parents and children, parents and teachers and the school committee and parents. As we dined and talked, each of these men had a long straw they called *'Muchich'* that had one end in a pot that contained alcohol known as *'buzaa.'* This was the maize roasted, mixed with millet and allowed to ferment for some days. The other end was in the other person's mouth. All these *"Michichas"* converged in the pot. They sipped the drink from one pot but using individual straws. Once in a while, a woman would come with some *'buzaa'* in a container and add to the already declining one in the pot. When I inquired about the use of *Muchicha,* I was told each one of them was sacking and drinking the buzaa through it (as a straw). They were not doing it continuously. One would sip for two minutes, then eat or talk and then sack again after four or five minutes.

What I noticed was that the more we stayed, the more their voices changed, indicating that they were getting drunk as time went on. I had stayed there from around 1.00 pm, and it was now 4.00 pm when I decided that I would go home. It was by then that a sized calabash of about two litres was placed in front of me. I was told that according to the Kipsigis culture, an honored guest had to conclude the sitting together with a special drink of "*buzaa.*" This is purposely for you, and before you share with anybody else you have to drink two or three cups.

These were cups with a capacity of a glass's content. I immediately protested, "*Oh, no, no, mimi situmii pombe*" (*No, no, I don't take beer*). From there, each man took the turn to explain to me the importance of drinking, even if it means one glass because, as one put it, "*Ukikataa ni kuonyesha wewe hukufurahi na sisi*" (*if you refuse, it is an indication to us that you didn't like our hospitality*) and even as he said that he was pouring some to my cup and he very persuasively placed it in my hands. I then closed my eyes, took one sip as if I was tasting, and I said, "*Sasa nimekunyua*" (*now I have drunk*). Then one said, "*Hiyo ni bora kuliko kukataa kabisa*" (*that is better than total refusal*). I then left for home feeling very bad that I had tasted beer. But I kept on comforting myself; after all, I did not swallow much. It then happened that every weekend, I had an invitation. I then made sure that to every invitation I responded, I would be in the company of a person or persons who took buzaa. Of course, almost all the men on my staff were drinking, so I used to go with them at different times. Our visit gave more honour to the parents because they had found favour with the headmaster.

It was from the pressure of these teachers and especially my deputy headmaster, whom I had known since the Thogoto College days, that I finally yielded to taking at first one-eighth of a cup, then a quarter, then as me went on half a cup and finally, I managed to take a full cup. This was of much joy to my hosts because they could now at least see my appreciation for their invitation.

By now, the news was spreading among the parents that I was now taking a glass of *"buzaa"* willingly. As me went on and very unconsciously, I was able to manage four or five cups. By the time I was doing my three months, I had become choosy of the invitations I received. When a child was sent to extend the invitation to me, I would enquire, *"Do you know the things they will have for me as a guest?"* Where *"buzaa"* would not be part of the menu, I would drop that invitation and opt to go where buzaa was available. I was no longer mindful of the *"Nyama Choma"* (*roasted meat*); my blood yearned for alcoholic drinks, including another one known as *"Kangara."* *"Kangara"* was more yellowish as it contained more millet and sorghum; it was a little more burnt, had more sugar and fermented more days than *"buzaa."* I no longer wanted to use the cup for drinking; I insisted that I use *"Muricha,"* which, of course had no control over. So long as your straw was in your mouth and the other end was in the pot, and so long as there was *"buzaa"* or*" Kangara"* in it, I could enjoy a continuous flow through my throat. This made me very popular among the parents.

I remember many times that I would go to visit riding my bicycle, but I ended up leaving it in the home of my host family or leaving it in the bush and then instructing a pupil on Monday to go for it. I remember Christmas day of 1973, in the company of a friend. We were very drunk, and we had to pass over a stream that was drying out, and it was all muddy. The bridge across it was a log that needed a lot of balancing. I had gone halfway when I lost control and in using my left hand to support myself, the hand went very deep into the mud. I struggled and finally managed to pull it out, but my very good watch was left deep in the mud. I never got it. My drinking had very negative effects on my family. Anybody who has ever been involved in this kind of drinking knows very well that one's wife is never happy, and she has a right to feel this way. I was very negative to my wife's corrections or comments and the way I responded left a lot to be desired. Thank God she had a strong will of perseverance. Nevertheless, this habit went on for the rest of the time while I was at Olmanyatta.

BARUT-RHONDA PRIMARY SCHOOL

It was one day in November 1974 when an officer's car pulled into the school compound. Out of it came the Area Education Officer (AEO) and his deputy. After greeting and congratulating me for the 'wonderful work' done over both academically and on the renewed structural progress, the AEO then said,

"Unfortunately, or fortunately, we have come to tell you that with effect from this coming January, we have transferred you to a school near Nakuru Town known as Barut-Rhoda Primary School. This will take place in a month's time. So, I recommend you give us a person who will take over from you since you know better the one who would fit in your shoes to continue with this progressive work you have begun."

He then handed me a letter. As we talked, I learnt that the powerful mayor of Nakuru by then, the late Mburu Gichua, was the chairman of the farm where Barut-Rhoda school was located. Many families had settled on that farm and they had bitterly complained to the mayor on their school's poor performance academically and even in terms of discipline. It was as a result of this that the mayor authorized the AEO to send one of his reputable headmasters there, someone who could uplift the standard of that school because it's academic and discipline situation was pathetic. As we parted company, the AEO said, *"So we are sending you there as our best; don't let us down."* They then left.

DRASTIC CHANGE

December holiday was the month of preparations, and come January, we moved to a very decent house, stone-built, self-contained, with electricity, clean water, flushing toilets, accessible decent transportation, tarmacked roads and a very friendly environment. It was a lovely estate known as Langalanga in Nakuru town. What a drastic change in life! Out of bushes to a flood of lights, supermarkets, and drinking places (bars) of all classes, where "*buzaa*" and "*Kangara*" were unheard of as they were considered primitive and outdated alcoholic drinks. Here, every drink was bottled with brand names like Tusker, White Cap and Pilsner. People drank in the floods of light, feeding on all types of food one would desire from fish, chicken, rice, fried beef - name it. People sat in well-arranged tables and chairs and even sofa sets. In case one was over drunk, there were lodgings attached to most of the bars, and after all, taxis were packed in plenty all over town. This was not just a professional promotion but also a lifestyle promotion as well. And with this promotion, I plunged into the newly civilized style of living.

It is obvious that there is nobody else who acquires a host of friends as easily and quickly as one who drinks in the bars. Now that my blood continuously yearned for alcohol, I would go to school, teach, and administrate to the highest possible degree. Before long, word had gone around, including to the offices of the mayor, that the new headmaster at Barut-Rhoda was of the best caliber that could manage and promote that school. I used to report to school by 7.00 am and stay in the school until 5.00 pm or even 6.00 pm. As usual, I would have the senior classes - standard six and seven - come by 7.00 am. I had convinced some teachers who would come in turns to take care of standard six classes both in the morning and evening. I personally concentrated on standard seven in those preparatory times. My administrative skills in approaching teachers, as well as the students and parents, in the right way quickly gave a new life to the school.

I quickly gained respect from all. Before long, the mayor decided to visit the school. I invited the parents, who then spoke highly of me and thanked the mayor for hearing their cry for, as one did put it, *"We have cried for many years and thank you so much, Your honour"*. The mayor also thanked me for the very good beginning and promised to use his influence to have the school get even more modernized in its building and outlook. I also organized a sand-digging quarry, which was within the compound from which we sold the sand and improved the standard of the school and the life of the students, especially in terms of improved school buildings, discipline and academics.

But sounding as good as it can be, I had a black side of my life. Every day, as soon as I finished school, I would go home, drop the books on the table and head to the bar. Usually, I drank un l around 9 pm to 10.00 pm. Possibly, I would never have become such a heavy drunkard if I never met Mr. Karia (not his real name). Karia was in the DEO's office, heading the salary section. Being in this office, he had access to all the teachers in Nakuru District which comprised of two hundred and fifty-eight schools. Every challenge that touched any of the teachers' salaries was to come to his table. He had a wider circle of influence both in the DEO's office and the Teachers' Service Commission. Thus, he could influence the transfer of teachers, house allowances, promotions, renewal of contracts, referrals of interdiction cases and other disciplinary areas.

This position had placed Mr. Karia (not his real name) in a strategic position of getting gifts/bribes from teachers who needed his help in straightening their life concerns. The gifts, in this case, were bottles of beer. So, what he did was that if a teacher came into his office with a request, whether relating to a transfer, salary ratification, promotion or any other, he used to tell the person, "*That is not a big deal; report here on such and such a day.*" When the person came back, in most cases, he/she would find the problem solved, and Mr. Karia would say, "*Your problem is over,*" and then he would tell the person to go and leave a number of beer bottles, depending on the income of the person and the seriousness of the case involved. Cases involving salary ratifications and transfers demanded a higher scale of appreciation. He would then refer the recipient of the favour to a certain bar in the town, asking him/her to go there and pay for the agreed number of beer bottles. He called it his '*beer stock.*' He had this kind of beer stock in almost every bar in Nakuru Town.

Now, for whatever reason, Mr. Karia came to like me so much. He had a Volkswagen car, and every day, as I arrived home, I would find him having packed his car next to my gate. I could then get into the house, drop the books and then leave immediately. It then turned out that I never bought beer. In most cases, Kuria never used the old stock. Teachers with problems kept on following him in his drinking places to present their cases to him. This way, they bought him a lot of beer. Others were cementing ties with him; others were seeking favors of different kinds, while others were normal fans but with money. Any place he went, in many instances, he had his stock added as he could not cope with all the beer he was offered. After every day's drinking spree, Mr. Karia would drive me home. We spent most of the weekends together eating and drinking. When I was not with him, I was in the company of other teachers or businessmen in the town. Again, in all these endeavors, my wife was an obvious victim. She could hardly have time with me and I hardly thought more about home. My mindset was in the school's work and drinking. I was both a workaholic and an alcoholic! Our firstborn, Githii, was around two years old at the time.

THE TURNING POINT

Now that we had moved to Nakuru, and it was nearer to Njoro than Subukia. In addition, Njoro was a more productive area with more openings to communication, I set my focus on doing some farming there at Mukungugu farm. My father was a shareholder of Mukungugu Land Buying Company. Mukungugu Farm was located at Njoro location. I therefore approached the officials of the farm, who then allocated me a portion of land on which I intended to carry on some farming and, at the same time, construct a house for my family.

Life in town was somehow expensive, hence the need to move my family to the rural area. I had already approached my father, who had made it possible for me to take a loan of ten thousand shillings from my bank using the title deed of the plot at Gikambura as the loan security. This money was meant to help me put up a house. Ten thousand by then was a good amount of money. In any case, putting up a house was easy, for in our neighbourhood, there was a very prosperous timber sawmill, Beeston Saw Mills, which produced tons of timber per day. The house was to be constructed in sections using timber within the Beeston Timber premises, and upon completion, it was to be transported to the site and the sections were put upright and then joined together. The whole process of constructing the sections and putting up the house took at least a week. In preparation for this new home, I regularly visited Mukungugu Farm so as to buy the materials required and also landscape the site where the house was to be occupied.

I really liked the surroundings of Mukungugu Farm. First of all, it is near this prosperous timber sawmill located in the south walls. It borders Egerton University to the East, and then to the North and the East there was a big forest.

It was on the Saturday of October 1976 when I had spent the day at Mukungugu making the final touches of the home setup, as I had finished the day's schedule, I started walking towards the main road to embark on public transport. In the neighborhood, I passed a pick-up truck packed not far from my piece of land. I had walked a short distance when I was overtaken by that pick-up. It stopped, and I was ushered in. The truck was being driven by a good friend, Mr. Kahuro, a teacher, an old friend of my father and the secretary to Mukungugu Land Buying Company. He had become a good friend of mine too. The front seat could accommodate two people only, and therefore, I had to sit at the back. The seat of the co-driver was occupied by a person by the name of Maracera. Mukungugu is about thirty kilometers from Nakuru town and ten kilometers from Njoro. Upon arrival at Njoro, my friend pulled to a bar, and I wondered because I thought we were heading directly to Nakuru town. They asked me to alight, and we sat around a table as they ordered some beer.

For reasons beyond my comprehension, lately, I had developed a spirit of dislike for alcohol. In the last three weeks, my mind was getting stirred by the things of God that I had learned during my Sunday school days and the Bible lessons I had learnt in the school Bible classes. In short, my mind was reverencing towards Godliness. Thus, it was not a pleasure that we had stopped at a beer joint. My desire was to go home and relax. I was not interested in drinking. I had the feeling that I should go straight home; hence, I asked the teacher friend, *"How long will it take us to be in this place?"*

He said,
   "David, we will be here for a while; in any case, you have done enough for the day. Why do you want to go home? Men are not meant to be home until late in the night. Weekends are meant for enjoyment."

Then he called the waiter and demanded for six more bottles to be placed on our table, two for each one of us. Before long, we were joined by two policemen who seemed to be well-known to my friends. We left there at about 8.00 pm now to head for Nakuru. But just before we got into the inner town, the driver took a turn, drove to the right about two hundred meters and parked next to another bar.

Again, I was reluctant to get out, but the teacher came back and called me a few nasty names, which really compelled me to get into the bar. Again, we sat around the table. This was a more elegant bar with different colors of flashing lights and some loud music, which made people speak the loudest possible. The bar was packed. This time, it was decided that each of us had to order what we used to call 'a round', i.e., one person ordering enough bottles for each person around the table. This meant that after each one had finally bought the round, each person would have taken 4 x 3, which was equal to twelve bottles. Someone offered to buy what they called '*Muchanganyiko maalumu.*' This was a mixture of meat ranging from beef, chicken, fish, tomatoes, boiled potatoes, carrots etc. And so, we ate and drank. I guess I got totally drunk.

The last time I remember checking on my watch, it was midnight. After that, drunkenness overwhelmed me. It was not until possibly 2.00 am that my friends decided to leave. By then, I was so drunk that I lost my sense of bearing. I still wonder how I got into the truck. What I learnt later was that I was placed at the back of the truck, for I could not tell them where my house was. They went to look for it, hoping that when they got there, they could inquire about my home's whereabouts from the people they would meet, including the watchmen. Unfortunately, as much as they inquired of people who might have known me, it all proved futile.

Finally, they decided to go to Sababit area, hoping that they could get a lodging where they could have me accommodated and then drive back to Njoro. Unfortunately, they could not find accommodation at Sababit, so they decided to leave me in the hands of a watchman. In other words, they left me lying on the ground without shelter or a cover. I was totally exposed to the cold. It was around 6.00 am when I discovered myself in the midst of nowhere. Then I lifted my head, which felt like a big heavy stone; as I struggled to rise, I noticed a man next to the door of a building who was now coming towards me. He held my hands to help me sit up. I now opened my eyes fully, looked around and noticed that I had vomited on myself and was surrounded all over with puke as I as well sat in the midst of it.

All the *'special mix of alcohol and food'* (*muchanganyiko maalum*), actually litres of beer, were spread on the ground. The place was really messy smelling horrible. The man went into the building, which turned out to be a hotel/bar and came back with some napkins, which he gave me to wipe my mouth, head, arms and legs. I also used them to wipe some parts of my trousers and the shirt. It was then that I asked him, *"Where am I? What was I doing here, and how did I get here?"* The man then explained to me how two men came with me, checked in the lodging for a vacant room and when they could not find any, one of them suggested,

"Let us leave him here and give this watchman something to take care of him, to which the rest agreed? So, I agreed, and this place is known as Shababu."

Then I told him, *"I know Shababu, but tell me, which side is Langalanga Estate?"* He then pointed to the South East direction and said, *"Langalanga is just one-and-half kilometers from here, is that where you live?"* *"Yes,"* I responded. I was already shivering terribly. My whole body was invaded by the night's cold weather. I therefore inquired from him where I could have a cup of tea, upon which he directed me to a hotel/bar. My body was filled with extreme cold and hunger. My throat was paining because of the vomiting.

First, I checked my pockets for any remaining money. I found a five-shilling note which by then was enough money for a cup of tea and good-sized slices of loaves of bread and would be left with some change. I was really shivering from cold and physical weakness.

After eating breakfast, I came to my senses and I now recognized where I was. I then started for home. No sooner had I taken the first step than my mind seemingly turned on a replay of my life's tape. It flashed back on memory lane. Memories of how my father was jailed for seven years with hard labour and how God saved him, possibly for the purpose of my life. If he never came back, I would not have attained education, and I could have either died or my life could be one of a vagabond. Pictures of the young men with whom we used to collect firewood in the forest and draw water for selling came so vividly into my mind. I remembered how those who never got an education were leading miserable lives. I realized that I could be like them, wrecks in life! I remembered how much I hungered, sometimes going for days without food, how for many years I slept in the sack, how I used '*ndongus*' to wash my torn clothes, the way I got almost killed in the forest, that dangerous experience with my mother that fateful night, and now, here I was a P1 teacher and a headmaster, totally lost in self-destructive habits. What a shame!

This revelation went on even as I got closer to my home. When I finally got home, God clearly paused a question to me, "*In doing all these things and in saving your father and you from the death, is this the kind of life I was preparing you for?*"

This was a very disturbing question from my creator. To make it worse, the tape continued playing in my mind. I remembered my dedication when I attended both the catechism and confirmation classes. I also remembered many others who gave up going to the confirmation class because, after all, they were after a baptismal name and persistently pursued knowledge about God. Deep thought engulfed my mind as I remembered my obsession and zeal to have my marriage solemnized in the Church, of my craving to be a teacher, a passion triggered by my Christian values, one that would act as a bridge to help me participate in the Lord's vineyard as I would promote Christian values to the children administered to in school. With a bang, the story of the prodigal son retold in my mind; it tormented and galvanized my soul. Under normal circumstances, before, I would have cried to God, but now, I had foolishly abandoned the God who had carried me through a most difficult childhood and career.

I felt so ashamed for having taken a path that was a betrayal to my savior, to my wife and our three already-born children, Benson, Sammy and Amos and to others to be born later and their offspring. Benson, the firstborn, was around four years and Ndicu, the last born by then, was around one year old. God reminded me of Christ's words that my body is the temple of God and the children He had given to me and those others likely to come and entrenched in my DNA were the greatest gift God had to bestow upon me.

Upon reaching home, my wife noticed my horrible condition. She then gave me some water to bathe after which she gave me some food. I then retired to bed. Inside the blankets and for the first time after a long time, I offered a personal prayer to God. I said quietly under the blankets;

"God, I am your child, as you forgave the prodigal son, please God, forgive me and stabilize my life. It will be my will even to serve you through whichever path you direct me. Thank you for protecting me over the years. Thank you for the children you have given me. Help me never to shame them through my unproductive life."

I then fell into a deep sleep. I woke up late in the evening, had supper and then went back to sleep.

The following day was a Sunday. For the first time, I woke up with a lot of peace of mind. This, I believe, was the first Sunday of October 1976. Also, for the first time after over four years of non-Church attendance, I felt my spirit being moved to go to the Church. I then took my breakfast. I got dressed up, and I decided to go to the Presbyterian Church, whose location I had known, PCEA Dr. Arthur Church. I knew the location of this Church because I used to pass by it on my drinking spree. After I went out of the gate, I had to decide the way to take it. If I walked along the main street, chances were that my friends would entice me to get in and have '*one for the road.*' So, I took a long course, seemingly going a little bit outside the estates as a way of avoiding falling into the temptation of falling into my usual profile of Sunday life. I finally got into the PCEA Doctor Arthur Memorial Church. The environment stirred a lot of memories. It took me back to those days when I used to attend the Church of the Torch in my primary school days and how much I appreciated the sermons and even wished to one time have an opportunity to stand there and address the congregation.

There were memories of the catechism and confirmation lessons, the many Sunday school lessons, and the much learning of the Biblical teachings from both my primary and secondary school's Christian Religious Education lessons. I remembered the prayers my mother used to offer during the critical times of our lives. How she often prayed, "*God, do not let these children die in my hands.*"

When the song '*Murigiti e haha riu ni Jesu Murigi*' (*The Great Physician now is here*) was sung, it stirred memories of my childhood when I used to hear my father sing as he prepared to leave for his teaching job at Ngong early in the morning. So was the memory of how my father was rescued by God on that night he was arrested in the forest. As these memories surfaced, tears started wetting my eyes. The wetting continued even as the sermon went on, reminding me of the purpose of Christ emptying Himself from the heavenly glory. It was so that I have life and have it abundantly. Yes, the memories of how many times I had heard that and the many times I had read it in the Bible clouded my mind, opening a wide door in it to allow the Word of God to penetrate through and shade a light that pricked the core of my soul. "*My heart bled*"

I could not wait for the end of the sermon as I expected the preacher to call forth to anyone who felt called to accept Jesus as his/her Lord and Savior. It then shocked me when the preacher concluded his sermon and never made an altar call. The service, like any other Presbyterian traditional service, came to an end without the altar call. I then watched as people left the Church compound, and to my surprise, nobody, noticed nor greeted me. This was so different from the beer joints where people jovially greeted even strangers. I then wondered why people were not saying hi to me or giving me a word of encouragement. I seemed to miss that joyous gathering in bars. But I immediately came to the realization that that was the whispering voice from the enemy. At long last, I left for home.

That week was the very week my family was to transfer from Nakuru Town to Njoro. I hired a truck that transported some of the furniture to our new home.

I had already worked out on my wife's transfer to the nearby school, Beeston Primary School. The family then settled in Mukungugu, and my wife reported to Beeston-Cheptoroi Primary School. As for me, I remained at Nakuru, carrying out my teaching duties. Thanks to God, I no longer felt the urge to go on the drinking spree. Every time I came back home from work, I just relaxed at home and actively read the Bible and other spiritual-related literature. The next Sunday was here with me, and I decided to go back to PCEA Dr. Arthur Memorial Church. As usual, I woke up, had breakfast and headed for the Church. I was now feeling acclimatized to the spiritual lifestyle. By now, the burning desire to surrender my life to Jesus was highly puffed up in my heart. I felt that if there was no altar call to be called out, I would try by all means to stand and then go in front of the Church and declare my acceptance of Jesus Christ as my Lord and Savior. Upon getting into the Church, I took a seat in the second row in front. The service went on, and the sermon midwifed my desire to be born again.

As the preacher seemingly was coming to the end of the sermon, I was getting myself ready to immediately take the earliest opportunity to make the declaration. In his conclusive words, the preacher said,

"The Lord has spoken. Let then those who have ears make their decisions as to whether one will take the line of God's decrees or the line of the enemy. Let us then pray."

He then offered a conclusive prayer and then proceeded to sit down. My heart was filled with a spirit of disappointment. How on earth could this man not make an altar call? I felt tempted to wake up and stand in front of the Church and make that eternal declaration, but as the preacher was going to sit down, the service leader was already on his feet, even as he said, *"It's time for offering and as we do so, let the choir sing our usual offertory song."* The choir responded immediately, and before I knew it, we were through with the offertory, which was prayed for, and this was immediately followed by recitation of the final benediction. The service was over. I felt like I was left with a big stone blocking my heart, a stone that needed to be rolled out.

As I went out of the Church door, I recalled that in those early days of my childhood when I used to worship at the Church of the Torch, there used to be men and women who, after the service, formed a big circle outside the Church and sang songs while raising up their arms as each individual went round greeting the rest, with women hugging women but shaking hands with men, and likewise the men hugged men but shook hands with the women. I then remembered that these people were referred to as 'ahonoki' (*The saved ones*). With that kind of memory, I felt excited because I would just wait for the circle to form, and then I would get in the middle of the circle and announce my new commitment to my creator.

I then stood at the corner of the Church watching and expecting to see a circle of people forming, but to my surprise, before long, everybody had gone. I then got quite grieved. It was then that I saw a person whom I had noticed being active in the front of the Church at the time of the service. He was busy organizing the front part of the Church as he removed the equipment and put them elsewhere. I went to him, greeted him and then introduced myself, saying,

"My name is David Githii, and I am the headmaster of Burut-Rhoda Primary School. I feel a lot of interest in the Word of God, and I would like to hear it more."

In response, this man said,

"Well, my name is Daniel Gatawa, and I am the Parish Evangelist. I am excited about your willingness to know more about God and his kingdom".

He asked for the details of where I lived. I then explained to him the location of my home, which was at the corner of Langalanga Estate, facing Rhoda and opposite councilor Njotheki's home. Gatawa then promised that he would definitely pay me a visit that evening. As usual, I never went anywhere. I kept on waiting for the door to be knocked, but nobody came.

The next day, nobody came. It was on Wednesday evening when Gatawa came accompanied by another person whose name I learnt as Maina. The two people gave me their testimonies, expounded the gospel and finally said, "*This is the best time to give your life to Jesus Christ.*" Yes, for them, it was the best, but not for me. I felt like if I confessed my sins to only two people, the confession would be too minimal. I wanted a place where I would confess to a crowd of people. I felt that for the past four years, my life had got too messed up and this could not be downloaded in the presence of the two people. I did not tell them what was in my heart, but after some quite lengthy persuasion, they prayed and left. But they did not labour in vain. Their preaching to me and prayers made my heart look like a dam that was so full and so ready to burst out. It became like a tube so pumped up that just one more pumping and it would explode!

THE DEVIL IN THE WARDROBE

The coming Saturday was the 30th of October, which was at the same time as the end of the month. I had, in the previous night, programmed myself to go to the bank the next day, withdraw part of that month's salary and then go home. I woke up early, read the Bible and prayed. I then made some breakfast, ate and took a bath. I needed to get home early so that I could handle some things. The bank used to open at 9.00 am and close at 11.00 am. Usually, there was a big queue, and I needed to be there as soon as possible. I also contemplated how much money I ought to withdraw, what to buy in town, what to buy at Njoro and how much money I would carry home. I had also figured out the previous night that I would survey the location of PCEA Church in our new home environment, and I was to worship there that coming Sunday, hoping that there would be an altar call then.

This was my third Sunday after I started the struggle to get an opportunity to declare Jesus Christ as my Lord and Savior. I comforted myself by contemplating that unlike the town Churches, possibly the rural Churches gave an opportunity for those people who felt called to repent their sins. At least, rural people's life was not so hectic and they spent more time in a Sunday service. It was quarter to nine when I closed the door to the house and headed for the gate.

I was just opening the gate to go out when, from the other side, someone was trying to open it. It was a very smartly dressed girl with well-kept hair. She had a broad smile. The girl said to me, "*Good morning, sir. I just felt an urge to visit you.*" This was a schoolgirl who was in the senior class in my school. I taught science in their class. She looked jolly in class, and any time I asked a question, or she raised her hand to ask or answer a question, she would do it with a big smile. When I saw her, I kind of moved, indicating to her silently that we could walk while talking. I suspected that she had a school problem, but holding tightly to the gate, she said, "*Mwalimu, nimekuja kukutembelea*" (*teacher, I have come to visit you*). As if her words and smile were magnetic, I also noticed that she was accompanied by a small girl. Thus, the three of us got into the house.

I offered the lady the chair, but she said, "*Mwalimu hebu nitazame nyumba yako, inaonekana safi.*" (*Teacher, let me have a look at your house. It looks neat*). As she said that, she was moving towards the kitchen and I followed her. She pretended to admire the kitchen, and then I said, "*Si nikutengenezee chai?*" (*Let me make you a cup of tea*) but then she said, "*Lakini hebu kwanza nione bedroom*" (*but let me first see the bedroom*). Then she moved quickly to the bedroom, but this time holding my hand tightly as she got into the bedroom. She sat on the bed and said, "*Ni sawasawa Mwalimu*" (*It is okay, teacher*). Then she sweetly smiled at me and continued, "*Hata kwa darasa mimi ujaribu kukwonyesha eti ninakupenda lakini inaonekana huelewi, au haunipendi*" (*Even in the class, I try to show you my love, but it's like you never understand my moves or simply you don't love me*). She sweetly explained. Although unlike all the other male teachers, all the pupils know that you do not like school girls. This is why I have decided to bring myself, for I have always admired you.

By then, the Holy Spirit illuminated my mind. I realized that the scheming over the past three weeks blocking me from having an opportunity to openly confess my sins was now setting the final assault. The power overwhelmed me. I started sweating. I felt two strong spirits fighting over my soul. I am not sure what I was saying, but I murmured, *"But you see, there is this little child; let's not do anything; she will go and report."* With these words, the girl went quickly, gave the child a coin and told her to go and buy bread. As I followed her, I heard what she told the little one, who immediately left. Now, the girl locked the door. She held my hand to take me to the bedroom, but my hand unconsciously resisted. I pulled her onto the sofa set, which she resisted as she kept on saying, *"Mwalimu, let us go to the bedroom, tafadhali, tafadhali..."* (Teacher, let us go to the bedroom, please! Please!).

I followed her as she pulled me, holding my hand tightly as if I were just a small boy. She threw me in the bed and quickly started undressing herself, but alas, as she was preparing to plunge into the bed, a woman neighbor called out, *"Ithe wa Githii!"* I hesitated to answer, and she called even louder, *"Ithe wa Githii (father to Githii), it was then I answered 'ii' (yes); she continued, "Niui mwana uyu urarira haha akiorataga gwaku?"* (Might you know whose child this is, who is crying here as she points to your house?). By then, the girl was already out of bed and hurriedly dressing up. It was then that I also quickly went to the door and said to the woman, but not without shame, *"Yes, she was here and went out."* Even as the little girl came in, the other followed me to the sitting room where the main door was. She now looked so calm and frightened.

As for me, the spirit of God was with me, and I felt like Samson after his hair grew. The Lord now gave me the way of escape. I told her,
  "You know what? Nothing will work; that woman will come to know now that she has seen this child. Now you just go and come in the evening. I will be here any time from 6.00 pm. What a night we will have! She complied with a wide smile."

But in reality, I was playing a game on her. I had to leave for home if I had to dodge the devil and cling to God's path, as it was my desire to leave the world of darkness. I knew this was the worst of the devil, for I was known as the headmaster who was very protective of school girls against sexual abuse. I strongly fought against men who took advantage of these naive and emotion-driven girls. All the same, I wondered why this temptation. Why now? I knew that it must be the devils doing to make me fall.

As soon as she was out, I locked the door and hurried to the bus stage that was to drop me near the Kenya National Bank, where I was to withdraw the money after which I would go home and never to come back until Tuesday.

As the bus moved towards the town, the urge to get saved as quickly surged into my heart mightily. I felt like I would stand on the bus and confess my sins. As soon as the bus stopped, I rushed out, taking wide strides towards the bank, but when I came to the main door of the bank, I pushed it but it was locked. I looked inside, and the gatekeeper came, opened the door and said, "*I am sorry, the bank closes at 11.00 am on Saturdays. I am sure if you are a regular customer, you should have known that.*" And then he closed the door on my face. Now, the spirit of God was grazing in my mind; I automatically realized that the devil was really after me; he wanted me to go back and be in my house in the evening. I put my hands in my pockets, searching for the bus fare. By God's providence, I had ten shillings, which was enough to take me to Njoro town. I boarded a bus and finally alighted at Njoro. I had to walk home as I did not have any more money. I began my walk to Mukungugu. Although I arrived home empty-handed, my heart was full of treasures.

God had empowered me mightily; I had a lot of peace of mind - my only concern was that the tomorrow seemed to drag too much. It was on the morrow (Sunday) that I wanted to declare the devil defeated.

I went to bed at around 10.00 pm. I soon fell asleep and woke up in the morning. My wife gave me the water to bathe, after which I took the breakfast. All this time, my wife was quite pessimistic about my change in behavior. After all, I am now alone at Nakuru. If I could not be trusted while she was with me, what about now that we were living separately? I then got dressed up and went to the Church. This was a smaller PCEA Church congregation that worshiped in one school classroom at Beeston Primary School. The service went on in the Presbyterian way of worship that included singing, prayers, announcements, reading of scriptures etc. The sermon was delivered by an old man from a village known as Gitiro. He preached well, but he first gave his personal testimony of how he lived in a different world, a hopeless world, but the grace of God found him, and he confessed his sins and he is now a forgiven saint. This was exactly what I needed, here is a preacher who understands and who will definitely give a chance to those who would like to confess like him. To me his sermon was too long because I wanted him to finish and give the chance that I would grab to move to the world of his experience. Finally, he brought the sermon to a conclusion and said, "*Let us pray,*" after which he sat down. The leader then called for the deacons to collect the offertory, then the hymn and the benediction. The service was over – no altar call. I felt so much cheated.

As I went out of the Church, I comforted myself that possibly they have the old Church of the Torch style. The born-again Christians will assemble outside, form a circle and then I will grab the opportunity to declare my only burning desire that Jesus Christ is my Lord and Savior. I then moved and stood at the corner of the classroom and watched as the people left one by one. I was now already depressed. I could not understand why it was taking me so long to have an opportunity to confess my sins. The images started coming into my mind: what if that lady comes back and finds me with no testimony? Will God defend me against the many demons she will bring this time? By then, I had my head down with my mind deeply involved.

It was then that the man who had preached noticed me as he came out of the vestry. He came and touched my shoulder and said, *"Niatia wethikira?"* (*Why do you look distressed?*) And he immediately continued by introducing himself to me and then went on to say,

"I am a born-again Christian, which means Jesus is my Lord and Savior. Tell me, what is your name? Do you really live here? You somehow look a stranger."

I then told him my name and the fact that I was a teacher at Nakuru but recently moved to Mukungugu. And I then asked him with eagerness, *"What is it that I heard during the time of the announcement? Something like the fellowship is as usual in the afternoon?"* The old man responded, *"Oh yes, this is the fellowship of those who profess Jesus Christ as their Lord and Savior. Such people come back in the afternoon to get organized teachings to help them sustain their salvation as they travel in the world."* This was a great relief to me. It dawned on me that the long-awaited time had finally come, and no wonder the devil had to try his last kick the previous day. After some discussion with the old man, I left for home. On arriving home, I was given some Ugali with vegetables. I tried to eat, but I could not eat a lot. My mind was set and yearned for salvation. Before long, I was on my way back to the Church. As I walked, I unconsciously found myself singing a hymn that we used to sing those past days at the Church of the Torch.

Sang;
"*Ndi mwihia ona wanyona*
Ithe witu wa iguru
Kinya guciarua gwakwa
Nii no njikaga uuru
Ndiratuire nduma-ini
Na ndionaga uuru wakwa
Ndironaga ta ndimuihia
Kana ngamenya wimwaga
(I am a sinner in the eyes of God
Our heavenly father
Since my birth
I continuously sin
I have lived in darkness
I couldn't see my faults
I didn't see myself as a sinner.
Or attained the truth of your goodness.

I sang:
Nariu uhoro waku
Niutonyete ngoro yakwa
Niuthecete ta i mu
Na ngaigwa na ngamenya

Ti itheru nguigwa ruo
Baba mwega, na ngathina
Rora maithori mwakwa
Ngiririra wihia wakwa
Njagiriiruo ni guthuura
Maundu maaganu mothe
Njagiriiruo ni gutiga
Indo cia shaitani ciothe

189

Unjiare ringi baba
Njikira roho mutheru
Atheragie ngoro yakwa
Na anjikire hinya mweru

But now your word
Has penetrated in my heart
It has pierced it like a spear
And I have heard and have a new revelation
For sure, I feel the pain
My good father and feel poor,
Look at my tears
As I weep for my sins
I ought to hate
All sinful acts
I ought to surrender
All satanic ways.
Make me a born-again.
Put your Holy Spirit in me.
So, he will be cleansing my heart.
And put in me a renewed strength.

As I continued singing this hymn, the more my heart yielded to salvation and the more my eyes were wetting with tears. As I finished the last stanza, drops - warm drops of tears were rolling down my cheeks. The surprising thing was that I had not sung this hymn for years, but it flowed in my mind in a very mysterious way. The Holy Spirit was upon me, ready to blow out all the bad stuff that had clogged my mind. As I approached the classroom where the brothers and sisters in Christ had gathered, I noticed that they were just starting the first hymn.

As I sat down, I felt nervousness attacking my body and the more as the service progressed, the more I became nervous. Of course, as one would expect, the devil had mobilized all his battalions to do their final assault on me, for it was now or never. At last, the one who was conducting the service said, *"Now we will give this time to whoever has greetings, a testimony or even one who would feel called to accept Jesus Christ as his/her Lord and savior."* Of course, the leader, in saying the latter, was targeting me as I was the only one in the group whom they did not know, and I am sure the old man had passed a word that I was likely to come back as I hinted to him that I would do that.

Two people gave testimonies, and three others gave greetings. As each one talked, it was like each added fuel to my nervousness. Thus, by the time the fifth person spoke, my body was vibrating and profusely sweating, my throat had become very dry, and something seemed to have blocked me so that I was made to feel that my voice could not come out in any way. It was like I had become paralyzed.

With the sixth person having given a prayer request of someone who was bed ridden, the leader then seemed to prolong the chances. He kept on pleading, *"Anybody else who has something to say? There is still time; I would hate someone to think that I hastened the time."* He was now kind of making the last call when I then stood up abruptly trying to force my way against what I felt as pressure pressing me down. Surprisingly, I immediately stood up; the sweating, the fear, and the clogging in the throat all went. I just felt myself so easily and unstrained, say,

"My name is David Githii. We are newcomers at Mukungugu farm, and I am the headmaster of a School in Nakuru known as Barut-Rhoda Primary School. For some years, I have been so much enslaved by the devil. He has made me do and say things that my God would hate to see me do, but today, October 31st, 1976, I now declare that I have accepted Jesus Christ as my Lord and Savior. Since these thoughts of salvation were first planted in my mind, I have been under constant satanic attacks, but at this moment, the devil has lost because God is more than a conqueror. He has redeemed me."

Even before I had finished the declaration, I was already surrounded by both brothers and sisters, three brothers embraced me simultaneously, and they hugged me as a born again even as the common hymn *'Tukutendereza'* went on. *'Tukutendereza'* has its origin in Uganda. This hymn was a kind of National Anthem of the East African Revival Movement.

The three brothers then released me, and all others in that fellowship either hugged me or shook my hand. The men hugged me, and the women shook my hand. Then everything went back to normal. We then sang the last hymn and the benediction. We all then left the classroom and formed a big circle outside. As the East African Revival hymn continued to be sung, each individual went around the circle, hugging people of his/her sex and shaking hands with others of the opposite sex. This kind of brothers and sisters greeting each other and forming a circle is what I used to see at the Church of the Torch in those early years of my childhood. It was their pattern of time that had changed. Instead of fellowshipping immediately after the service, they now decided to go home for lunch and they would then come back to their revival fellowships in the afternoon. It was called the East Africa Revival Movement, as its influence covered Kenya, Uganda and Tanzania (*formerly Tanganyika*). This movement became the foundation for my spiritual growth; hence, I find it important to highlight its origin, growth and development.

The East Africa Movement originated in Rwanda in the 1920s and finally found its way to Kenya in 1937. It acted as a catalyst for the reawakening of the Church. In Kenya, many of its members encountered severe persecution at the hands of Mau Mau, who accused the members of being loyal to the British colonizers. Also, in 1969, when there was an oath-taking among the people of Central Kenya, those who adhered to this movement were greatly persecuted. One by the name of Gathinji was brutally murdered.

MY ZACHEAUS CONFESSION

As soon as the greetings were done, the whole group accompanied me to my home. It was a large multitude. As we walked and others sang Christian songs all the way, the only image that flashed through my mind of who to best liken myself with was that of Zacchaeus. There were these people accompanying me to my home as they did with Zacchaeus. Truly, Jesus had called me from a tall tree whose branches of sin had hidden me from God's wonderful creation and salvation. Like Zacchaeus, salvation had come to my home. Finally, as we approached my home, my wife (as she testified later) was surprised, and she panicked when she saw the big multitude of people coming.

At first, she never saw me, but as the crowd moved closer, she identified me. Her immediate conclusion was that I had gotten drunk, fought and possibly had badly injured a person. But as the people came closer, she could hear them singing Christian songs, and finally, we came to my homestead. The neighbors brought the seats quickly, and before long, we were all seated. I then, like Zacchaeus, stood to give my personal testimony. I highlighted some of the dark places in my life and concluded by saying,

"Today, Jesus Christ has rescued me from the eternal condemnation. I am now a born-again Christian." I then made a request, *"Please pray for me so that I will win this battle that the Lord has today recruited me into."*

This was followed by a prolonged singing of '*Tukutendereza*.' After this a brother and a sister in the Lord spoke, each encouraging me to trust the Lord, for now that I had enrolled myself, the battle was the Lord's. One of them quoted the book of Judges 7, where Gideon was called upon by the Lord to lead the Israelites in fighting the Midianites. Gideon trusted in a big army, and he therefore recruited an army of thirty-two thousand strong men. But somewhere along the way, the Lord said:

> *"The people that are with thee are too many for me to give the Midianites into their hands, lest Israel vaunt themselves against me, saying, mine own hand hath saved me (Judges 7:2).*

When Gideon called upon the fearful and afraid, twenty-two thousand returned' as if this was not enough, the Lord said:

> *"And the Lord said unto Gideon, the people are yet too many; bring them down unto the water, and I will try them for thee there: and it shall be, that of whom I say unto thee, this shall go with thee, the same shall go with thee; and of whomsoever I say unto thee, this shall not go with thee, the same shall not go"* (Judges 7:4).

With such encouraging portions of Scripture, the speakers spoke. A lady spoke, directing her speech to my wife. She reminded my wife that it was by God's grace that her husband had a U-turn in his life and this was more for her and the children's lives. She called upon my wife to consider becoming a born-again Christian as well. At one time, she told my wife,

"You might wonder what sins you have committed for you to get born again, but remember, we are born with the sins of Adam. After all, you are a human being and the way your husband behaved made you hate him. You have been having a lot of anger that you have harbored in your heart and mind. Biblically, these are enough sins to make you reconsider your relationship with the Lord."

All this did not seem to ring any bells to my wife. She had undergone a lot of psychological torture, and she wondered, *"What if he renounces the salvation and goes back to the world?"* No wonder my wife never gave up that resistance until some years later when she finally declared to be a born-again Christian. By this time, she had assessed and was fully convinced that I was a born-again Christian and was there to stay. What followed was a life characterized by involvement in Christian activities. I was in Barut-Rhoda primary school only in the month of November. The schools closed for the December holiday. I had felt a great need to stay with my family; hence, I approached the office of the District Education and was easily given a transfer and also allowed to continue with my headmastership at Beeston Primary School. This was the school nearest to my home at Mukungugu. It was in this school that I reported in January 1977. This was the same school from which I had received Jesus Christ as my Lord and Savior, and it was also the school my wife taught. This school was known by two names, that is Beestons and Cheptoroi. Beeston was the corrupted name of the settler who had owned the farm prior to independence. His name was *"Bigstone,"* which Africans pronounced as Beeston. Cheptoro was the Ndorobo tribe's name for pigs.

5. CHEPTOROI (BESTONS) PRIMARY SCHOOL

It seemed like every school I was posted to had problems. Like in Olmanyatta School, they had a pattern of the academic results, which were mainly EEE, DEE, EDE, etc. On the best performance, there would be a student with two D's and an E. Thus, out of the maximum 36 points, the best candidate would have attained 5 to 10 points. There were many reasons for this, such as all the male teachers in the school spent almost all the days of the week drinking homemade beer from a nearby village, the Beestons village. This village mainly hosted the employees of Beeston Saw Mills, which was one of the largest sawmills in Nakuru District. All the homes had thatched houses. These employees were paid so little that the authorities allowed them to make homemade alcoholic drinks like the ones I used to drink. This means the teachers hardly taught. The parents of the pupils never discouraged teachers from drinking because they were the people with money, hence, their best customers.

The teachers owned small scattered farms, most of which were an average of five miles from school. These farms surfaced after trees were harvested in a given forest. The cleared area was subdivided into half an acre, one acre or two acres. The forest guards gave those portions to forest workers and even non-forest workers. Even teachers were able to acquire portions of land in the forest. On these farms, people grew pyrethrum, maize (corn), potatoes and beans. Would you believe that some of these teachers never knew the real spots where their farms were? All it took was for a teacher to offer those forest guards a drink and then agree that that teacher send a pupil who would be shown the land. The reason for that is because they used the children as their labour force. When the pupil reported back to the teacher that he had seen the land, the teacher would call the class and tell them, *"Tomorrow, all of you come with pangas."* In the morning, the teacher would inspect the pupils to make sure each had their panga. He would then instruct the pupil who had earlier seen the land to take the students there so that they could cut down the bushes. This activity would take two to three days. The next step was for the students to go with hoes so as to have the land cultivated. Another day, they would each bring some of the seeds to be planted there. When the time for weeding came about, the students would go and do the digging. They are the ones who did the harvesting and made the produce ready for marketing. The teacher would then negotiate the price and then pocket the money which he further utilized in drinking and reaching out to harlots. Remember, this is just an example I have given; otherwise, every teacher owned an average of five of these portions of farming land in different locations. Thus, the pupils were kept busy throughout the year. This was done every year and every season. Again, the parents benefited from the proceeds because after the teachers had sold the harvested produce, they used that money for drinking. Thus, the higher the yields, the better it became for the parents. Of course, there were parents who were opposed to this, but the School Committee, the teachers and the village elders rendered them voiceless.

As the teachers engaged in their drinking spree, their main work was to discourage parents from the need for education. This was an easy game since every child who had completed school was at home for none had qualified to rise higher in education. As the children turned to adulthood, they joined the drinking community and enjoyed the company of their former teachers as they drank and talked about the useless education. These former pupils turned into parents, and the vicious cycle continued. This had, over time, turned into a chronic situation in the surroundings.

Coincidentally, many of these male teachers were not married. They used school girls to cook for them, wash their clothes and do other domestic work, including drawing water. They turned the school girls into wives. One wonders why the parents saw no problem in all these evil activities - but one reason was that these teachers, in their drunkenness, boasted to the parents that they would marry their daughters. This was something every parent looked forward to - having a teacher for a son-in-law. Someone with money and education. Thus, one would never have dared to discourage either the daughter or the teacher from their superficial relationships. The parents would even advise their daughters on how to win over the hearts of teachers in order to marry them. This would also mean a good dowry.

There was another disadvantage in that the headmaster, unlike the other teachers, never lived in the school compound. He was the only one who commuted from Njoro town, which was ten miles from the school. He had to cycle a longer distance when going home since the way to school was almost hilly throughout. The teachers took advantage of this since the headmaster arrived at school late, at around 11.00 am and could leave latest by 3.00 pm. In this case, the headmaster was an old man with less education as compared to the teachers who were much younger and more educated. It was very easy for them to manipulate him. They also had an upper hand with parents and pupils for the headmaster was not able to report to school every day. He used to miss office attendance two to three days a week, especially when he had to attend some headmasters' meetings or visit the DEO's offices for some school matters. It was also unfortunate in that his deputy headmaster used to be bribed with favours by the staff, and he never used to mind their daily endeavors. He was also a beneficiary of what was going on in the pupils'/parent's manipulations for early marriages. This was the situation I had to face and deal with, a real test in my administration.

STAFF MEETING

Soon after my arrival, I called for a staff meeting. In the agenda, there was an introduction of the school staff to the headmaster and methodologies for improving the learning environment and students' education sustainability/performance. The introduction agenda went on smoothly but when we came to the second agenda, someone immediately said he did not see the relevance of the agenda as the academic life of the school was in good order. Everything in regard to the school was dictated by its environment. He concluded by saying,

"This is the way the school is, and not even an angel would change anything beyond its present condition, and I think the headmaster should be careful how he approaches the running of the school - we are the old-timers. We have had a grip on this school lifestyle over the years. It's wrong for the headmaster to think he is a new broom that will sweep cleaner than how we have swept so far."

I then took time to explain that I had looked at the school files as per its history, including the government examination results going back over ten years, where no child had been admitted to any secondary school, and that was the reason I thought it was a high time we thought of other different approaches to the entire life in the school. I explained that I did not in any way deny the fact that I was too green in the area and school, but I had a concern for the school and the community as well. I also stated the fact that there is no organization that is so much rooted in its environment that it cannot change; it is people who make traditions, and it is people who break or alter them. It seemed that the more I tried to convince this staff, the more we parted company. I lost control of the meeting. I could tell that some of these teachers were drunk, for they started talking in sarcastic language. For example, one teacher addressed me and said,

> *"What a new broom to sweep clean! We have seen many headmasters, and you will not outwit us; rather, you will join us. You are pretending to be a staunch follower of Christ. We are also Christians and what we are doing is biblical. Paul told Timothy to be taking beer."*

When some of them started walking out of the meeting, I had no alternative but to call an end to the staff meeting.

The next morning, I called all the kids for the assembly. I led in some Christian singing, did some Bible reading and teaching, and then prayed. Then, the time for announcements came. In a voice betraying me as angry, I gave them the following instructions from that day onwards;

1) No schoolgirl was to be seen anywhere within 100 yards of the teachers' living quarters,
2) No girl was to draw water for the teachers.
3) No girl was to cook or wash the teachers' clothes or be in their houses except for pressing reasons, and for such, only the headmaster was to give permission.
4) Henceforth, no student was to work on a teacher's farm or do any non-academic task for a teacher unless he/she had permission from the headmaster.

5) All pupils were to be in their classes at all class times, and silence was to be observed whether there was a teacher or not.

6) No pupils were to be seen roaming about during school days.

7) Every pupil should think academically, act academically and talk academically. For standards six and seven, they had to come back to school for the evening studies from 7.00 pm to 9.00 pm. This was mandatory.

8) All pupils were expected to respect all teachers as they spoke and behaved as they dealt with them, maintaining a respectable body distance to avoid provoking the male teachers by girls, either knowing or unknowingly. Woe unto him/her who would be brought to me on this issue or on accusations of fighting, abusing others or stealing something from other pupils.

9) All schoolchildren were expected to respect all other people in the community, irrespective of their age. Any pupil caught misbehaving or being disrespectful to the community was to be reported to me.

By then, many of the teachers had come from their houses and standing far, they were listening to what I was telling the pupils. I could see them turning and talking to each other after every announcement I made. Then came my final announcement that;

"All the parents were to attend a parents' meeting the coming Saturday, which was three days ahead then. I emphasized that

every parent was to come and whoever failed to turn up should accompany his/her child to school on the coming Monday."

My speech and announcements that morning acted like a matchbox that set the fire aflame. The teachers spent the whole day speaking angrily in small groups of two, three or four. As for me, I went into the various classes speaking to the pupils and especially encouraging them to love one another by sharing books and other things they had. I also encouraged them to love education, for it was a hidden, precious treasure.

Finally, I got into standard seven, which was the final class. I talked to them at length and then started teaching them English, focusing on how to write the compositions. I spent the rest of the day working on the class timetable. The next day, the teachers who were to take the lower classes (standard 1-3), mostly women, reported to their classes and followed my advice to prepare their timetables.

Women were showing some positive responses, especially following my announcement that girl pupils should not visit the male teachers' houses or draw water for them, and also the call to pupils to respect the teachers. This applied to teachers, especially the female teachers who had suffered insults from schoolboys who even called them names. Only one female teacher was really arrogant. Her eyes had become quite red with anger. Sometimes, I could see her in the midst of male teachers, angrily raising up her arms and writing on the paper what I thought were the teachers' plans for the next steps they were to take.

PARENTS' MEETING

On Saturday, the day scheduled for the parents' meeting, the parents started showing up at 9.00 am as the meeting was scheduled for 10.00 am. I could see parents forming groups as they engaged themselves in serious discussions. Meanwhile, I was meeting with the members of the school committee. I was enlightening them on the various ways I thought we could use to improve school life. Some looked very enthusiastic in supporting me, but a few who drunk with the teachers were looking at me defiantly. Nevertheless, I explained to them the strategy that I had already committed myself to and the fact that I needed their support. The more I talked, the more I seemed to convince even those who seemed to be against me. Their perception of me took on a different viewpoint from what they had heard from the teachers. After all, all these stories were told in drunkenness by the same teachers who bought beer from them and for them. It now seemed that, as we all went out to begin the parents' meeting, we were speaking in one voice.

I started the meeting by reading the Bible. The text was Luke 13:6-9 where Jesus talked of the parable of a lazy employee. The owner of the tree expected fruitfulness of the tree but for three years, it yielded nothing. I explained the fact that the tree was of a good breed and could produce like any other tree, but what it lacked was the care it needed - manure, thinning of branches, watering, cultivating around it, and even spraying it to kill the pesticides. I then likened the school to this tree. Even as the caretaker asked for one more year so as to give it the necessary care, I challenged the parents to take up the tools and join me in taking care of the tree, and they would be surprised as a result of the school's academic and discipline outcome. I explained the fact that I was well trained in the job and I had the ability to change the life of the tree if only they gave me the support. I did my best to convince them that their children were not born different from other kids in other schools and that their children were the best kids I had so far. They had great potential academically, but they needed some pruning, watering, fencing and cultivating around them. The more I talked to them, the closer I drew them to me and broke the cords of the negative thoughts with which they had been fed for years by the teachers.

I tried to help them visualize the pupils coming from some government school smartly dressed in school uniforms. I showed them how these children would later be supportive of their families and even lead a better life as they shaped their future. I could tell from their faces, some with wet eyes, that I had a battalion behind me - an army to fight to the end. It was then that I laid down the announcements I had made to the children and said,

"These are only ideas; there is nothing I am dictating. You have the room to air your opinions on the same. This is your school; these are your children and you have a say on how it should be run. I then asked the chairman of the school to take over the floor. The chairman, Mr. John Ngugi, was a fine Roman Catholic Christian. He began addressing the parents by reminding them of the way the children of Israel had lived in bondage for many years and how God sent Moses to rescue them from slavery.

He concluded by saying."

> *"Finally, God has sent us a Moses. We have lived in Egypt for many years. For so long, no child from this school - only one in 1975 has passed exams. And he had done the examination three or four times - let us rally behind our Moses. With God, all things are possible."*

Even as he was coming to the conclusion, all the parents were standing up and clapping with the women, ululating.

The chairman went through my performance and discipline; he read them out one by one, taking me to explain how each one of them had adversely affected the school and pupils. As he came to the last one on the list, he said, *"I do not know any other children that have suffered abuse like our children,"* and having said that, he became too emotional to continue speaking; hence, he sat down. He called upon the vice chairman to give a brief comment and then open the ground for the parents to make their comments.

The vice chairman echoed emphasis on what the chairman had said and concluded by saying, *"I feel so relieved. I have prayed for this school for so many years, and for me, God has at long last answered our prayers."* He then gave the parents a chance to individually air their views.

One parent after another blamed the fate of their children on the teachers, and one of the women said,

> *"Our daughters are their wives! What a shame! They have even helped our daughters to abort after impregnating them. They have been selfish and not given our children a chance to learn and be teachers too. Let us unite and support our Moses.*

He is also a God-fearing man for recently, he accepted Jesus Christ as his personal Savior right here in this school. I trust that the same God he has accepted is the same God who can use him to bring about tangible reforms in the school."

The parents adopted all my ideas and added two more. That any parent who would sell beer to the teachers would have his/her children expelled from the school, and at the same time, such a parent would face the wrath of the chief. The second one allowed the headmaster to deal with both pupils and teachers as he deemed fit. The school committee reaffirmed their support. They also passed a resolution to buy books for the children.

The meeting came to an end at around 5.00 pm. It was closed by prayers from three parents. One of them prayed in pain and tears, calling God to give the headmaster the 'Mosaic Staff 'with which to touch the *"Red Sea"* so that the children of Cheptoroi Primary School would cross and get into the academic Canaan. Her prayers sounded like an expression of the rest of the parents. As the parents left, you could feel the changed charged atmosphere. They were talking with excitement and hopefulness. I overheard one say, *"Truly, God can make a way in the wilderness."* The following day was a Sunday. As usual, I went to the Church. Many people congratulated me for all that transpired in the parents' meeting. Their talks indicated that the parents had already seen the light at the end of the tunnel.

Monday seemed to come with some light. The children, unlike other days, came to school much earlier than the usual time. One could tell their joy as they talked to each other. I noticed the excitement, especially from the standard seven class, who, until the bell for the parade rang, were involved in a jovial discussion outside their class. In the parade, I read the Word of God accompanied by some singing. In my speech, I commended the parents for their availability on the previous Saturday and also thanked the pupils for the initiative they had taken to persuade their parents to come. I praised the pupils for their understanding and their eagerness to learn and I promised my support for their good future. I also made an announcement that standard seven pupils would be reporting for school at 7.00 am for their morning studies. The students then broke up for their respective classes. It was by then that I noticed the number of teachers with a positive attitude was increasing one by one. Quite a number of them were frequenting the notice board to check on their classes' time table.

But there were six among the staff who really portrayed the spirit of rebellion. Their faces reflected anger. These included: (Chegu, Lisca, Nderito, Amenyu, not their names), Nyambimba, and a woman teacher. They categorically refused to get into their classes. Instead, they held a meeting in one of the teachers' houses and strategized on how to deal with me. Otherwise, the rest of the school felt silent. Only the voices of teachers could be heard as teaching was progressively going on well. Meanwhile, I went to each of the classes which were taught by the rebellious teachers. I gave each class some work that kept them busy. The day slowly gave way to 4.30 pm when that day's school time was over. After making sure that all classes were closed, I then left for home. The following day started well. I was in the standard seven classroom by 7.00 am, busy teaching them. Then came the parade, after which the children got into their respective classes. I then went on with the first lesson that ended sometimes after 9.00 am. Then, I went to the office to attend to the few parents who had come to consult with me. From there, I started my lesson plan and then carried out the marking exercise on the work given to the standard seven pupils that morning.

I had earlier noticed that four of the rebellious teachers were aimlessly moving about in the school compound, but I had decided not to pay much attention to them. I thought that, before long, their anger would subside, and I would lovingly talk to them in an effort to win them. But alas, fifteen minutes to lunchtime, the door of my office flung open. The force used was too much that its back hit the wall, which was fixed with a big bang. The arrogant woman headed to me and shouted in her highest voice, saying,

"You think you are a bishop? You, useless man! Are you really a man? Come on, if you are a man; come out you, toothless dog."

By then, she was attempting to jump on me, but I was seated behind a table whose one side touched the wall, giving no entry from that side. Plus, my chair had occupied all the space behind the table, so it gave her no room to accelerate the completion of her mission. She was now shouting and yelling, and to the surprise of my eyes, she was trying to lift up her clothes, revealing her pink underwear as she continued to haul words at me, *"Come on, you impotent man."*

She was reaching for my jacket, trying to pull me out of my sitting position. It was at this critical moment, with the woman's clothes fully pulled up and trying to pull me towards her, that Mr. Chege, who was one of the rebellious teachers, stormed into the office, and as he got in, he shouted, "*What is wrong? What is wrong? What is happening here?*" He then pushed the arrogant lady towards me instead of pulling her away from me and trying to pull the clothes further up as he shouted, "*Does it mean that this evil man was trying to rape you?*" Immediately, three of the rebellious teachers also came in. They started shouting he was a rapist; he wanted to rape her!

On hearing this commotion, one of the good teachers came in and held the rebellious lady, forcing her to have her clothes lined up in spite of the other teachers trying to block him from doing so. A pull-and-pull commotion filled the office. All other teachers came, and a confrontation ensued between the two groups of teachers. One of the teachers, Mr. Njuguna, tried to block the woman's mouth as she was vomiting out very sexually abusive words. I then had a chance to rush out of the office. Immediately, the negative teachers followed me, seemingly wanting to beat me up, but they were blocked by the supportive group of teachers. I heard one of them say,

"*What do these teachers think they are? Let any of them dare to touch the headmaster, and we will deliver them to hell's gate. We will not allow you to live that evil lifestyle anymore. All teachers have no choice but to change and adopt the new ways spelt out by our school head.*"

It was then that the bell for lunch break rang, and children came out running to go home for their lunch. Soon, the negative teachers started walking away towards the teachers' quarters in the compound. They seemed regretful that their plan had not worked.

It was after two days that one of the teachers' revealed to me that the strategy had been laid out by the opposing team to have me jailed for at least seven years, which according to Kenyan laws, is the sentence for rapists. One of the schemers was the lady's boyfriend. They had just had sex. The plan was that the arrogant woman would come into my office, jump on me and force me to the ground, then tear up her underwear as she shouted for help. Then one of their own who would be standing just outside would have come and forcefully placed me on top of the woman and simultaneously shouted for people to come and witness my attempt to rape the woman. Then, her comrades, who were strategically placed not far from the office, would respond quickly and pretend to have caught me red-handed raping her.

I also learned later that one of these teachers, who was said to be her boyfriend, had already gone to bed with her even before she came to my office. Thus, having falsely ascertained that I was caught in the very act of rape, they were then to act very quickly by taking the lady to Njoro Police Station, where she would make an entry in the OB (Occurrence Book) and at the same time, have the woman visit a doctor who would then verify that the woman had actually been sexually molested and refer her to get a P3. In the process of all these undertakings, some bribing for false entries would take place for their case to win. As soon as the verification had taken place, the police were to immediately order my arrest, and then I would have been arraigned in a court of law and be condemned to a jail term according to Kenyan Law for seven years with hard labour. They had also stage-managed the episode to coincide with the time the children broke out for lunch so that they could take the news to the village during the lunch break.

I thank God that the woman was not able to get hold of me; hence, their plans backfired. But even though this was the case, these teachers never gave up on opposing me in all my endeavors to give the school a new face. They were determined to fight me until they had me maimed and dethroned to get rid of me from the teaching profession. Thus, after their first plan had collapsed, they continued to meet for the next few days. They were still plotting how to block me from succeeding with my plans. They now took the option of beating and maiming me.

There is this morning I came very early to carry on the teaching before the scheduled time of class lessons. It was around 7.00 am. I got into my small office. This office was a room that was subdivided into two sections. There was the inner section where the books and chalks were kept and it had its own door and a window that faced the main door through which the books were given out. When I entered the office, I went straight into the inner room to get some exercise books and chalk.

No sooner had I entered this inner room or bookstore than one of the rebellious male teachers hauled very abusive words to me like;

> *"You dog, how long do you think you will bark at us? You wild pig, do you think you can do anything to us? Today is your last day to live; we are going to skin you alive."*

By then, he was trying to get in through the bookstore door, but I had already locked it up. He banged at it with his feet and fists, trying to open it as he yelled progressively and vomited all kinds of insults;

> *"You think that this is your kingdom? This is our kingdom, not yours. Today is your doomed day, you son of a bitch…you must get to know whose kingdom you are trespassing. We shall take you to hell and have you baptized by the devil himself."*

By now he was trying to get through the window, but he was having difficulty, as it was small for him. He sought alternatives to reaching me with his feet and, other times, stretching his hands aggressively to get hold of my neck.

But unfortunately for him, I was squeezing myself into one corner. In spite of the small space, he persistently squeezed himself through the window, and it was when his shoulders were almost through that he gave a very sharp demonic cry that seemed to be the sign of telling the others that it was now time, they should come.

Instantly, I had some quick movements in the adjacent classroom for pupils who had come for a lesson. Then, there was a commotion outside my office. I heard the voice of the class prefect say, *"Let anyone touch our headmaster, and his blood will quench the earth today."* This was followed by many other voices rejoining, *"Yes, attempt it, and you will die."* x 3

Already, the big boys were upon Nyambimba, pulling him out of the window. From his whining, I could tell that he was in great pain as his shoulders were stuck in the window, and he was now pleading with the students not to hurt him. Some of them were already raining blows on his back. I heard one say,

> *"This is why they spent all the night drinking. They must have been strategizing on how to attack our headmaster this morning. Let us beat them and teach them a different lesson today. Comrades, tighten your grip on whatever you have in your hands!"*

At that point, I came out of my hiding place. I heard the pounding of feet on the ground as the teachers were trying to escape from the irritated students but they were encircled. It was timely. One muscular student, Kariuki, had thrown down one of the teachers, Mr. Chegu (not his real name), who was already worn out by the weekend alcohol drinking. He could hardly stand on his feet. He was already on the ground, and Kariuki had his hand in the air to strike him. Upon seeing this, I called out to the boy, *"Kariuki, don't touch him! God will deal with these people in His own ways."*

I then went closer to Mr. Chegu (not his real name). I noticed that his shirt was torn, and he had a bruise on one of his legs. I also noticed a club, four large and thick sticks, a sword, a whip and a knife on the floor. I asked, *"Whose weapons are these?"* Kariuki, the Head Boy, responded,

"These are the weapons the teachers had carried to attack you. We are so very grateful to you for you have taken us out of Egypt, where these teachers had enslaved us. We cannot allow any of them to harm you."

Another one interjected;

"Yes, they want to take us back there; we will not accept. We shall protect you with our lives, for you have given us hope."

With all the noise made by the students and the ensuing commotion, it reached far to the village, attracting the attention of the villagers. Some being parents in the school, they responded to what seemed like an emergency happening and they came to the school compound. After hearing the ongoing conversation, they understood what was transpiring and became part of the happenings. A parent retorted,

"These teachers think that they can wreck our school again, no way! If they are not careful, we shall ambush them from their drinking sprees and beat them thoroughly. We need to teach them a lesson."

By then, many more students had already reported to school. They had joined their colleagues in craving for the blood of the rebellious teachers.

It was then that I called upon the students to observe silence. I addressed them and reminded them that what was happening was a result of my endeavor to prepare them for a better future. So, as much as they were ready to defend me, they should, in the same zeal, take their studies seriously, I cautioned them, saying,

"But as much as you do all these things, let us cultivate love for one another. Let us show respect to our teachers and parents. They carry God's blessings upon our lives".

Then, turning to my *"enemies,"* I said,

"I just thank God for having saved me within the last three months. Otherwise, if it were not for that, I would have caused serious injuries to Nyambimba when he was stuck in the window. I was a well-known fighter when it came to physical fights. It is God who has changed me, and I would pray that He will also have mercy on each one of you so that you will come to respect your bodies and not pollute them with poisonous drinks and hard drugs."

Turning to the students and the parents who had already formed a crowd, I said,

"I thank you for being good and responsible parents. You have made my day by rescuing and defending me from my colleagues. I will live to treasure the events of today in my heart. Let this be a row model of how we are to defend the education of our children, all united for our success. We must all jealously protect them and secure their future by resisting all forms of negative energy, no matter the source. Schoolchildren need protection in every sphere of their lives. Your coming to rescue the situation has greatly motivated me to do all I can to hasten the promotion of this school in matters of academic, spiritual, discipline and any other important matters. I have come to realize that I am in good hands, for I have the support of both students, their parents and the community at large."

Having said that, I called upon one of the parents to lead us with a word of prayer, after which all the students dispersed into their respective classes, and before long, silence prevailed in the school compound once more. Only the teacher's voices were breaking the silence as their voices came out through the windows as they taught. I went into the office, took a few exercise books and got into standard seven class, where my English subject was scheduled for. I watched from the classroom as the three attackers left the school compound, this time individually. Two of them headed for their houses and Nyambimba, my aggressive attacker, seemed to be very much confused. He was behaving like Judas after Jesus was crucified. He headed for the road, and throughout the morning session, I could see him walking up and down the road, sometimes sitting down in a melancholic mood. A few times, I saw some villagers talk to him. He looked so depressed.

Three days after the morning *"drama,"* two teachers, Lisca (not his real name) and Nderita (not his real name), came to my office. They looked very calm and in a regrettable mood. One of them said to me,

"It has really become impossible for us to work under you. Nevertheless, history will tell what good or bad you will inflict upon this school. Meanwhile, we are asking you to do us a favor. We want you to recommend us for transfer from this school. Will you do it?"

Before agreeing or disagreeing with their request, I took a little bit of time to explain to them that it is important that they understand that my concern was the call of duty and ethics that demanded for preparation of the children for their future, but it seemed they had little regard for that. I said;

"I know you are not married, but assuming that you had children, would you like them to be treated the way you have treated these kids for years?"

To this they did not respond, but Mr. Lisca (not his real name) said, *"We are just requesting you to accept to sign our transfer documents."* I then said,

"Well, if you have the forms, then bring them, and if you don't have them, then you have my permission to go and get them from the DEO's office, and I shall sign for you."

As soon as I said this, the two left my office. True to their words, they went to the DEO's office, had the forms filled, and I signed them. They then brought them for signature, and indeed, I signed them. The following day, a truck pulled into the school compound and headed straight to the teachers' housing compound. Meanwhile, they returned all the school books that they had and went back to direct the loading of their luggage into the truck. They did not have much property as all their money went to drinking. As they left, the truck stopped at the school gate, and Mr. Nderita (not his real name) came straight to where I was standing outside the office and said to me,

"I have gone, but I will make sure that I come back to shame you on this year's examination results, for the poor performance will beat the record of all the years we have been here."

He then quickly rushed back to the truck as the driver was already hooting for him to go. I soon got them replaced by two very industrious teachers, Mr. Odongo and Mr. Kirikiru Kanina. Odongo taught Geography and History, and Kirikiru taught Math in standard seven. They were also good Christians.

Meanwhile, Mr. Nyambiba and the lady who was being used to falsely scandalize me with the rape allegation did not ask for a transfer. The female teacher was already at loggerheads with the other teachers in the opposition. She had come to feel guilty for the scandal she had involved herself in. She accused them of having misused her in their plans to have me falsely accused of carrying out a treasonable act of raping her. No wonder then, even before the other two had left, they were no longer birds of a feather.

She later came and explained to me the whole plot and how it had been hatched to destroy me and my teaching career. As she narrated the story, she broke into tears. In the midst of her sobs, she said to me, "*Headmaster, forgive me; I abused you too much, showed you my nakedness and tried to negatively expose you to even pupils, villagers and parents... and even to the possibility of having you jailed on false allegations. I thank God for the teachers and students who intervened, for I would have hanged myself, and I could not be alive today.*" As for Nyambiba, he sent a lady teacher to come and talk to me. This lady came to my home the evening of the day he wanted to attack me. She explained to me the fact that Nyambiba was so much regrettable for what he did. According to her, Nyambiba was only misled by the others, who had even made him drink most of the night so that come that morning, he could face me squarely in his drunkard state. Even when I told her that my conscious was clear and I had forgiven him that very moment, she seemed to want me to affirm more. She said;

"Please, headmaster, don't go to the DEO's office tomorrow, don't report him. This is his fear that tomorrow, you will not even report to school in the morning. We all think that you will go straight to the DEO's office to report on your victimization by the teachers. Please, please, forgive him."

It was then that I told her of my experience at Barut-Rhoda school, where the school was comprised of many women whose husbands held high government positions in the nearby Nakuru Town and how they rebelled against my administration and how I had reacted by writing many letters accusing them to the Area Education Officer (AEO). I told her how, one day, the AEO called me in his office and told me:

"David, I have called you because of two things. One is to congratulate you for the good work at Barut Rhoda School and to tell you that we are happy because you are not letting us down. The second and most important is to advise you never to write a letter accusing a teacher to the higher authorities when you are angry. Always give yourself time, even if it means one full week, so that when you write the letter or take a drastic action, your mind will not be clogged by anger. Then, your action will be carried out with a sober mind. I tell you, if you do this in your life, you will never find yourself in great problems. Anger exaggerates the way we feel and act. I have regretted many things I had done before I came to embrace this theory. It will surprise you that, at the end of the one week, in

most cases, you will find no need to write a letter. It has happened to me several times."

I then explained to this lady the fact that this advice from Mr. Nyagah is the catalyst in my administration as I try to overcome the obstacles that I encounter, not emotionally and, in this case, there was no way I could go to the DEO'S Office to report them. In response to Nyambimba's threats, I told this lady to go and read to him the Scripture. I remember trying to console her and explaining that if it were not for salvation, I would have been in for it because I could not have tolerated all those abusive words she had thrown at me. I took the opportunity to preach to her, we prayed together and she then left. She became a very good supporter of my administration, supportive in teaching and even also very helpful information to me;

"Do not be afraid of those who kill the body but cannot kill the soul. Rather be afraid of the One who can destroy both soul and body in hell" (Matthew 10:28).

In this case, I told her to let him know that I was not afraid so long as what I was doing glorified God. And true to my word, the following morning, I went to school at 7.00 am as usual. After the assembly, Nyambimba came to my office and so gently and politely knocked on the door. After I said, *'Come in,'* he came in with his hands at the back and, somehow bowing, said, *"Good morning, Mr. Githii."* I responded, *"Good morning, Mr. Nyambimba. Please, have a seat."*

Mr. Nyambiba then, very apologetically, spoke, narrating how he was misled by the other negative teachers, especially Lisca and Ndirito (not their real names). He described how he and the other teachers had really wrecked the school by discouraging the parents not to be serious in educating their children, and even further discouraging the pupils from being aggressive in their studies. He even told me how they used to give the big boys money so that they could talk or organize strikes by the pupils. He told me how they had the school girls in their houses during game time and how they kept others in their houses while others went to work in the teacher's farms. He told me how they fed some members of the school committee and some parents with beer so as to silence them, and he said,

"It is not until now that I have come to realize how much damage we have done to this school. I am sincerely asking for your forgiveness. I am also, in the same breath, promising you my full cooperation in all school matters, including academics."

He continued,

"I also want to thank you for not having gone to report me to the DEO. Surely, as an untrained teacher, I am more vulnerable to being interdicted than the others because they are already trained teachers. I thank you more for not anchoring on my foolishness."

I told Nyambiba that until the previous year in October, I had had a lot of foolishness as well. And I told him that the reason we were talking face to face with him was because of the undressing of that foolishness from my heart by Jesus Christ. The moment I accepted Him as my Lord and Savior, the curtain of the unforgiving spirit fell off me making it possible for me to control my emotions of anger. I got it replaced with the spirit of love and tolerance. I took time to explain to him the negative consequences of taking beer. Among other things, it distorts the mind and drains one financially. In response, he said,

"Thank you so much. I have learned a lot from you, and henceforth, I will pursue a deep understanding of my relationship with God. Meanwhile, from now on, I shall not consume any alcohol." We then prayed together, and he then left my office.

From then henceforth, in him, I had one of the most devoted, trusted and respectable teachers. As he was already addicted, it was hard for him to stop drinking at once, but he seemed determined to quit alcohol. He remained a very faithful teacher until I left that school.

The following day after my meeting with Nyambimba, I called a staff meeting. It was the most peaceful staff meeting that I had ever had. Everyone was so humble and respectful. Each spoke in a very apologetic voice. Nyambimba and the formerly negative lady championed the peaceful atmosphere. Their contribution was notable, appropriate, progressive and positive. On the agenda on working and living in unity, the lady said,

"Of course, you know how much Nyambimba and I have retrogressively opposed the headmaster and we now regret our actions. Let us, with one accord, join hands with our devoted headmaster and make this school to be a school of choice."

After a few other teachers had spoken and as we were coming to a close, Nyambiba said:

"I am sure you are all aware of my satanic activities in trying to finish the headmaster. I thank those of you who came to speak to me, especially after that morning I had championed the headmaster's attack. I had been fed with beer almost the whole night, and even now, when I look back, I cannot understand what had led me to behave in that manner. I was just misused and I am really thankful to the headmaster, for were it not for him, you all know that today I would not have been here with you. Let us, with one accord, support the learning and teaching in the school." The meeting ended with a word of prayer."

THE MOTIVATING STRATEGY
GOAL SETTING

Now with all the teachers on my side, it became so easy to run the school. It did not matter whether I was in school or not. The teachers felt guilty if at any time one came late, left late, or even failed to mark books or even failed to say 'hallow' to me. The school became like a beehive where both teachers and pupils worked hard and harmoniously. The standard seven teachers, the class that was to sit for that year's examination, were really kept busy, especially by the three of us. That is myself, teaching English and science; Odongo, who taught Geography and History; and Kirikiru, teaching Mathematics.

One of the strategies I took in the quest to have as many kids pass the examination was to construct a library for individual students. Thus, in one of the parents' general meetings, I managed to convince parents to contribute money that could be enough to buy three textbooks per child, although not for them to buy the books but to give me the money to do so. I knew that if I had asked the parents and pupils to individually buy the books, then books on Mathematics and English would have dominated the overall list, leaving scarcity in other subjects like History, Geography and science. Otherwise, with me managing the sorting out and with 30 pupils, each having three books, it meant the class would have 90 textbooks of different categories. Thus, I bought like 20 Mathematics books, 10 English, 10 History, 10 Science, 10 Geography and 10 books of questions and answers for some past years' exams. I made sure that a pupil with a Mathematics book did not own an English book so that they could exchange the different subjects text books. Thus, a pupil, let's say with Mathematics, Geography and science books, would use the same to exchange any of those books with another one who had none of the above. This then created a big mobile library and academic interactive sessions in the class. The other strategy that we came up with was to stress the importance of evening preparatory studies. All teachers combined their efforts in this one. Each teacher would be on duty every evening to supervise the pupils in standard six and seven as they worked in groups of three or four. Some evenings, one of us – Odongo, Kirikiru or myself would be teaching. As there was no electricity, the parents had bought some pressure lamps and they had contributed money towards the paraffin as well. The standard six and seven pupils also came for studies on Saturdays from 8.00 am to 1.00 pm. During the holidays, as other Kenyan schools went for holidays in the months of April and August, these two classes had a break of two weeks only. In the school days, they had to be in class by 7.00 am to 8.30 am before the morning assembly and the beginning of the programmed lessons for the day. The afternoon lessons ended at 4.00 pm. But as already stated, the two upper classes came back for the evening studies.

ADVANCED LEVEL OF EDUCATION

Meanwhile, I continued with my personal academic studies. I did not want to leave any stone unturned until I further advanced in education. I had a very strong desire to climb the mountain of education. The sky was the limit. Thus, as much as I was busy, I hardly had a day go by without spending at least two hours doing my studies. I used to wake up very early for personal studies, mainly based on the subjects I was to sit on the Advanced Level (A-Level) examination. They included History, Geography and Religious Education. I hardly ever lost my vision and goal of attaining the doctorate level of education. The peaceful school environment helped me to concentrate on both teaching and my personal studies. Thus killing two birds with one stone.

I was really determined to sit for the Advanced Level examination at the end of that year, 1977. This meant that I was practically overworking myself as I had to use every available time to fully teach the Standard Seven class. At the same time, carry the school administrative duties and pursued my own studies for I strived towards my personal vision. I had a strong urge to accomplish it without delay. I always knew that an opportunity lost would never be recovered. That was the best me for me to carry on my studies before our children advanced in age and, hence, needing more resources and attention.

CERTIFICATE OF PRIMARY EDUCATION (CPE) RESULTS

November was the time that examinations were taking place, and so as the students sat for their examinations, I also sat for my A-level exams. December was a month full of anxiety for me. I could not wait to receive both the students' CPE results and mine as well. The time seemed to drag far too much. There were so many of us waiting for the standard seven examination results. At the same time, there were so many 'Thomases' who did not believe that any miracle would rescue the school from the usual E's and D's that had characterized the school results over the years. There were even those parents and teachers who had come to associate the poor performance of the school with a *'curse.'* But for us, especially the three of us who taught that class, we were so optimistic that something better than the previous school performance was coming. It was just a few days to Christmas Day when, early in the evening, came out the news through the radio that,

"The 1977 CPE examination results were out. The headmasters were asked to collect the results from their respective District Education Officer's offices."

Consequently, that was the longest night I can remember. Many images kept flashing through my mind. (*What if some of the pupils never wrote their identification numbers well? What if the pupils panicked and, as a result the usual E's and D's would be decorating the results slip paper?*)

But then, there was the other side of the coin. (*What if the performance surpassed any other within the previous ten years?*) Then, I could imagine the jubilation that could come out of this. I kept on tossing and turning all night long in the bed. I never slept a wink. As the cock crew at 3.00 am, I was still tossing in the bed and then came the morning light. I woke up, took a cup of tea and did not even care for anything else. I then walked the six miles to Njoro, got into public transport and by 8.00 am, I was among the other few headmasters who were waiting for the DEO'S offices to open. As we waited, a headmaster and a friend of mine introducing me to another said, *"Meet Mr. Githii, the headmaster of Cheptoroi/Beeston Primary School."*

In response, the other headmaster said,
>*"Oh, you are Githii? News has spread far and wide about how you have transformed that school; I am sure the results will favour that transformation."*

I then said, *"Well, I have tried to do my best, but as you know, with God, all things are possible."* The man then asked me, *"Are you a Christian?"* I said, *"Yes, a born-again Christian."* As I said this, the DEO's door opened, and he quickly said, *"I will be with you soon."* By then, there was a big crowd of headmasters of the 258 Schools that constituted the Nakuru District.

The DEO first addressed us. He said that there was a general decline in many schools, but he was however pleased with a few schools particularly with one school that for many years had humiliated the District. My heart was awakened by joy, for I realized that somehow that school might turn out to be Cheptoroi, but my joy was short-lived, for he continued to say, *"We hope that other headmasters will emulate this school which is located in Molo."* My heart sank because my school was in Njoro. He continued to say that he would soon call a headmasters' meeting to evaluate the performances and even encourage the headmasters to learn from each other.

The schools were called one by one as each headmaster took the results and went his way. It reminded me of the Kikuyu proverb that says, '*Ciathanaga ikigwa no ikiumbuka*' (*the birds of feather harmoniously land together, but when a disturbance occurs, each goes its way*). At last, I heard 'Cheptoroi/Beestons Primary School.' I moved forward, and with hands somehow vibrating with anxiety, I held up the sheet, and through the transparency of the paper, I spotted many Bs and Cs and I thought I saw an A. I left the hall and went behind the building to see the results alone undisturbed, only to find many other headmasters doing the same. I opened my sheet, and my eyes could hardly believe what I saw. The paper carried at least three A's, some B's and C's, and, of course, some D's. Then, as I looked at the paper, I closed my eyes and said a short thanksgiving prayer, *"Father, thank you for the good fruits of my labour; thank you for using me to glorify your name."* Even as I had the last word of my prayer, a headmaster from a neighbouring school tapped my shoulder and asked me, *"How is it?"* I responded, *"It's great!"* as I showed him the paper. Upon his eyes falling on the paper, they gorged out in wonder and thundered;

"I now believe in the transformation people have been talking about. I cannot believe that there could be a grade A in that school's CPE results. They hardly had a good C in the past years. Bwana headmaster, what is the secret?"

He said this so loudly and full of wonder that the other headmasters were attracted, and like bees seeking the nectar, they converged on us, surrounding me as they all looked on with excitement at my school's results.

Then one of them coming towards me said,
"Cheptoroi Bestons should be the school the DEO had referred to. He must have confused Njoro with Molo. I have just consulted him on this for having come from Molo, I was curious to know that good performing school in Molo".

He then whispered to me saying;
"It is Cheptoroi Bestons, whose headmaster is David Githii. He is the one we had taken to Barut Rhoda School when we were authorized by the Nakuru mayor to take a good headmaster there."

One headmaster in the small crowd said,
"Mr. Githii, I will seek an audience with you; I really need to know the secret behind your administrative and teaching skills."

At this juncture, I left for the bus stage. My legs seemed not to carry me fast enough to where I was to catch the bus to Njoro, and even when I got into it, it seemed to move sluggishly.

Finally, I arrived at the school. Even from afar, I could see a big crowd of people. It seemed like pupils of all classes in our school had come to school yet it was holiday time. The whole village, teachers and others from a nearby village too had assembled in our school compound. What I had not known was that one of the headmasters who had seen my results had immediately telephoned the school chairman in the Beeston sawmill, and the news had quickly spread and reached all workers and the village like wildfire. No wonder all these people had gathered wearing very cheerful, jolly faces. As I came closer to them, I could see their smiles.

I restrained myself from talking to them; instead, I went into the office and transferred all the results on paper (as there was no photocopier), after which I hung the results on the notice board. People somehow scrambled as each wanted to have a glance at the results. Soon, people were talking in small groups, and one could tell the joy that puffed up these people's hearts. I then went to the office.

Before long, I came out of the office and interacted with some people. To my surprise, I overheard a person who had not spotted me saying,

"I really do not believe in what this headmaster has pinned on the notice board. I was born and raised here, and now I am a man with a family and I have never seen such results in this school. Call it a miracle but I cannot believe in it. There is no way Cheptoroi Bestons school could produce such results."

I overheard another one saying,

> *"The headmaster cheats to be a born-again Christian. Have you ever heard of a born-again Christian who can put such lies on the noticeboard? He is a liar, a cheater and a pretender."*

Another one was in the habit of saying,

> *"The chairman of the school collaborated with the headmaster to cheat this community, and there is no way this school could score A's, B's and C's! There is no way! No way! Nothing like that at all! What we have on the notice board is nothing but cooked CPE results!"*

It was unfortunate because many parents became victims and joined with the increasing number of 'Thomas's.' The negative propaganda was now quickly spreading among the pupils even as the schools opened in January.

Luckily, three weeks after the results, the first letter of John Mwangi arrived, admitting him to join one of the most prestigious boarding high Schools situated in the City of Nairobi, actually the Starehe Boys High School. As soon as I got the letter, I called for a school assembly. I then summoned the school prefect in the front of the parade. I handed him the letter and asked him to read it loud and clear. He read it,

> *"To John Mwangi, Congratulations on your excellent performance in CPE-Kenya. We are pleased to inform you that you have been admitted to Starehe Boys High School... This is one of the most prestigious schools in Kenya."*

Both pupils and teachers were left with their mouths wide open in shock. I took advantage of the opportunity to talk to the pupils encouraging them to study hard. As a way of counter-attacking the Thomas's, I told the pupils to go home and let their parents and the community at large know that Mwangi had been admitted to Starehe Boys. This by itself was enough. The community needed no further evidence. One such case was enough. The news of another pupil being admitted to a government school came, and each time, I would call an assembly and ask a pupil to read the letter after which I encouraged the rest to read smart and also to spread the good news. A total of seven pupils who had attained 32 out of 36 points joined very competitive national and provincial schools, while a few others joined district-level high schools. But the greatest achievement was the position the school was placed. Out of 258 schools, it took position 3 as compared to the previous years, when it used to be among the poorest performers in the District.

The Churches heard of the goodness of the school. The government administrators came to know my name. In two months, people started coming, some from very far just to witness the good things happening within our school. With this spirit, the teachers, pupils and parents were becoming addicted to the spirit of academics. All pupils thought that I acted academically. We were all dreaming of moving the position of the school from 3rd position that it had attained to number two out of 258 schools in the district. So, we worked hard. The evening studies, Saturday holidays and morning studies. Standard seven pupils were seen reading and asking each other questions as they went to the farm, to draw water, to fetch firewood and during their free times at home. Teachers were joyfully giving assignments and marking them. Even those who never taught in the senior class did all they could to give a helping hand.

A LEVEL RESULTS

End of February the same year, news came on the Radio that, "*The 1977 Advanced Level results were out. The school headmasters and the private candidates were advised to collect their results from the Provincial Education Offices.*"

Unlike the night of the announcement of the CPE results, this time, I had no problem sleeping. With the good performance of the pupils, I felt relaxed. After all, I can always re-sit my A level, but the CPE results could not be repeated. In any case this was an individual's case, of which possibly nobody even remembered that I had sat an examination.

In the morning, I first went to school as usual and taught my morning classes. I then headed for the PEO's office, where I was given the results and what a joy! I had obtained two principals and one subsidiary, a principal in History and Religious Education and a subsidiary in Geography.

But, the best ever CPE results in the history of Cheptoroi Beston Primary School and more so, taking number 3 district-wise made me a house-to-house talk. All the dwellers of Njoro heard about me.

The spirituality that characterized the school had permeated to both teachers and pupils. Some teachers came to accept Jesus as their Lord and Savior. Among these were Odongo and Kirikiru. Many pupils, especially girls, who did not initially confess to Christ became very good

Christians. In later years, they became Church leaders. I have met some, like Kibiru and Karanja, who are playing big roles in the Church leadership. Karana was very brutal before I came to Cheptoroi. He became a Church leader within the Full Gospel Church. Mungai is a Presbyterian Church elder. Kibiru became a pastor. The school qualified for the description of a God-fearing school. The pupils could hardly miss attending Sunday services in their respective Churches.

SPORTS

In sports, I had divided the school into houses. These were Mt Kenya, Mt Kilimanjaro, Mt Elgon and Mt Kilimambogo. The games on my table were laid in such a way that at the time of games, different houses practiced the sports by themselves. This meant if the house was playing football, they would take a group of twenty-two, with each side having eleven players. Then they would have another twenty-two. After the four teams had played, each group would be asked to give their best five, who would then combine with another five from one of the other teams. So, it would be the case also with the other two teams. Then, the ten would play against the other ten. Then, the next time, each of the teams, composed of ten people, would be asked to give their best six and finally, the house had their best soccer players and a reserve person. After every house had come with its best twelve players, the next level was what we called knockout. In this Mt Elgon would play with Mt Kenya, then Mt Kilimanjaro would play with Mt. Kilimambogo. The winners of each played together. The winning house got a cup. Meanwhile as the four final teams played, the games master and I (the soccer coach) were picking out the best players in the different positions. For example, the best goalkeeper among the houses or the best Center Forwards or Full Backs.

If there were others better than some in the winning house, we would replace those in the winning team. In this way, we were able to come up with talented players and no wonder our soccer team championed from zone, location, district up to provincial level.

The same pattern was used in the athletics. Each house practiced an event by itself. For example, when one house was practicing individual throwing of the shot put, another was doing the long jump, another was running 100 metres while yet another was running 220 metres etc. As each house practiced, they were taking the names of their best in each event. After three months, I organized what is commonly known as an 'inter-house competition.' This was an important day, and there would be a guest of honour and all parents. The best in each house and in each event would compete.

Each of the competitors had to do the best as his/her parents, relatives, brothers, sisters, the guest of honour and the teachers were there. Therefore, a word of praise even at home, in the neighborhood and in school was important (we all want praise when we do well). Thus, all the events were held. Such included 100m, 220m, 800m, 4x400m, 1 mile, 3 miles and 12 miles, throwing of javelin and short put, the long and high jump. Each house cheered their competitor and the parents joined in cheering whichever of their children was participating. After the end of the competition, certificates were given to all competitors who attained positions one to three. Trophies were also given to the first three houses. After giving out the certificates, the guest of honour delivered a speech of encouragement. The vital aspect of these inter-house competitions was that they encouraged the pupils to discover their talents and to tap into their potential. All those who held positions one to three represented the school in the interschool competitions. Our pupils proved to be very competitive. They got a lot of certificates, and our school, mostly in the lead, got many trophies.

1978 CPE PERFORMANCE

The year 1978 was the second year for Cheptoroi Beston School to do the CPE examination while I was the headmaster. After witnessing the excellent results of the 1977 class, we doubled our efforts. Then came the month of November. Together with the entire school, I escorted them to the examination centre, which was one and a half miles from Cheptoroi. The centre was Nesuit School. The kids went singing Christian songs. Other times, they talked and laughed. The non-candidates encouraged the candidates, even as they joked about the easy exam. I overheard one say,

"You know last year's lot had our headmaster for one year. If they performed so well in the exam, then for us having been with him for two years, we shall all pass with flying colors."

Before we set out for the examination centre, I had prayed with candidates and in my prayers, I tried to make them visualize each one of them scoring A's and B+. Also, in my lessons, I did take time to encourage them to set their mind on a positive note - nothing was negative in their minds. On the morning of the exam, all the candidates looked eager and ready to excel.

We finally made it to the examination centre. The kids went to the examination room with a lot of confidence. The invigilators were ready, the hall all set and only the class masters of standard seven and headmasters were allowed in to affirm that the examination papers were not tampered with. After this, we left the examination hall. I remember I went and lay on the grass somewhere; one of the invigilators saw me and noticed the fear of the unknown on my face. I remember him saying,

"David, if there are those who should worry about the performance of their pupils, you should not be among them. Your children are doing everything with confidence; never in my life did I see such kids who even smile as they do the exam. They even have very impressive handwriting."

That statement gave me a lot of relief. It is true these kids had good handwriting. My trick was that before a pupil qualified to join standard seven, he/she had to satisfy me that they had good handwriting. I picked eight to ten best handwritings of the previous standard seven and asked the standard six pupils to practice any of those handwritings for six months before joining standard seven. Thus, knowing good writing was one of the qualifications to join standard seven. Each of those pupils in standard seven had good and legible handwriting. I knew that good handwriting was a catalyst for good marks in an English composition, which carried 30% of the total English examination paper.

The first paper was Mathematics. The bell rang at 10.30 am, indicating that the first paper had ended. I was eagerly looking at the door where the kids would emerge for the 15-minute break before taking the second paper. The first to come out looked at me, smiled and raised his thumb up, and so did the second, the third, etc.

When the bell for the end of the English paper rang, the students rushed out, hoping that I would still be there. They then raised their hands up as they held one another and then held up their thumbs. Many were writing A's in the air, showing me that they expected an automatic A. Finally, the pupils entered for the final paper. Since whatever has a beginning has an end, the CPE examination of 1978 came to an end. The pupils went home discussing cheerfully as they talked about different questions, and when a group found that they got the same and the correct answer, they could break into laughter. They confirmed what one of the invigilators had said to me as he got into the car holding a bunch of exam papers, *"Mr. Headmaster, your kids are really smart; we need to learn from you. Start celebrating."*

The anxiety to know the exam results grew as the month of December trekked on its path. Two days after Christmas, the radio announcement came;

"The 1978 CPE examination results are out. The headmasters are advised to collect the results for their e-schools from their respective District Education Offices tomorrow."

That night the whole talk around Beeston village was about the truth coming. Many spent nights talking and even betting on their expectation in the year's examination results. As for me, I could not sleep much as my mind was full of excitement for the next day. Unlike the previous year, this time, every thought was positive. I woke up early, had quick preparation, and by 8.00 am, I had arrived at the AEO's Offices at Nakuru Town. I joined a group of headmasters who had already arrived. No sooner did they see me than I realized that I had become the immediate subject.

When I reached them, they were somehow competing to shake my hand. As they shook my hand, each was saying something like;

"Congratulations on the last year's CPE results. I will invite you to talk to my teachers; I need to borrow a leaf from you. I am sure you are going to give us another surprise this year. I will not be surprised if your current pupils outdo last year's class."

I was just responding to them when a lady at the DEO's office summoned us to draw nearer to the office. As I drew near, I saw the DEO's eyes gazing at me with a smile. I also responded with a smile. He then started addressing the headmasters, covering many areas, but with what looked like a conclusion to his speech, he said,

"This time, I would not hesitate to praise Cheptoroi Beeston School for their continued good performance. I would really encourage the headmasters to borrow a leaf from Mr. Githii, who is the headmaster of that school. The school has taken the second position out of the 258 schools in this district. St Mary's Academy in Molo has maintained its unrivaled position, but I caution them that in Cheptoroi School, they have a determined competitor. Let them work harder; otherwise, they face a big challenge next year."

He went on to say, *"All in all, this year's performance in the district has shown a lot of improvement."* He then read the results of the first ten schools, of which my school was number two out of two hundred and fifty-eight schools that comprised Nakuru District. After this, he handed in the individual school's results to the corresponding headmasters, and then we were dispersed.

As I went aside, a big group of the headmasters were following me curiously waiting for me to open the envelope. Upon opening the envelope, not even my eyes could believe what I saw. The result slip was decorated with A's and B's. My heart got puffed up with joy. Meanwhile, the headmasters were pushing for each wanted to have a glance at my results. The first name was Lucy Wairimu Chege. She had obtained all the marks to accumulatively score untainted thirty-six points. That was the highest mark. It was the apex of the total marks. She had obtained an A in every paper. The whole sheet was decorated with A's, B's and C's. Yes, this time, I could believe my eyes, for it was no more mythical. Both the teachers, pupils, parents, and the school committee had worked hard for it. There was a tag of sacrifice from each of us, a true trend for any successful accomplishment of any mission, for there is always a price tag for any sacrifice. I was just returning the sheet to the envelope when one of the education officers tapped me on the back, saying,

"We are proud of you; you are really helping this district in maximizing its mean score. You are now among the few headmasters we are counting on; keep on keeping on."

He then addressed the headmasters who were eagerly studying the results but, most important, admiring the girl with 36 out of 36 points, having cleared every question set in the examination. He told them,

"You can see for yourself. It is not by luck, accident or coincidence; it is through teaching and admirable administration. Go and do likewise."

There was a prolonged clapping, which was brought to an abrupt silence when one of the senior headmasters interjected,

"My colleagues, this is not a laughing matter; it's a matter of some of us feeling ashamed of what our results sheets show. The officer is right, there is no luck here, and what one man can do we can all do it. Let us put pride aside and invite Githii to come and talk to our teachers, or the DEO can organize seminars in which Githii can be the facilitator. What makes me give credit to Githii is that unlike St. Mary's School, which has taken number one in the district, St. Mary's is a boarding school, but Cheptoroi is only a day school that borders a big forest. St Mary's is located right in Elburgon Town. It has installed electricity next to a tarmacked road. Cheptoroi has none of these. In fact, in their studies at night whether in school or at their homes, they use paraffin lamps. Unlike St Mary's School, whose surrounding community is made up of established farmers and business people, the Cheptoroi area comprises very poor people who just depend on the produce of small gardens that they are temporarily given after some parts of the forests get cleared."

At this juncture, we dispersed, and I headed towards the bus terminus. Meanwhile, one of the headmasters joined me, and as we walked, he told me that the suggestion that I be invited by the headmasters to facilitate seminars was not well taken by the officer. He said;

"This is what I figured out when looking at his facial expression. Immediately, it was proposed that headmasters invite you for seminars or the DEO's Office to facilitate such, the officer's face had a negative expression."

He went on to explain why the officer's face would negatively change;

> *"Such a move would be jeopardizing the officer's position. Such an appraisal would be an indicator that you are better than all those others in the DEO's office."*

He even felt that some headmasters would not accommodate such an idea because some of the officers were their godfathers, people they easily corrupt by buying them beer so that they could maintain their headmastership positions and, more so, remain in the big and well-financed schools. They would hate that someone would outshine them. Before long, we parted company, and my friend headed for the bus stage.

As for me, I got into a hotel and asked for a bite, but the main purpose for getting into a hotel was to have time to write down the school results so that upon arrival at the school, I would have them pinned on the school's notice board. Thus, having compiled, I boarded a bus and arrived at the school by 1:00 pm. I went straight and had the results pinned on the notice board. Meanwhile, there was a big crowd of people who had been eagerly waiting for the results. No wonder even as I hung the results on the notice board there was a lot of jostling as each wanted to see the outcome. The first person to have a glimpse exclaimed, *"Thirty-six! Thirty -Six! Thirty- Six! Thirty-six! Lucy Wairimu, thirty- Six!"* Another one shouted, *"It is the thirties."*

The news spread like bushfire such that before long, there was a throng of people streaming from Beeston's Village,

Mukungugu Farm, Beeston Sawmill employees and the surroundings as far as Nessuit and Ndoswa. There were streams of people coming to see for themselves.

As I sat in the office compiling another list for the teachers' notice board, I could see people discussing in groups, some shedding tears of joy, others laughing uncontrollably, and before long, all the pupils were jumping and clapping their hands as they sang joyfully. As I left the office to go home, I could not control the forest of hands that wanted to shake my hand - from pupils, parents and other people from nearby villages, some I had not even seen before. After shaking a large number of hands, I then silenced them and addressed them for about ten minutes. I thanked the pupils, parents, and the school committee and extended the same to the teachers. I thanked them for the role each had played. I further encouraged them to love God, for the fear of the Lord is the beginning of wisdom (Proverbs 9:10).

One week after the results, I do not remember what I had exactly gone to do at the provincial education offices, but it so happened that as I walked along the office corridors, I met one of my good friends with whom we were classmates at Thogoto Teachers College. After some chat, the man said to me,

"By the way, do you know that Muriu, who was our former lecturer at Thogoto Teachers College, is presently the Rift Valley Provincial Primary Schools Inspector (PPSI)? Why not get into his office and say hi to him? I am sure he will be excited to see you. I saw him a week ago, and he was really welcoming."

I responded by saying, *"Oh! You mean Muriu is the education boss in Rift Valley Province? That is great. I will go to his office just now."* I went and knocked on Muriu's door, and he responded, *"Come in.* On seeing my face, he said, *"Is this Githii? You mean this is where you got posted to?"* By then, he had a tight grip on my hand as he shook me. In response, I said,

> *"Yes, in fact, I am the headmaster of Cheptroi Beeston Primary School, which has made great news as a result of its wonderful performance in the recently concluded CPE results for this year."*

I could feel further tightening of his grip as he said,

> *"Congratulations, congratulations. I am very excited about this. I was looking forward to meeting that headmaster of that school with such excellent performance that greatly promotes not only Nakuru District but Rift Valley Province as well."*

I have learned that the leading student with 36 points comes from the Cheptoroi Beeston school.

Muriu then directed me to a seat that made me directly face him. He then narrated how the Provincial Education Office had learnt of the wonderful performance of Cheptoroi Beeston Primary School in Nakuru District. He further said,

> *"David, I am really proud of you, but this is not a surprise to me. You said it in your life both in class and outside the class at Thogoto College. I can remember how you paid attention as I taught your class; your work was good. In fact, you are among the few people I can remember in your class, though I still remember some for their crooked life."*

Yes, Mr. Muriu was one of those teachers I respected in the course of my two years of training at Thogoto Teachers College. He was a dedicated and loving person. On top of teaching, he made us realize the challenges facing teachers outside the college after their completion of training. He used to expound to us how one could overcome some of these obstacles.

Thus, in response to his compliments, I said,

"I am not as well surprised that you now hold this big post of being the Provincial Primary Schools Inspector. I learnt a lot from you at Thogoto College. I am happy to learn that you are the one holding this position."

Then he said,

"Yes, this is my second month, and not even many of my friends are aware of my present promotion. But one thing I want to tell you, David, is that when you do your work with all sincerity and devotion, those above you will one day say, 'Look, here is a man who has made a difference through a positive impact on the community. This is one catalyst of God touching the heart of people to bring a difference in one's life, and then before you even know it, you would have moved from one glory to another."

We were by now sipping a cup of tea that he had requested the secretary to bring. We engaged in a long discussion, more so on many of life's memories of those days we were at Thogoto Teachers College. The discussion stirred a lot of memories, including the many different characters of both students and tutors. We talked of some very nice teachers but also of a few teachers who were addicted to alcohol and some who even came to class drunk, something that was setting a very bad example to the students. I, however, also shared a bit of my life after college, which, though somehow negative in some ways, had drastically changed me for good. Before I left Muriu's office so as to give him a chance to attend to other people waiting to see him, I said to him, *"I wonder whether you would be willing to come and visit my school. I would really appreciate that."* He responded, *"Of course, David. Why don't we fix a date now?"* He took hold of his diary and said, *"What date do you propose and it has to be on a Saturday?"* After some consultation, we settled on the second Saturday of January of that year, 1979. I then left for home. On the way, I kept on meditating on how I was to strategically organize a wonderful reception for this great man in the education sector.

The following day, I called an urgent staff meeting. I explained the fact that the Provincial Primary Schools Inspector was to visit our school. The teachers were not only very happy but got very excited about this news and, more so, because it was very rare that a person of such caliber visited a school and, even more so, at the invitation of a headmaster. Such an officer's visit is usually organized by his juniors, who include the District Education Officer (DEO) and the Area Education Officer (AEO). In one accord, the teachers adopted the idea. The teachers also passed an agenda to organize parents' meetings so that the idea and the urgency of the matter could be passed to them. But this idea was the first to be adopted by the School Committee. I, therefore, called a school committee meeting that joyfully adopted the idea. The committee also advised me to call for a parents' meeting. Likewise, the parents adopted the idea. From that time, the school turned into a beehive of activities. A lot of cleaning was carried out; scientific tables for the pupils' demonstrations were all set. Each student knew what to do. The Friday before the visit was a free day so that in the morning, the pupils could go and clean their clothes, and in the afternoon, they came to school wearing home clothes to clean the school. The teachers also came to do the final touches on various areas of preparation, including final touches to the songs, drama and recitations that were to be presented by the students and even teachers. Of course, being the PPSI, Muriu was to be accompanied by other senior officers from the province, including the DEOs and AEOs and District Inspector of Schools (DIS) and other government officials, like the Area Chief, District officer (DO) and Njoro police commanding Officer.

THE BIG DAY

The awaited Saturday came. All the teachers and the parents were in school by 9.00 am. Most of the kids were in by 8.00 am so as to do the final rehearsals on their folk and Christian songs, the scientific demonstrations, all drawings of the subjects, charts, projects, name it. I had placed a pupil somewhere outside the school compound with instructions that as soon as he spots the motorcade of the chief guest from afar, he should run very fast and report it to me. No sooner had the report come than all the pupils lined up on both sides of the road leading to the school compound. They were under instructions to wave cheerfully to the guests and, at the same time, clap their hands as the vehicles moved into the school compound. Some were to hold placards bearing writings like, **"PPSI WELCOME TO CHEPTOROI, WE LOVE YOU."**

And so, the vehicles drove through the queues with kids portraying the highest degree of discipline and joy. The children were also under instructions that, as soon as the guests got into the school compound the senior classes were to move quickly and stand silently in their respective show stands. One group of pupils was to stand very near to where the guests would be signing on the visitors' book, singing softly. Likewise, another group of students would also be singing softly from a distance as I continued to introduce the guest to the staff and the school committee members. Everyone was smartly dressed including some of the invited guests like the government representatives.

As expected, Mr. Muriu was accompanied by some of the education dignitaries, including Nakuru District Primary Schools Inspector, Mr. Gaitho, Deputy Nakuru District Officer, Mr. Gachunji and other officers from the Provincial Education Offices. As I introduced them to the teachers, the children's choir appetized the atmosphere. Then immediately, the teachers joined us as we now moved from one stand to another. The kids were very highly skilled and motivated in all their demonstrations. I could tell from their look that our guests were really moved as they listened to these kids' presentations.

They were especially excited when they got to Lucy Wairimu, who had topped the CPE examination not only in Nakuru District but was nationally among the top performers. They really admired her skills and congratulated her for her incredible performance. It was like they all wanted to hear more and more of the pupil's presentations. We had planned that phase to take forty-five minutes, but it took one and a half hours. As we left the stands, all the parents stood from their seats and clapped warmly as they progressively said, "*Karibu Mkuu wa Elimu Katika Rift Valley. Karibu Mgeni Mheshimiwa…*" (*Welcome the head of education in Rift Valley Province; welcome our guest of honour*). Other local guests included the manager of Beestons Saw Mills, H.K. Patel and the Forester, Mr. Kinyanjui. Mr. Patel was a good friend of the school. He gave a big party for all the school kids at the end of every year.

Finally, the time came for starting the meeting. The deputy headmaster stood up and requested all to stand for prayers. A lady's parent said the prayers. We then sang the National Anthem. After which, the deputy said,

"It is now my privilege to call upon our beloved headmaster, Mr. Githii, to come and welcome our guests and also to give a brief history of our school".

With the usual confidence that I had built over the years, I began my speech by saying:

"Our honored guests, the Rift Valley Province Inspector of Schools, the Nakuru District Deputy Education Officer DEO, the Nakuru District Primary Schools Inspector, the parents, pupils, teachers and all protocols observed, it is my honour to welcome you all to this happy and memorable occasion in our school. This is a day we will treasure and never forget. As you are aware, due to protocols and a very busy schedule, it would have been almost an impossibility to get a person of Mr. Muriu's caliber to visit our humble school. And if this could be possible, it would have taken a long time before the bureaucratic system got through. I just met you in your office, and you gave me the date. I want to let you know that I truly appreciate your acceptance when I requested that you pay us a visit. On behalf of the Cheptoroi Beeston community, I thank you and, in the same breath, welcome you to our school."

There was a prolonged clapping of hands. After the clapping subsided, I talked a little bit more, highlighting the past achievements and challenges, both physical and then handed back to the deputy headmaster, who was the Master of the ceremony of the day. He called upon the teacher who was to invite the school entertainment teams. For one hour,

257

the kids presented very entertaining songs compounded with interesting, educative poems. There was also a play that depicted the life of the school slightly before I came in as the headmaster and the life after my arrival. It, in particular, portrayed the academic dwarfness for ten years and then the academic revival after my arrival.

Mr. Muriu and others did not need a handout to read about the progress of the school. The kids demonstrated it all through the drama. After this, the chairman of the school, Mr. John Ngugi, talked and emphasized all that had been portrayed by the pupils in the presentations. Two more parents and a teacher also spoke. To wrap it up, I spoke, highlighting the secret of our success, and somewhere I said,

"Our guests of honour, there is a great need for a Secondary School here. Last year not all our students who had qualified for the high school got secondary school admission. There were those with 20 to 25 points who never got places, yet they were good materials for high school. This year, so many of our kids have qualified to go to high school, but not all will be admitted due to the limited nationwide number of secondary schools and also accessibility of those in existence. I can only talk with surety of at least 24 who will join national, provincial and District schools. In voicing this, I am not advocating only for pupils from this school but also pupils from the surrounding schools like Nessuit, Ndoswa, Egerton, Mwigito and Ngonogeri. Unfortunately, some of these schools do not get even a single pupil admitted to a high school, not because they do not have qualified pupils, but they fall into the 20 to 25 points brackets".

As I finished talking about this issue, all four guests were engaged in what seemed a conceived discussion such that I had to hesitate in my speech for a while for them to complete talking, and I knew that my speech had hit home. I suspected that they were analyzing the possibility of coming up with a secondary school. The Forester was fully engaged in what seemed deep consultations. When I finished my speech, I called upon the deputy DEO, who really emphasized the issue of a high school. He revealed to the guest of honour that Njoro area, with more than 20 primary schools, had only two high schools, i.e. Njoro Boys' High School and Njoro Girls' High School, both of them at Nakuru District level. Hence, all the 258 schools were competing to get places in these two schools.

The next speaker was Mr. Gaitho who was the Nakuru District Primary Schools Inspector. He highly congratulated the staff, headmaster, parents and the school committee for the wonderful progress the school had made. He said,

> *"This school, for many years, had been a thorn in the flesh in Nakuru District. It had always contributed to the derailment of the district when it comes to the mean score."*

He explained that, after the CPE results, all the points of individual kids in each district were added together, and then the total was divided among the total number of candidates in that district. The resultant figure was termed as the district's mean score. The districts then numbered in order of their performance and due to the poor performance of Cheptoroi School and a few others in the past when Cheptoroi pupils got E's and D's. This greatly lowered the mean score of Nakuru district - no wonder Nakuru district had hardly been on the top list in the Rift Valley Province. He mentioned that the DEO's office was so pleased with what I had done, stating that I had done what they had failed to do for many years, that is, to take off the thorn that was deeply entrenched in the body of Nakuru District. This was followed by a prolonged hand clapping, accompanied by ululations. He hoped that other schools in that same category would follow in the footsteps of Cheptoroi Beeston School and come up with notable improvements.

On the issue of the high school for the vast area that surrounded Cheptoroi, Mr. Gaitho observed that they had talked about it for a number of years, but one of the main obstacles was insufficient funds to buy land in which it would be constructed, and also lack funds from the government in carrying out the construction of the school and the staff houses. He said, *"These factors, our guest, are the main hurdles we have for many years failed to overcome"*. Other speakers included Mr Patel, the director of the Beeston sawmill, Mr Kinyanjui, the forester and the area chief. They all congratulated me and agreed there was a great need for a secondary school in the area. I then called upon our area chief, who, after some talk, invited the chief guest, Mr. Muriu.

He started by saying,
"Words cannot qualitatively express my feelings towards the strides of achievement that have taken place in this school. I didn't know much about this school until I absorbed all its

history and development from all that was strategically communicated to me through songs, drama, all the speeches that have been poured here and the demonstrations by the pupils I first saw when I arrived here."

He went on to praise me. He talked at length about how much he knew me as his pupil at Thogoto Teachers College and my seriousness in whatever I set out to do, from academic work to sports. He said;

"I knew Githii as a very determined person. He also took his studies very seriously and never played with his book work. If you needed him, the wise thing was to not search for him in his room but in the library."

He talked at length about the academic achievements at Thogoto Teachers College. Now, referring to the pupil who had achieved 36 points in my school, Muriu conclusively said,

"Thirty-six points, thirty-six points, it is not a joke. This girl waving me is leading in the whole district, and nationally, she is among the top few."

Now lifting first the previous year's results sheet, he said,

"While 1977 was such a good performance, the 1978 CPE results are a wonderful performance that has placed this school second in the district out of 258 schools. I congratulate the headmaster and his staff."

With his jovial emotions rising up, he said,

"Thirty-six points... the highest in the district comes from here; what a performance! This paper is colored with A's and B+s and B's. English alone has 15 A's."

He paused as if he was searching for the secret behind all this, and then addressing the school chairman, he said,

"Mr. Chairman, stand with your committee, headmaster and your staff; stand up as well. I would hate to give you an oath but I now give you this challenge. We need a secondary school here. Otherwise, where will all the pupils who will not be admitted to the few secondary schools we have in the district go to? I am also aware of the fact that there are a number of kids from the surrounding schools who have qualified for secondary school education, but likewise, they will miss admission to secondary schools. I would like to inform you that Mr. Githii and Mr. Mungai here are qualified to teach in secondary school as well. They have good papers when it comes to academic qualifications. The ball is on your side. I don't see the reason why we cannot have Cheptoroi High School here under the leadership of Mr Githii with his able administration. He can easily handle the two sections of the school. He is a rare person to find, a person so highly talented, a person marked by high integrity. Give him anything that needs ratification, whether in politics, Religion, economics or social affairs, and I assure you, he will excel in it."

Muriu's speech was characterized by cheering, hand clapping, and ululations from the parents, pupils and all other guests, for we had invited teachers and committee members from the neighbouring schools. They had attended in great numbers and more so because of the presence of the Education authorities. They all wanted to see the Provincial Primary Schools Inspector. As the people were in this jovial mood and were now discussing among themselves, the guest of honour was involved in a deep discussion with the other education officers, after which he said,

"My comrades here have promised teachers if you build a secondary school, for we have faith in your headmaster Mr. David Githii. He is qualified and has the capability to teach in a secondary school. I also note that you have Mr. Mungai, another qualified teacher, to teach in the secondary school section. So, my work will be to give you two more teachers to begin with. This, then, means the ball is squarely in your yard. For you to score, you must erect some structure that will be used as classrooms".

He then talked a little more, encouraging the community to come together and save their children from ignorance. He reminded them that time lost will never be recovered. He concluded his speech by quoting two English proverbs that is, *'Make hay while the sun shines'* and *'The early bird catches the worms.'*

One thing I noticed was that as soon as the guest of honour threw the challenge, the school chairman, the forester and the managing Director of Beestons Saw Mills got engaged in a deep discussion. It is important to let the reader know that Cheptoroi Primary School was located in the jurisdiction of the government-owned forest.

The last person to speak was the chief of Njoro Location, and among other things, he said,

"This is a great performance. No school is comparable to Cheptoroi, for it has been champion not only academically, but it has led in the areas of athletics and soccer. It is a school with some peculiar excellence. And for this man, David Githii, I will

never be surprised to hear that he has been elected a member of parliament. He has a great passion for community service and the transformation of the life of the common person. He has a very good name in our society where many take him as a role model in any given community."

He went on to say,

"On the government side, we will render any help to this school so long as it is within our reach."

And for sure, there is a yearning need for a secondary school here.

After this, the deputy headmaster gave a vote of thanks, and then the ceremony was closed with a word of prayer. Everyone headed for the reception to enjoy the food and drinks, including Kikuyu traditional homemade porridge. It was a great celebration where people talked of their pride in the school's performance and the possibility of having a secondary school, something that was so foreign to the community. That area was considered as one of the most backward places in Nakuru District and it was for that reason that many were wondering, *"Can something so good come out of Beeston?"*

As we were heading for the reception, the chairman whispered to me to announce that both the Forester and Beestro Saw Mills Director would like to meet the school committee members, so these should remain behind for;

"Things are shaping up. We will have quite some surprises. All indications are that God is on our side. This is what I gathered from the brief discussion I had with the Managing

*Director and the Forester. They are very excited about the
project."*

After the reception and having bade farewell to our guests,
the school committee, Beestro Saw Mill Managing Director
and the Forester sat down to discuss the way forward for
the proposed secondary school buildings. The school
chairman started by saying in Kikuyu language, *"Maundu
maitu moru"* (on our side, things are not bad). He went on to
say how delighted he was for all that took place in that day's
program. He said,

*"And what really excited me was the challenge to start a high
school here. At first, I was possessed by a spirit of unbelief,
finding such a move impossible, but then I remembered words
that our priest has always quoted, 'With God, all things are
possible.' Then I got the full light of this secondary school idea
as a possibility after we had a brief discussion with the Beeston
saw mill director and the forester."* He went on and said,
*"Allow me to invite the forester to say something about this
new and surprising venture."*

One could tell from his facial expression that the forester
was equally excited. It was not a surprise that as soon as he
stood up, his first words were:

*"What a good thing to be associated with this kind of school!
A simple school, but it has commandeered the many giant
schools not only in this district but nationally. I am really
proud of the headmaster and his staff, and also the board
members. Mine is to say that I am very ready to champion the
process by allocating the land to put up the secondary school.
In fact, I will make sure that the land surveyor is here by
tomorrow. This is not something to be delayed; we need to*

move fast and hit on when the iron is hot. We anticipate the intake of the first secondary school students immediately. My congratulations once more to you, Bwana headmaster, and your staff."

Now, it was the turn of the Beeston Saw Mill Director. As I said earlier, the sawmill produces tons and tons of processed timber per day. He started by saying:

"I have great regard for this school, but that happened after Mr. David Githii became its' headmaster. Otherwise, prior to that, I hardly wanted to be associated with it. I was so discouraged by the poor examination results that it used to attain and also the Indiscipline of both the staff and the pupils. I hereby confess that, for a long time, I have not walked near the gate of this school. I first came to appreciate the work and the determination of the current headmaster when he came into my office to ask me for some help in buying the pressure lamps that the kids could use in their evening studies. I remember asking him. But why do you want to do this, and it is not something the kids are used to?: He then responded and said, "If the children have to do well in exams, then we have to move away from the old way of doing things. In fact, I want to challenge all the traditions that have dictated the life of this school, including kids working in the teachers' gardens, cooking for them and some sexually abusing the school girls. I also want to do away with the alcoholic lifestyle of the staff. In this case, and where possible, I would love to have your helping hand."

The director went on to say:

"For the first time in my life, I saw a very determined teacher who, unlike many others, was not working for the sake of

earning a salary. He is after making future leaders of a nation. It was then that I decided to give the best I could for the school. I have been giving prizes to the best performers in every class at the end of each term. No wonder then, I am hereby promising full sponsorship in the building of four classrooms to become Cheptoroi Secondary School. And with the headmaster's and school board's help, I want that work to start tomorrow. Even before the forester has shown the ground, the building materials will be placed somewhere where the land is likely to be allocated. The idea of constructing Cheptoroi Secondary School is so exciting that I feel tears of joy bubbling in my eyes. What a moment for the people of this area! Congratulations to you all."

The three requested me to fully involve the parents by making them own the project and in digging the trenches that were to lay the foundation of the buildings. Otherwise, before the timber work is done, a five-course of stones to protect the timber from being destroyed by the white ants must be laid. This message was to be relayed to everyone in the community so that all persons could participate. The message was to be announced in different Churches within the area. The office of the area chief was charged with the responsibility of passing the message to the community, even if it meant calling an assembly or a public baraza. That night, I wrote a note to all the surrounding Churches, a note that stirred excitement in the community. In the note, I requested them to encourage their church members to report at the school on the following day by carrying working tools like spades hoes and digging forks and axes.

The day after the meeting, the forester came quite early, accompanied by H.K Patel (the sawmill director), the chairman of the school board and all the members of the school committee. The forester indicated where the beacons of the proposed secondary were to be put. This greatly expanded the school compound. No sooner had the manager returned to the Saw Mill than tractors started following each other carrying building materials. There were stones for laying the foundation of the classrooms so that they could also be cemented, and the timber - especially the 3x2 for the construction of the walls. By the end of the third day, all materials were in place, and consequently, the carpenters, the architects and all required labor force were busy. The parents finished their work on that first Monday. This was because the chief and the forester used their offices to have all in the community involved. Therefore, the parents were not working alone. The leveling was done by use of the saw mill's tractors.

The sawmill director would come twice a day, and the manager (school chairman) would constantly be visiting the site. There was a united focus on the buildings among the Beeston Saw Mill leaders and workers. The entire focus was on the construction of Cheptoroi Secondary School. Within a period of thirty days, the four classes including all the required facilities like books, desks, blackboards, etc, were all done. In other words, all that was necessary for a Secondary School was all set, including laboratory equipment. The next move was to visit the District Education Officer to report on the completion of the project.

When I got into his office, on seeing me, he stood up and enthusiastically shook my hand and said:

"David that was a wonderful day, a day I will ever cherish. Your kids did wonderful, and I was particularly amazed by the discipline instilled in those children, their skills in presentations etc and that explains the secret behind the wonderful Examination results. Your community, the Cheptoroi community, gave me great joy. Keep on keeping on. It is my prayer that in the future, you will manage to have a secondary school."

In response, I said,

"O, thanks, Sir. You have also done a lot by helping me in my administration. If you had never come to my rescue in those early days when I was struggling to settle in the school, a time the teachers really resisted my administration, then I would not have done much - hence, the good results are a product of our combined efforts. Meanwhile, I have come to let you know that the secondary school facilities are ready. The ground is all set for the form one intake. It is important that you and possibly other senior officers come and witness. You will really admire it."

But now, I could tell from his facial expression that this officer was in total disbelief and no wonder he asked this rhetorical question;

"Are there angels helping in your working mechanism? Do you mean, and on a serious note, that there are buildings representing what I assume will be known as Cheptoroi High School?"

In response, I said,

"You know the Bible talks of doors that God can open and the fact that if He opens a door, none will close it. What I am telling you all, and also, mind you, it is not one class but four classrooms, which also include an office."

He then grabbed the phone and at the same time murmuring, *"Unbelievable, this is unbelievable."* He summoned the deputy District Education Officer (DDEO), the District Primary Schools Inspector (DPSI) and the Area Education Officer (AEO). He made it sound urgent, and so within five minutes, they converged in his office. Then he said, *"Mr. Headmaster, can you repeat what you have told me in front of these officers."* I then repeated what I had said with an emphasis, *"The school is complete, and it now awaits your inspection."* It was then that the PPSI said,

"I am sure David means what he has said. Let's get a date; it's like there is a divine power working within him because even the way his school performed seems quite like a miracle as far as I am concerned."

The date was fixed for three days later. On the appointed day, the three officers came. They marveled at what they saw. Everything was so good-looking. After finishing the inspection, we gave them a cup of tea over which they gave us further advice on the running of the Secondary School. Finally, the DEO said:

"Now Mr. Headmaster, the completion of this school is quite timely because it is next week that the headmasters of schools in Cheptoroi High School's category are doing the selection. Now, I have given you the authority to go ahead and do the selection for this school, and I have also mandated you to be the

headmaster of both Cheptoroi Primary and Cheptoroi High School. Today, I will communicate with the Provincial Education Officer (PEO), and everything will be streamlined. I also think it is high time you are considered for some upgrading. In fact, we have almost no other teacher as determined in his/her work like you, one who, if I quote the Bible, is so devoted to working in season and out of season."

THE BEGINNING OF CHEPTOROI SECONDARY SCHOOL

To my surprise, I did not go to do the selection. The news of the establishment of a High School in Cheptoroi spread so fast that parents from the surrounding areas flocked to the school seeking admission for their children to form one class. In fact, my dilemma was in the selection of the best candidates, not only with good grades but well-behaved. I was looking for both academically qualified and talented students in other areas like sports. I also did not want to take a huge number of students and especially this time the school was in its initial stages.

I was also looking forward to that time the school's first class would sit for the Ordinary Level (O level) examination, pass well and therefore act as a catalyst to advertise the school. I finally managed to admit twenty students who soon started their classes. It did not take long before the government posted three teachers into our school. Now that I had a good A-Level examination certificate, I took the teaching of Christian Religious Education and History.

No sooner were we settling in the secondary section than I received a letter from the DEOs Office informing me that things were already in motion with the aim to have me promoted from Primary Teacher One (P1) to the grade of Secondary Teacher One (S1). It incidentally also happened that, at that very time, my mind was drifting from teaching as a career to service in the Holy Ministry. At one time, the

DEO had whispered to me that I was already good material for the Area Education Officer but said,

"Let us first deal with your promotion from P1 to S1. You will need to pass these seemingly divine teaching skills to others."

6. CALL TO THE HOLY MINISTRY

It was while I was at the height of my teaching career and enjoying a good salary and many other benefits that I felt the call to the Holy ministry. This was not a premeditated thing; it just occurred, for I had never thought of it or premeditated on the Church Ministry. All along, I was fully focused and settled on my career of choice, that is teaching profession, which I was very good at.

The revelation and acceptance to go to the Holy Ministry took just three weeks. Otherwise, as much as I was involved in the running of both primary and secondary schools, my mind got hijacked in the spiritual grazing world. Something was pulling me more and more to the involvement in Church life, but at first, it had not occurred to me that it was the call to join the Church Ministry. I just started experiencing a heavy burden about the Church.

For me, I sincerely knew nothing about Church ministry and had never taken interest even after I received Christ as my personal Saviour. I had never even lived close to people who were fully involved in the Church work, like pastors or elders. Those priests that I could remember were the ministers who examined me for the catechism class and confirmation, also the ones who baptized me and the ones who solemnized my wedding. All this had taken place at

Thogoto Parish, which was also my home area. Thus, I had no knowledge of how the PCEA church functioned.

After graduating from Thogoto Teachers College, I was posted to Subukia, which was somehow a remote area, and there were no Churches nearby, let alone the Presbyterian Church. Even when I moved from Subukia to Nakuru Town, I never took an interest nor concentrated on Church life. It was when I went to Cheptoroi School at the very time that I received Jesus Christ as my Lord and saviour that I could count as the time I came to be involved with Church life. But then, between the time I got saved and the time I felt the need to be involved with Church ministry, it was a duration of around two years. This means I had almost no experience as far as Church life was concerned. I had not even come close to Njoro parish priest, whose name was Rev. Waithaka. Sometimes, it took him four months before coming to our Church, for he manned over 32 congregations that comprised his parish. The said congregations were also miles apart. In many places, there were no good roads and he used to get red as he moved around riding on an old bicycle. Although, even if he had come to our church, I had no business with him, for my only relationship with the church was on Sunday, to attend the routine service. The PCEA Beeston Church, where I worshiped, was a small congregation manned by two elders and six deacons. We held the service in a classroom, and it was here that I announced the change of my life and putting my trust in Jesus Christ as my Lord and savior on October 31st, 1976.

Until I joined Beestons PCEA Church, I hardly knew the real role of an elder and deacon. At Beeston, I learnt that both Mr. Kiongo and Thuo were elders. They made most of the decisions regarding the life of the Church. Sometimes, they held joint meetings with the deacons, but they also talked of another parish elder's joint meeting that they called as '*Kaka session.*' It was only after I became a theological student that I came to learn what they pronounced as "*Kaka session*" was a distortion of the English word "*Kirk session.*" They were somehow unschooled. Like their pronunciation of English words, I had likewise a very distorted image of Church life. Yet, it was in the midst of this ignorance that I felt the call to go to the ministry.

When the call became so persistent, I decided to go and share my feelings with Rev. Waithaka because he was the parish priest. He lived about six miles from where I lived, and his office was located in Njoro Town. Upon arrival, I knocked on the door, and I was let in. He directed me to a seat. I introduced myself as a born-again Christian and the current headmaster at Cheptoroi Schools. He also introduced himself to me, after which he asked me,

"*What can I do for you?*" *I then said to him but in Kikuyu language, "Ndoka tondu nindirenda gutwika muhunjia"* (I have come because I have received the calling to be an evangelist).

I had been seeing some people carrying the title '*Muhunjia*' (*Catechist instructor*) coming to teach catechism to some kids in school. I also remembered that the person who taught me catechism prior to my baptism was also '*Muhunjia.*'
Rev. Waithaka then stated,

276

"If I am not wrong, I understand that you have already started Secondary School, which means you are heading both primary and secondary school. "I responded, "Yes,"

Waithaka then continued,

"This has then placed you on a very high status as far as the education career is concerned. But then, by telling me that you are looking for a way to be an evangelist, do you mean going for a Church minister's training college or being employed by the parish to be an evangelist?"

I found myself confused. I did not know the main difference between a priest, a Church minister, a pastor and an Evangelist. I had never in my life talked closely to a priest. The times I saw a priest in a Church, he/she would be speaking from the pulpit and serving the Holy Communion from the Altar table and never move to the people. After every service, the priest left by following a procession headed to the vestry and I never saw him again. Rev. Waithaka seemed confused. He could not understand how on earth such a learned person with such high responsibility could not know the difference between a pastor, Church Ministry, clergyman and an evangelist. When I noticed that he had some internal struggle, I said to him,

"Since I don't seem to know much about the Church, I would appreciate it if you could advise me on how I can be involved in serving God in the Church because I feel a persistent urge to take that direction."

As a way of discouraging me from going towards that direction, Waithaka said,

"But you seem not to understand the great role you are playing in the Kingdom of God through your teaching. You are making such a great number of pupils pass their examinations. Furthermore, you have paved the way for this community to have a new secondary school. Personally, I feel that that is a big calling, and if I were you, I would concentrate on that. Many of these pupils will end up being doctors, teachers, engineers, politicians and even priests. In fact, yours is a wide ministry. I just feel that, you should pursue the work you are doing now. Otherwise, what do you think of my advice?"

In response, I told him that, for me, teaching does not qualify as a calling since I did not feel its satisfaction as a way of serving God. I feel that going to be an Evangelist is what will fill that yearning that has started growing in me. He then said,

"But are you aware that the salary a priest like me gets is peanuts compared with the salary you are earning as a headmaster of both a primary and secondary school? Make sure you are not acting emotionally."

I replied to him,

"This is a decision I have taken and I feel that God is directing me that way."

Waithaka kept silent for a while and was seemingly submerged in deep thoughts. In opening his mouth, he said,

"Well, if that is what you have decided, I feel that the next move is to share your feelings with the officials of Nakuru Presbytery, under whose jurisdiction we are. So, today being Tuesday, let us meet at the bus stage on Thursday so that I can

go and introduce you to these officials; possibly, God will speak to them differently."

Having come to that conclusion, Waithaka offered a prayer, and then I left for home.

On the agreed Thursday, I joined Waithaka at the offices of Nakuru Presbytery which was part of PCEA Nakuru West Church located at Sababu. This is the same locality in which I had spent the night prior to my salvation, being totally drunk. As we got into the presbytery premises, I noticed a signboard that read '*Presbytery Office.*' The word Presbytery did not make any sense to me. Rev. Waithaka first got in, and after like ten minutes, he invited me in. I was given a seat next to the person who was referred to as Presbytery Clerk. Waithaka went on to introduce me to the two officials. The person he referred to as the Moderator of the Presbytery was known as Jacob Mugo and the Presbytery Clerk's name was given as Patrick Rukenya. Looking at me, the moderator said,

> *"It is good to have you. Rev. Waithaka has briefly introduced you to us in your absence. Nevertheless, you can tell us who you are and what has brought you to the offices of Nakuru Presbytery."*

I then introduced myself, indicating that I am a teacher and also a headmaster of a school known as Cheptoroi School and I am a born-again Christian. I then explained the fact that I had received a calling to be a pastor in the PCEA Church, and it was for that reason that I had gone to

Waithaka's office, who then advised me that we come and see you as the presbytery officials. Then the secretary asked,

"Could it be that you are the headmaster whose school had one of the best performers in this year's primary school examination?"

Before I had even responded, Waithaka said,

"This is the person whose name has become a household name in my parish where the school is located."

Then the moderator said:

"Congratulations, you are the kind of people God wants, people who will work diligently not because of money but because they feel the need to uplift the image of God. And how we would love to have you as one of us laboring in God's vineyard? Nevertheless, having said that, my only concern is that we have already carried out the interviews at the presbytery level, and we have already submitted the five names that the PCEA Training and Personnel Committee had asked us to send. The thing is that this committee will never accept a name outside the required number. This then means that we have no leeway to include your name. So, my suggestion is you wait until next year when another interview will take place. One thing I am sure of is that a person of your caliber should be well-versed in our denomination's practices and procedures. Meanwhile, we thank you for coming."

The Secretary-General, Rev Rukenya, then spoke, saying,

"Yes, I do agree with our Moderator that Githii is a very good material for the Church. It is unfortunate that we cannot send your name. I just wish you had been with us when we were sorting out the names to be forwarded to the Training

Committee. However, as the Moderator has said, let us try for the possibility come next year."

At that juncture, he offered a very moving prayer over my life and that if it were God's will, a door to open not necessarily next year but at His timing. We then left for home. As we went out of the gate, Waithaka told me:

"Jacob Mugo, the moderator, is a very learned man. He took his studies in America. He is also a very understanding man, and I could say the same about Rukenya. He loves people, and he is a true man of God. I was amazed by the way they received you and even the fact that they never asked me whether the interviewing protocol had been followed. You might not know, but for you to come this far, the elders of PCEA Beeston Church should have recommended you, and also, the Njoro Parish Kirk session should have interviewed you and forwarded your name to the presbytery with supportive minutes proving that the right procedure had been followed. I think they saw something peculiar in your call, but then we have to accept the way things have turned out for the moment. I love Romans 8:28, which indicates that "all things work together for good to them that love God and who are called according to his purpose."

In my heart, I felt a lot of peace. I was telling Waithaka how much I appreciated meeting the two officials and how I loved their attitude towards me. By then, we were getting to Sababu Round About. A few steps diverted from the road that led to Nakuru West Church. I saw someone in front of us but heading in the opposite direction, trying to draw our attention to a person who was beckoning us, making the sign that we go back. It was Rev Rukenya. Waithaka said,

"That is Rukenya summoning us to go back." We then turned back, and as we were walking back, Waithaka engaged me in some talk.

He was saying,
"We have a very good and understanding Presbytery Clerk, and he was excited about your academic and leadership qualities. It is also important to note that ours is the largest presbytery. In fact, this presbytery is commonly known as the Great Rift Valley Presbytery. It extends from Naivasha to the East, Nyahururu to the North East, Lodwar to the North, to Lake Victoria."

When we finally arrived at where Rev Rukenya was, he ushered us into the office. Having taken our seats, the moderator said,
"You know what, Rev. Waithaka, we have thought with Rev. Rukenya that, since we have a Presbytery meeting this coming Saturday, which is only in four days' time, we should invite David to be interviewed by the presbytery and if he qualifies, we will forward his name to the Training Committee with a presbytery minute attached to it. I think this would work, and if it doesn't, we would have done our best."

As the moderator was saying all this, I kept on thanking the Lord for the rejuvenation of this matter, which we had thought had come to an end until the following year. In response to the moderator's suggestion, Waithaka said, *"That sounds a good idea. Let us then wait for their Presbytery Level."*

Then Rukenya said:

> "David, we wish you all the best. As the Moderator said, a person of your status is well versed with our traditions and contents of practice and procedures."

The two officials bade us farewell, and having walked some distance, Waithaka said,

> "Now that you have known, the Presbytery office, be there on Saturday at 9.00 am. Have I not told you that we have very understanding Presbytery officials? Let us both keep on praying so that God will do according to His will, but my desire is that you go into the Ministry. It had not occurred to me of how strong your calling is, but having seen the reception accorded to you by our presbytery officials in regard to your calling, I have taken it as a confirmation that God has called you. Bye for now."

Upon reaching the DEO's office, where my presence was highly respected, I met one of the junior officers and in a whispering tone, he said, "A recommendation for your promo is at an advanced stage. I am sure you will learn about it soon."

THE PRESBYTERY MEETING

Come Saturday, I reported at Nakuru West Church at 8.45 am. I met some smartly dressed people taking tea. I hesitated to sit down, but Waithaka, who had already arrived, beckoned me to sit on one of the chairs as he poured a cup of tea for me. Within thirty minutes, a crowd of very smartly dressed Church elders and ministers had flooded the premises. Never in my life had I seen such smartly dressed Church people. They were all in ties, while the pastors wore clerical colors. Never in my life was I so close to pastors, some of whom shook my hand, possibly thinking I was one of them because I was also in a tie and suit but of poor quality. They were all talking, but I was not able to connect with much of their talk because it was all based on Church terminologies. Then, someone I knew came in; his name was Gachango.

Gachango was a teacher who, in the years past, taught in a school at Subukia, the same location as Olmanyatta School in which I was the headmaster. In this case, we used to meet in many school sports competitions especially in soccer and athletics. When he saw me, he excitedly hugged me and asked me,

"*Githii, where are you teaching now and what has brought you here?*" I said, "*I am teaching at Cheptoroi Primary and Secondary School in Njoro.*" He continued, "*I remember you very well because of your very well-coached soccer teams. Many times, you defeated my school. Anyway, enough of that. Are you still a headmaster?*"

I then narrated to him about my life in Subukia and Nakuru town and how I came to accept Jesus Christ as my Lord and Savior after undergoing some lifestyle challenges which had jeopardized even my health. I then told him how my relationship with God had undergone transformation such that I now felt a deep sense of calling to serve God as a pastor. I told him what had taken place between Rev. Waithaka and how it had led to my being there that day. With amazement, he said,

"Oh, Githii, I just wish your name had reached us earlier. I am the chairman of the interviewing committee, and we carried out the final presbytery interview two weeks ago. I immediately forwarded the required five names. Oh no! What can we do now? I would have had your name among the five names I forwarded. Now tell me, is it the presbytery clerk who told you to come today or the moderator?"

I then explained to him how I went to see Rev. Waithaka and how he led me to meet the two officials of the presbytery. He said, *"In that case, it is both of them. We will see what will transpire in this meeting."* In fact, it was getting late for Gachango. All the people were already gathered in the Church and they were singing the opening hymn. But as he hurriedly left, he said to me,

"David, I wish you all the best in your interview. Don't panic; you are a wise man."

The meeting started at 10.00 am. I was, therefore, left in the office waiting for the time I would be called to get in for the interview. This was the presbytery office, and therefore, the secretary was busy doing her work. At times she could engage me in some conversation and then concentrate on her work. There was an inflow of Church members who kept coming to enquire about some issues, occasionally interrupting her. When it reached 12.00 noon, I started having some anxiety as the time I had expected to be called prolonged. But I was not worried, for my expectation was that the interview would involve Biblical questions, for I had attained a *"principal"* in the Religious Education paper at my 'A' level exams. Little did I know that I was to be there for a long time. It was around 4:00 pm that I heard the gathering singing a hymn. The secretary told me that that hymn was an indication that the meeting was over.

And true to her words, no sooner had the hymn ended, followed by a concluding prayer, that people started coming out, some coming out hurriedly. I asked the secretary why some were leaving hurriedly, and she said, *"Some will travel around a hundred miles to get to their destination, and as you can tell, it is already late for that kind of long traveling."* Instantly, I overheard one person in a mood of complaining say,

   "Why do we have to deal with issues that have already passed? That issue has taken us so long, and we already had the required number of candidates sent. Many of us will not make it home."

The secretary told me that that kind of complaint was based on me, which means my agenda was handled, and it consumed much time. But there were many who shook my hand in excitement as they went out. Finally, Rev. Rukenya and Waithaka came to me and advised me to go home until

I heard either from the Training and Personnel Committee or from the presbytery. Again, I did not understand all this, but I said, *"Thank you; mine is to praise God in every venture."*

As we went home, Rev. Waithaka told me that my case was handled with quite some emotions. There were quite a number of people who felt that my issue had been overtaken by time as the presbytery level interview had already taken place and the five required names forwarded to the Training Committee. Of course, there were others who did not believe in your call because they could not understand how you could leave such a well-paying job plus that headmastership position unless you wanted to use the ministry as a means to advance your education or as a bridge to go overseas. Also, there were those who think you are too green in your spiritual journey, having become a born-again Christian less than three years ago. But thank God, there is this man called Gachango who spoke very convincingly on the importance of recommending you as a trainee candidate, basing his argument on your good academic qualifications, your experience in leadership and your willingness to sacrifice a good job for the sake of the Kingdom of God. He said that he has known you in the past and your work in the teaching profession spoke for itself. Of course, there is the added advantage that he is the chairman of the presbytery interviewing committee. Hence, his argument was well received by many such that when the vote was taken, the majority voted in your favour. It was decided that your name be forwarded without carrying out the interview for there was no time for that. So, what remains now is for us to keep our fingers crossed as we wait for the decision from the Training Committee. We went direct to the bus stage to board a bus to Njoro, and before long, we were on our way back home. Finally, Waithaka got to the bus stage where he was to alight and we therefore parted company.

THE INTERVIEW

Two weeks after my encounter with the presbytery meeting, I decided to go and inquire about any outcome from Rev. Waithaka, who promised me that he was sure someone would communicate not later than two weeks. The two weeks had passed. One day, at the school, three of us were relaxing in the school's Staff Room and just talking casually when I said, *"There is a letter I had been expecting, but I haven't received it."*

And then Mr. Kirikiru said:
"Wait a minute, I remember a pastor handing over a letter to me, but I was so busy cutting out the loaves and opening soda for the kids. The last time we had taken the soccer team to Njoro, was the day we got that trophy (pointing to the trophy on the wall). Oh! I don't know where I kept the letter the pastor gave it to me. I remember taking it from his hands but my mind was so much on feeding the kids because the driver of the vehicle taking them home was threatening to leave, and if you remember, it was approaching seven in the evening. In fact, I remember the pastor telling me that I should hand the letter to you as soon as possible as it was urgent. Let me go to my house and check in my jacket that I had worn that day."

Kirikiru came back with the letter. When I opened the letter, it was inviting me to an interview taking place at the PCEA Lay Training Institute the following day. All the candidates were expected to report this very day I got the letter. This then took me by surprise, but one thing I felt in my spirit was that this was not by coincidence; it had taken the hand of God and more so because usually, we are never together in the office at break time. Kirikiru used to go to his house for a cup of tea as his house was located in the school compound, and so were some of the members of the staff.

Others used to go to a nearby restaurant to have a bite. Yet, this time, Kirikiru and I happened to be in the Staff Room. As for me, many times at break time, I would be attending to pupils' concerns or attending to parents who came at such a time to present their concerns to me. So, how did it happen that things worked differently that day? If God never intervened, it was just five minutes remaining before the bell rang for the resumption of the classes. That would have been the end of it. Having received the letter and the urgent attention it required, I had therefore to act quickly. This was because I had to travel to the Pastoral Institute that day. I, therefore, rushed to my office, wrote a few things for the deputy headmaster to attend to and then summoned him to my office. I told him,

"I have something urgent to attend to, something that requires that I be out of school for the next two days. I have written a few things you will need to attend to while I am gone."

I then handed over the note I had drafted and left immediately. I went straight home, took a bath, got dressed up, and went to the bus stage and off I left. I had expected to have a word with Rev. Waithaka before attending the interview, but it was now too late. In any case, my comfort was in the fact that this would be a written test based on the Bible, and I was well-versed in the Bible. So, I decided to go anyway.

It took me four hours to get to Pastoral Institute where I arrived around 5.00 pm. I found many more people than I had expected. Everybody seemed to know everyone else. They were talking with excitement. They talked in groups of five, ten, two, six, etc. I learned that almost all of these people were very experienced in Church life. Some were Church Elders, Deacons, Evangelists, etc. Their talk was focused on the expectations in the forthcoming interview and the kind of questions expected. Unfortunately, they were using some terminology I could not make head or tail of. Socially, they were well interacted and they seemed like comrades. I was the only one who looked out of place, the only one who seemed not to know what was going on, the only one who was not making any contribution to the debates, something that made me look like a fool as I did not contribute or make any comments. I must have seemed a fool, for some kept on casting a quick glance at me, and I am sure to many I looked confused and an unschooled Presbyterian.

As we ate our evening meal, there was a lot of loud talk among these candidates. As for me, I was not talking. Instead, I kept my ears attentive to what the people around me were saying. They talked of their many years of experiences as elders, deacons and evangelists. Some talked of their involvement in Kirk session meetings because they were elders. They also talked of Presbytery Church committees. They talked of the many seminars and retreats they had attended. There were those who talked of being youth members and leaders for many years and even being Sunday school teachers and leaders. They continued with such talk even when we went to the hall where we were to be addressed on the next day's program, and even when we finally went to the rooms where we were to put up, they talked of the times the presbytery moderator, the presbytery clerks or the moderator of General Assembly said this or that. They talked of issues that were passed by the Business Committee, the General Assembly or the Head office officials. They talked about the document that they referred to as the custodian of the PCEA powers, a document they called the Practice and Procedure.

One of the dominant speakers in this debate was a person whom people referred to as Ngoima. He told stories about the Church and his experience (of which he had a lot). Other people who spoke of their great experience in the Church were Gatua, Gathairu and Solomon. At one time, they seemed to have kept quiet to listen to me since it was expected that everyone around the table had to say something. I felt like jumping and rushing out like Judas Iscariot because I felt like a total intruder. But darkness had already invaded the entire external environment, and I could not even make it to Gikambura, where my parents lived. I only introduced myself and then said, "*I have a lot to learn about PCEA Church. I am hoping to learn more about it if only I qualify to join a theological school.*" The talk went around the table, and before long, we all retired to our beds. Two of my roommates continued to talk about the expectations of the interview as I listened to them attentively, but before long, they fell asleep. At long last, the whole campus was quiet. Everybody had fallen asleep. I did not sleep immediately. I took time to meditate on all that I had heard since the time I got onto the campus. The more I thought about it, the more I felt like I was in total confusion. Everything sounded so foreign from the little I had known and what I had learned since getting there. It was while inside my blankets that I came up with a final decision. I would wake up very early in the morning before anyone else, take a bath and head to the bus stage, board a bus for home. This I would do early in the morning by 6.00 am. It was the best time to catch a bus. Soon, I fell asleep. I was awakened by some of the candidates who spoke so loudly to take a shower, some with a little bit of pride, indicating that, after all, the forthcoming interview was not difficult. Others talked of people they knew in the interviewing panel, and hence, the chances of passing were very high. I then overheard one saying,

"*You people are taking things for granted. I had the same mentality of having known some people in the interviewing panel, but believe it or not, this is my fourth time coming for this interview. It seems the people in the panel do not favour anyone, even if one is the brother. There is some fear of God in them.*" Another person said, "*I concur with you because I had the same mentality, but this is my third time to come for this interview.*"

The words of these speakers seemed like a confirmation that there was no way that I should have attempted to get involved in the interviews. Their words seemed to agitate me to "*pack and go,*" for this was not a place for me. Psychologically, the environment was quite hostile to me. Only a fool could go ahead to take this forthcoming interview. I got out of bed, took a shower and then took my bag, now determined to go home. I had just stepped out of the room when the bell summoning people for breakfast rang. I dropped the bag on the bed and went hurriedly to the dining hall had a cup of tea and a piece of bread that was sandwiched with a fried egg. I ate quickly and then rushed to my room, took my bag and headed for the bus stage. It was a cold morning, and I did not have warm clothes. I kept on wishing for a bus to come, but it took around one hour before one showed up. When the bus appeared from afar, I got ready to stop it. The more the bus speeded towards me, the more I got excited now that the interview ordeal was over, but alas, this bus flashed the lights, indicating to me that it was full. As the bus passed, my heart sank with despair. It took a while before another bus showed up. I tried by all means to stop it, but like the first one, it flashed the lights and speedily passed by. I kept my bag down and cursed myself for having come all the way only to be in this kind of predicament. I even had to use my money as I was not to wait for the end of the interviews to have my money reimbursed. I kept my eyes focused on the horizon so that I would be in a position to spot the bus from afar and then apply all kinds of signs that would make the driver stop. Another bus showed up after another hour.

At first, I stood at the center of the road. I was raising all my hands trying to show the urgency in my travelling. I even used hand signs to indicate that I was traveling far. At first, the driver flashed the lights giving the usual indication that the bus was full. I did not give up. I persistently made signs to the driver pleading with him to sympathize with my travelling urgency.

Finally, the driver had a second thought, and he made the bus slow down, but not without much application of breaks. It finally stopped some distance ahead of me. I then ran as fast as my legs could carry me. The conductor was already on the ground, and he was shouting at me, saying, "*Where are you going?*" I hesitated as I was already red and breathing heavily. I was now a few steps from the bus when the conductor, with a note of impatience in his voice, asked me, "*Where exactly are you going?*" I said, "*I am going to Nakuru.*" Then the conductor said, "*Sorry, our first stop will be at Eldoret.*" Even as he said this, he gave a big blow to the boarding side of the bus, a signal for the driver to leave. I then walked back to the bus stage, feeling discouraged and hopeless. I tried to stop two long-distance trucks that came by, but none stopped. I tried a few personal cars, but none of the drivers responded positively. I had come to that bus stage at 6.30 am, and now it was a few minutes to 9.00 am. An idea came to my mind: what if I go back to the Pastoral Institute, not so much to do the interview, which, after all, I was already a failure, but to have time to relax because even if I got transportation at that time, it was already too late for me to make it to Cheptoroi School to do any teaching. The faculties of my mind came to a unanimous agreement; hence, I started to go back to the institute to relax, have lunch and get my transport reimbursement. I had just got in my room when the bell rang summoning people to report in the hall to be engaged in the interview. I then rushed out of my room and joined the others. Soon, a pastor who introduced himself as Rev. Dr. Njoya and also the Secretary to the Training and Personnel Development Committee came in, and what followed was total silence.

He then went ahead to explain the procedure that was to be followed in carrying out the interview. He said that there was first to be a written examination where each individual would sit alone and answer the questions as printed on the sheets. After this, there would be an oral interview where each candidate would face the interviewing panel. He further said that the interviewing would be a long process and therefore called for patience among the candidates. The interview was to take the whole day, and therefore, the candidates were to put up another night and leave the following day. Bus fare was available for everyone. That was the first time I met Rev. Dr. Njoya, and I had a lot of admiration for him. He looked intelligent with a good personality, one whose words carried some spiritual fatherhood, an honest personality and one worth emulating. Before he prayed and based his belief talk on John 15:16, where Jesus had reminded his disciples that, in matters of ministry, it is Him who chooses the person to work in His vineyard. In this case, Jesus said, "*You did not choose me, but I chose you, appointed you to go and bear fruit-fruit that will last.*" To substantiate this statement, he reminded us that the interviewing personnel had no power to choose. Each member of the personnel listens to the Holy Spirit, who then gives the discernment indicating who has the call. He said'

> "*More than anything else, the personnel focus on who has the call. It would not be unusual for the personnel to interview all of you and conclusively find none who has been called.*"

He went on to encourage the candidates, telling us not to lose heart if one does not qualify this time, for there is always a next time. One thing I noted as Dr. Njoya explained all this was that the candidates were very quiet, and by looking at them, one could see the nervousness that had invaded each one of them. Even when Rev. Njoya left after saying a prayer, there was total silence and it was like they were no longer birds of a feather.

Even those who spoke did so in whispers. I noticed a few taking out handkerchiefs to wipe what looked like sweat from their faces. This was one thing I could not understand: why were they nervous? Why was this interview so important to them? As for me, I was very relaxed; after all, I had come back to relax, sleep and catch a bus the following morning to go home. Before long, Rev. Njoya came and said, "*You can now come and take your written exam.*" I joined others, whose heavy breathing, in close proximity, one could now hear as an indicator of the anxiety that had overtaken most of the candidates. One could tell the degree of panic in many of them as they searched for their names on top of the desks. I easily noticed where mine was because they were listed alphabetically. Before long, everyone was busy doing the exam. Apart from a few ecclesiastical questions, I found the paper very easy as most of the questions were Bible-based. Nevertheless, there was the statement I heard the previous day around the table as we took supper. Someone had said,

"*The written exam is not a big deal; it carries at most 10% of the total interview; what matters is the oral interview, which carries like 90%.*"

Thus, even when I found this exam to be so easy, I at the same time figured out that even if I got all the questions right, there was that dilemma since it would only account for 10% of the overall interview. The oral interview accounts for 90%. But then another feeling came in; after all, since the best I could get in the oral interview would be a good zero, I had to do my best. I quickly finished answering the questions, but I decided not to go out immediately. I fell into a meditative mood.

I felt like cursing all those drivers I stopped at the bus stage who refused to stop. But there was one thing I was to benefit from. I had a free dinner the previous night, then the breakfast and now there were other good meals coming in the form of lunch, dinner and tomorrow's breakfast plus the bus fare. I was the first person to hand in the papers, and I went out. As time went on, others kept coming out, and finally, all came out because time was over. The bell for the mid-morning tea rang, and we all went into the dining hall. As we took tea, a few people were talking but very cautiously about the exam. One of them seemed to confirm what I had heard the previous day when he said,

"*Don't be worried by that exam, it carries very minimal marks. The determining factor is the forthcoming oral interview.*"

Within thirty minutes, everyone was through with tea. Rev Njoya came and said, "*This will be the order in which you will come in for the oral interview.*" Then he read the order of names and then, he asked the first person to follow him. People kept going in one by one, with some taking more time than others. I also noticed that the more each person's name drew nearer to being called, the more one looked nervous. Some were so nervous that they were sweating

298

profusely and hardly wanted to talk. The atmosphere was like that of people waiting for a body at a mortuary. I really could not comprehend why these people were so nervous yet none of them was like me. When I asked someone why some people looked so nervous, he told me that such were the ones who had undergone this kind of interview a number of times, yet they were very eager to be pastors. Then he added,

"*It is as a result of such nervousness that they hardly make it through; otherwise, fear is the greatest enemy to human beings and their greatest downfall.*"

As for me, no change of heartbeat occurred. I felt so relaxed for one thing: I was so sure of having already failed even before I faced the panel. But then I saw Njoya coming just as he had already done several times and then he said, "*This time is for David Githii from Rift Valley Presbytery. Please, follow me.*" I then just walked behind him in confidence. I decided to face the panel with positivity and cheerfulness; after all, these were brothers in Christ. I knew that worrying would have made me look more of a fool; after all, I had prayed and left everything in the hands of God. I had, therefore, to continue anchoring my faith upon Him. It is Him who opens doors and closes those that He decides to close. I got in and with a wide smile and seemingly looking as if I knew everybody there or seemingly knew all the answers, I said, "*Praise God, my dear brothers in Christ?*" I expected a chorus in everybody responding, "*Praise the Lord!*" Instead, they all looked at me suspiciously.

They were around ten or more. A part from Rev. Chrispus Kiongo whom I had seen severally during my childhood as I attended Sunday services at the Church of the Torch, I hardly recognized anyone else. The first question then came, *"David, what do you do, where in particular do you live, and which Church do you worship and serve God?"*

I replied that I lived in Njoro, Nakuru District, and I worship at P.C.E.A Beeston Church, and I do not participate in the running of the Church, but as the headmaster of the school on whose premises the Church is located, I did help in making sure the classroom is clean for the Sunday use. The second question came, *"In which parish is Beestons Church?"* I had already known that Rev. Waithaka worked and lived in Njoro, so I said, *"It is in Njoro parish, sir."* The third question, *"David, are you telling us that there is no way you participate in your local Church, PCEA Beeston."*

In response, I told the panel that I did attend the Church every Sunday. Then one person asked, *"Is that all?"* I said, *"I think that is all."* Now, I could feel that the environment was changing. There was already a change of mood among the panel members. Other questions came up;

"David, are you telling us that you have never read the scriptures on any Sunday, you have never conducted the service on a Sunday, you have never taken part in making the announcements, you have never been a deacon, and you have never even taught a Sunday school class and so on?"

In answer to this, I said,

"That is true. I am speaking the whole truth, and I don't think there is any such question related to Church work and structure that I will be able to answer."

Another person shot this question;

"David, are you telling us that you even don't know the work of a deacon, or what is the presbytery or Kirk session for that matter?"

I said, *"For sure, I don't want to pretend; I know none of these Church terms."* What followed was a prolonged silence where the members of the panel were looking at each other in a mood of disbelief, and then some of the members got engaged in some conversations but in whispers. One other person asked me, *"David, were you interviewed by the elders of your Church, the Kirk session or the presbytery?"* In reply, I said, *"No."* The same person said, *"This is never heard of in the PCEA Church interview procedure."* As I answered these questions, I felt very relaxed. Then, what turned up to be the last question came. This time, it was from Timothy Njoya. Looking at me in the face, he said, *"David, can you tell us about yourself."* The fact that they continued to interview me took me by surprise. I had expected that having failed in all the questions they had asked me; the next thing was to release me. But here I am, they wanted to know more about me. But then something told me that they were possibly looking for a way to keep me busy so that I do not seem like I have finished the interview in far short a time compared with the others.

Nevertheless, I went ahead to explain my background and upbringing. I started by narrating how, in my childhood, I used to attend the Church of the Torch, where I undertook the catechism classes on the Lord's Table and Baptism. I told them the kind of hardship in life I faced as a result of my father being jailed for seven years with hard labour as he championed the struggle for independence. I told them how my mother tried to get me into school but could not manage the school fees for my joining class two; hence, I had to be out of school for the next two years until my father got released from prison. I told them how I seriously engaged in studies that finally led me to a teaching profession where I had been a headmaster of primary school in different locations in Nakuru District. I told them how I had lived a mismanaged life until I came to know the Lord in October of 1976. Now, the strong call to join the ministry despite having a good salary and the move to upgrade me from P1 to S1 and later appoint me as a primary school inspector in the Njoro location. As I started to talk about my life in Subukia, I expected them to tell me to stop, but I noticed that they were all very attentive to every word I said and almost all nodded as if they said unconsciously, *"Go on, we want to hear more."* So, I narrated my horrible experiences at Subukia, the way I had come to forget myself and got involved with drunkards, then my life in Nakuru and how finally I came to accept the Lord Jesus as my Lord and savior. By now, I had already taken the time for two other candidates. Then came the tricky question, *"That is very interesting, David, and now, can you tell us who is the moderator of the General Assembly?"*

This was a hard nut for me to crack. I now decided to create humor, and I said, "*I seem to forget, but it is one of you.*" Even as this laughter was going on, the chairman (*whom I would later learn was Rev. Gatu*) looked at his watch and sort of made a facial expression to the others as if signaling that they were running short of time. In a conclusive voice, the chairman, looking at me, said, "*Finally, David, what is your final word to this panel?*"

In reply, I said,

"*I have this request that you qualify me to go to a theological school, and after three months of my being there, just call me and ask me all the questions you will think of in relation to the Church life, and I will answer them all. Just give me a chance.*"

The chairman then said,

"*I am not giving you any hope of being one of the people who would qualify but if any miracle could happen and then you get admitted to a school, who would take care of your family?*"

I then explained that my wife was an untrained teacher, and we owned a piece of land in Njoro, which was quite productive. Food was not a problem. The final words came from the person who was being referred to as Secretary General, who then said,

"*Thank you, David. You will hear from the secretary to the Training and Personnel Committee about the results of this interview, and that is what we are telling all the candidates.*"

The process of interviewing all the candidates came to an end around 6.00 pm. We then assembled in the dining hall for dinner. We were all to board there and leave the following day. Thus, when the bell rang in the morning of the next day, we all went to the dining hall for breakfast. This time, there was not much talk about the interview apart from a few close friends who just whispered about it. After tea, we all assembled in the hall for the final word from Rev Dr. Timothy Njoya, the Secretary to the Training Committee. He delivered a speech part of which said:

"On behalf of the PCEA interviewing panel, I congratulate you all for having qualified from your presbyteries. I am sure you defeated many others before the five of you surfaced to be among the five candidates whose names were forwarded to us by the presbyteries. It's only the Rift Valley Presbytery that had the privilege of sending six names to us. However, the interviewing panel was concerned that not many of you were able to express yourselves. Many of you just gave very short forms of answers. If this interview was a secular one like the banking, many of you could not be identified as staunch believers who are even born again. People spoke more about their physical contribution to the Body of Christ than from the spiritual perspective. In reality, it is only a few of you who really dwelt on the spiritual perspective at length."

After this, Rev. Njoya called for a hymn that we all sang. He then concluded with a prayer. We were then given the bus fare enough for the journey each person was to undertake. We were then dispatched. I went straight to the bus stop, and unlike the previous morning when every bus I stopped never did, this time, the bus I waved my hand to just stopped at my feet. I had a safe journey that made me arrive at the school around 2.00 pm. I then got into the office only to find a letter on my table. The letter indicated that the

DEOs office had been impressed by my school administration and also my good teaching and has therefore come to the conclusion that I need to be promoted, and as a formality, an officer could soon be visiting my school to observe me teaching. This did not bother me as I felt that the chances of qualifying to work in the Church were out. I had already disqualified myself because, in reality, I did very poorly in any attempt to answer the questions the panel had asked me. After all, I could not even know the Church courts, which I later came to learn meant General Assembly, Presbytery and the Kirk session - something most of the Church youth could know. I was not even sure that I understood all the questions. I felt like I had just proved myself a fool. So, I went on getting myself ready, putting my lesson notes and schemes of work ready for the inspection by the Education Officer when he/she came.

There was this day that I got the greatest surprise. It was two or three weeks after the Church interview when among the letters brought by the mailman were two letters directly addressed to me. One was from the Presbyterian Church of East Africa, and the other from the DEO's Office. I started with the letter from the DEO's office, for I knew that it had good news for me. The latter indicated the day and time an officer from the DEO's office would come and assess me. Then, I reluctantly opened the second letter. It started with the words;

"Congratulations! I am happy to inform you that you satisfied the training and Personnel Development interview panel; by proving your strong call to the Church Ministry, you, therefore, passed the interview. You are supposed to use the

attached forms for the medical test, which you have to send back to the Training Secretary on the specified date. You proved to be the person with the best call."

The letter also went on to advise me to be ready to report at St. Paul's United Theological College by 7th January 1980 to do a diploma course in theology. I now had two wide avenues open. There was an automatic promotion. I am already a very notable headmaster in the entire Nakuru District. I was already a headmaster of both a primary and a high school. It had been well hinted to me by a senior officer from the DEO's office that the promotion was not only to place me in an acceptable position of being a high school headmaster but also to be a stepping stone to being made an Area Education Officer (AEO) in the very near future. But then there was also an ecclesiastical avenue that had now opened, a way for me to serve the Church. By now, I was more conversant with Church life than when I was first attending the interview. The candidates I had met and listened to at the pastoral institute greatly opened my mind. But I found myself in a dilemma. Going on in teaching meant more prestigious opportunities and hefty salaries. Going to Church meant earning a meager salary, walking long distances and, at times, being hungry and thirsty. In order to solve this puzzle, I visited an experienced clergy for advice.

This clergyman almost drifted me from the course of serving the Church. He pointed to my current well-paying job which at the same time commanded some respectable administration. After all, helping the kids to get good grades in their final years in primary school was a ministry that even Heaven admired. This kind of advice really confused me. As a last resort, I decided to share my dilemma with my wife. She was to act as my last mentor. I pointed to her the situation I was facing, including the fact that our last-born child, Njoki, was only two months of age. I also pointed out the fact that the burden of six children during my three years of studies could be too much for her.

To my surprise, she did not find it a dilemma. By the way Lucy just became a Presbyterian after I had married her. Prior to that, she was a staunch Roman Catholic. In answering me, she talked about her background. She told me that when she was in high school, she had opted to be a Roman Catholic nun, but she encountered a tough confrontation with her father. Her father denied her the chance on the grounds that if she became a nun, then she would not give birth to a baby named after him, meaning that his name would be lost in her linage. He also complained that by Lucy becoming a nun, he would never get a dowry from her marriage. So, with these observations, Lucy finally said,

"My desire is that you go and serve God. I will struggle with these kids through some farming and my meager salary, and these children will never miss food, school fees or clothes. That God who is calling you will provide for us."

That then became the final nail to solve the puzzle. My mind was hooked by an urgency to go for ministry. I made a covenant with God that never again will I look back, forward ever, backward never. The following day, I went to the DEO's office and explained the situation and the fact that I was to leave teaching. I remember the officer looking at me unbelievably and said:

"Do you know what you are exactly saying? Have you taken the checks and balances between your current positions as a prosperous teacher with a lot of potentiality of advancing to higher levels of administration compared with that humble job of being a pastor? Have you really studied what it means to be a pastor, the kind of life they lead? I thought with your well-organized administration and your good skills in teaching you could not have drifted your mind to another seemingly unproductive profession. My guess is that you really don't have much understanding as to who a pastor is, his income and his way of life. David, you have already built yourself. I insisted that, that was the way the Holy Spirit was leading me. He asked me again, *"Are you sure that you know what you are doing?"*

I stood my ground even after the officer took a long time to discourage me. Finally, he asked me, *"So you now want us to stop this officer from assessing you for promotion?"* I confidentially said, *"Yes."*

After some talks that were not fully based on my next move, he now congratulated me for the good work I had done in my short-lived yet notable career at Barut Rhoda and now Cheptorot Primary and Secondary Schools and the way they had counted on me as a near future Area Education Officer (AEO). The following day, I went to Nakuru General Hospital for a medical test. Having everything ready and with all documents well filled, I passed through the post office and mailed the documents to the Secretary, Training and Personnel Development. I also confirmed that I would be reporting to St. Paul's United Theological College on January 7th, 1980. This was around September.

I then called a parents' meeting and passed the news to them. They could hardly believe their ears. To parents and the teaching staff, it was like I had run out of my mind. They could not believe that I could leave such a prosperous career with the forthcoming promotions. There was a lot of talk in the whole area that I had run out of my mind and even some people stopped talking to me. The news of my departure spread far and wide but not without much regret from many who believed that I had left Canaan to go into the wilderness. Even many Church colleagues did not find the step I had taken appropriate. One said to me,

"My brother, hasn't it occurred to you to realize how much good your teaching ministry is doing for all of us? Don't you understand that by producing these clever pupils, you are already doing the wonderful work of God as these kids will turn out to be nation-builders? What ministry is better than building the nation? That is what the Church is already striving to do and by so doing, you are already in God's ministry."

I received a lot of such discouragements but my call was far much stronger and beyond any human understanding. I went on teaching and preparing to leave come January. The school was closed for the December holiday. I bid the kids goodbye as they closed the school. It was in mid-December when the mailman brought me a letter. The address on the envelope read, 'St. Paul's United Theological College.' I opened the letter and read it, but it had a different message from the one I had expected. In part, it read,

"I am pleased to inform you that your admission to the Diploma course in this school beginning 7th January 1980 has been cancelled. We have looked at your academic papers, and you qualify for the degree work. You are now to report in September next year instead of January to work on a Bachelor of Divinity Degree."

I went with the letter to the DEO's office and reported the postponement of my January departure. They, therefore put on hold the appointment of the incoming headmaster. As the year came to an end, the results of that year's CPE were announced. Like the previous years, I went to the DEO's Office to collect the results. As usual, I got into a hotel, asked for a cup of tea and had the results listed in a full scup. When I got to school, I found a big crowd of people, including students and parents, waiting for me with a lot of expectation. As I hung the results on the notice board, the crowd was squeezing me as each wanted to see the results. As usual, there were lots of A's and B's. The performance was very good, but the school still held the second position in the District out of 258 schools. I had earlier in the year expected to make the school attain position one in the district, but with the issue of my calling to the ministry and all that it entailed, I missed concentration on my part, which, of course, would also have activated concentration from the teachers and the pupils. The news of my possible departure had also somehow affected the pupils, teachers, and even the parents psychologically. Nevertheless, as I have said, the school retained its second position in the district, which by all means was a great performance. Many students got admitted to the government schools. Quite a number got absorbed in Cheptoroi High School.

When the news of my delayed departure was relayed, it was received with tears of joy by the whole community. Many wished that a miracle would happen that could make me not leave the school at all. In any case, I was to be in the school teaching and carrying out the administration until September of the following year. January came, and the schools opened. I now got to work. I wanted to prepare the kids such that by the time I went in September that year, the students would be well-tuned for the Exam in November. I encouraged the teachers, students and the parents morally, and to my joy, each was trying to do more than usual.

The year went fast. As the schools closed for the August holiday, I now officially bid farewell to the whole community. There was a farewell party. Psychologically, the community was now prepared for my departure. I handed over the school to Mr. Mungai, who was already a staff member. I was now ready to join St. Paul's United Theological College and therefore reported in September 1980. You cannot miss reading the next book covering my second phase of life in the book titled *"Relentless Life Bumps,"* which is an elaborative continuation of my autobiography. It is a must-read!

FORWARD EVER BACKWARD NEVER!
NEVER GIVE UP IN LIFE!

I. L.B. Cowman (Statements from: *"Streams in the Desert"* by L.B. Cowman 1st. Published in 1925)

a. *"Tribulations imprint is on every great achievement. It is the door to triumph."*

"No one wins the greatest victory until he has walked the winepress of woe."

"The footprints are visible everywhere; the steps that lead to the thrones are stained with spattered blood and scars. And scars are the prize for scepters."

"We will wrestle our crowns from the giants we conquer. It is no secret that grief has always marked the trail of the reformer."

b. *"The strength of a hurricane can be demonstrated only by the hurricane. On the same note, the power of the gospel can be fully shone only when the believer is subjected to some fiery trials. For God to give songs in the night, the day has to fade away, and then God brings in the night."*

II. Martin Luther King Jr.,

"The ultimate measure of a man is not where he stands in moments of comfort and convenience, but where he stands at times of challenge and controversy."-

III. Nelson Mandela

a."A winner is a dreamer who never gives up."

b.*"Difficulties break some men but make others."*

c.*"It is in your hands to create a better world for all who live in it."*

d.*"It always seems impossible until it's done."*

This book is part of the books that cover Dr. David M. Githii's autobiography. The others include;

1. Relentless Life Bumps (in the market)
2. Church Transformation Through Turbulence: Propelled Orchestration of Church (in the market)

Other books written by the author include;

1. Progressive Infiltration of Idolatry into the Universal Church and Nations: A Chronological Perspective (in the Market)
2. Kenya Repent or Perish (out of print)
3. How to Grow a Healthy' and 'Vibrant Church Through Small Church Groups (out of print)
4. Tithing: Principles and Practices (out of print)
5. Phases of The Church (out of print)
6. Exposing and Conquering Satanic Forces over Kenya (out of print)

Remarks by Githii's children on him:

1. **Nicholas muhia**
    I grew up knowing no other Hero, but my father.
    He has been a great father to us, bringing us in fear
    of God, in Christian life. He is a role model to me,
    to whom I admire many of his characteristics. He is
    a man of courage, God fearing, charismatic
    speaker, a leader, a teacher, full of wisdom, giver
    of the needy, and a man of the people. His heart is
    in the ministry, where he has served God
    truthfully.
    May God bless you father; may he give you
    strength and good health. May he give you many
    more years. May you be loved by your
    grandchildren and great grandchildren.

2. **Ben Muhia**
    Tribute by His Firstborn — Benson Githii Muhia
    They say a father is a mirror through which a son
    glimpses his future.
    If that's true, then I've been blessed to watch a lion
    walk through fire — unburned, unbowed, and
    unbought.
    Dr. David M. Githii is not just my father. He is a
    spiritual force. A reformer.
    A living sermon wrapped in courage.
    In a world drowned in noise, he dared to thunder
    truth.
    In the midst of storms, he danced with Scripture.
    And me? Well, as his firstborn, I once tried to argue

with him using logic—
I lost faster than Pharaoh's army in the Red Sea!
Lesson learned: never debate a man who reads
Greek, Hebrew, and Revelation for fun.
I've watched him plant seeds in dry seasons—seeds
that bloomed by faith alone.
Scripture says, "The righteous man walks in
integrity; his children are blessed after him."
I am that blessing. I am that witness.
Dad, you didn't just write books.
You wrote legacy—into the world, and deep into
our hearts.
—Benson Githii Muhia

3. **Mary muhia**

   A lot can be said about my dad, but I will keep it
   brief. He is a giant of faith—steadfast, unwavering,
   and unafraid to stand alone. He has often said that
   he is at peace even when others oppose him,
   because as long as God is on his side, nothing else
   matters. His strength and conviction have been one
   greatest lessons in my life.
   Dad, I am the woman I am today because of you.
   Your faith has been my foundation, your wisdom
   my guide, and your courage my inspiration. Thank
   you for introducing me to faith—it has shaped my
   life as a wife, a mother, and the very essence of
   who I am. I am forever grateful to you
   Wangari

4. **A. Muhia**

My father, Dr. David M. Githii, walks in integrity like few I've ever known. He doesn't just preach truth—he lives it. Transparent in his dealings, unwavering in his convictions, and unshakable in his faith, he has been a pillar in both the church and the community.

As a former Moderator of the PCEA Church, his leadership was marked by bold decisions and servant-hearted reforms. He helped launch church partnerships, invested in people, and gave generously—not just in sermons but in substance. From establishing a secondary school to founding El Gibbor Ministries, his impact is still unfolding. "Mūndū mūnene ti ūrĩ indo, nĩ ūrĩ wendo." —A great person is not measured by possessions, but by love.

Dad, your legacy isn't just in books or buildings— it's in people who now stand taller because you lifted them.

—Amos Muhia

www.ingramcontent.com/pod-product-compliance
Lightning Source LLC
Chambersburg PA
CBHW021215130626
46554CB00004B/1226